THE OFFICIAL RULES OF
BASEBALL
ILLUSTRATED

THE OFFICIAL RULES OF
BASEBALL
ILLUSTRATED

AN IRREVERENT LOOK AT THE RULES OF BASEBALL AND HOW THEY CAME TO BE WHAT THEY ARE TODAY

DAVID NEMEC

SPORTS
PUBLISHING

Visit our website at www.sportspubbooks.com.

10 9 8 7 6 5 4 3 2 1

Library of Congress Cataloging-in-Publication Data is available on file.

Cover design by 5mediadesign
Cover photograph: Getty Images

Print ISBN: 978-1-68358-323-3
Ebook ISBN: 978-1-68358-324-0

Printed in the United States of America

To Marilyn, whose book on rules is far more irreverent than mine

Contents

Acknowledgments

Twenty-six years have passed since the original edition of *The Official Rules of Baseball Illustrated* first appeared in 1994. In that time several baseball historians and researchers have imparted information that has been of considerable help in preparing the 2020 edition. The author would especially like to thank his editor, Jason Katzman, and fellow baseball historians and researchers Dennis Bingham, Rich Topp, Bill Deane, Ev Cope, Frank Vaccaro, John Thorn, David Ball, Dick Thompson, Al Blumkin, Pete Palmer, Don Malcolm, Dave Zeman, David N. Johnson, Stew Thornley, Ken Samelson, Bob Tiemann, Cappy Gagnon, Richard Malatzky, and Richard Hershberger for their invaluable contributions, along with Eric Miklich and Scott Flatow for fact-checking much of the updated material with their usual expert eyes.

Introduction

French historian Jacques Barzun is best known to followers of our national pastime for having written: "Whoever wants to know the heart and mind of America had better learn baseball, the rules, and reality of the game." Barzun's implication, of course, is that baseball epitomizes our nation and that its rules and rites spring from American roots. Yet that is not altogether true.

Europeans played many different types of bat-and-ball games for centuries before the earliest American colonial settlements. These informal divertissements gradually evolved into the orderly games of cricket and rounders that had circumscribed rules and games like one old cat whose rules were often made up on the spot depending on the size of the playing field and the number of players. What all these early games had in common was that they were ancestors of baseball. For our national pastime did not have the "immaculate conception," Barzun's epigram would lead us to imagine but rather developed by trial and error.

The Official Rules of Baseball Illustrated endeavors to track the evolution of a great many of present-day baseball's more interesting rules and rituals. To do so, it reports on key episodes that inspired the game's thinkers to reconfigure a portion of the rule book and, in the process, often cites examples of both the correct application and misapplication of certain rules. Many of its illustrative anecdotes come from the nineteenth century, when the rules were in an almost constant state of flux, but the baseball rule book is still far from a perfect instrument. George Will has commented: "The real powers behind the rule book are the people who balance baseball's financial books." His observation is dead on, and to a large degree has always been true. Throughout the last 150 years, whenever the unequal balance between hitting and pitching threatened to affect attendance—to say nothing of lucrative TV and radio contracts—major changes were made in the game's playing code. Arguably, the most significant one in 1893 lengthened the stretch of ground between a pitcher and a batter by moving the pitching slab to its present 60-feet, 6-inch distance from home plate, but just eight years later foul-hit balls with less than two strikes for the first time counted as strikes, and in our own time it recently no longer became necessary to pitch four balls to issue an intentional walk. Some observers are of the opinion that the game could soon arrive at a crossroads so radical that either the pitching distance is again lengthened, and if not, the possibility of the strike zone being shrunk. Others, particularly pitchers, believe the ball needs to be "dejuiced" so that every delivery in the strike zone does not boast home run potential. Fans in general indirectly agree that the ball is livelier, specifying the rash of spectator injuries of late by foul balls. The probability is strong, in any event, that a future edition of this book will depart profoundly from its predecessors.

But the rules are also continually being rewritten for other than financial or safety reasons. Each new season brings at least one occurrence that cannot be resolved by the rule book. The 1983 "Pine Tar Game" between the New York Yankees and the Kansas City Royals is a prominent example, and is discussed in this book. But there are literally hundreds of remarkable moments in the game's history when a player or umpire found themselves in a situation that did not have a rule to govern it.

One of the earliest came in an American Association clash in 1887 between Louisville and Brooklyn, when a Louisville baserunner, after scoring from third base on an infield error, began wrestling with the Brooklyn catcher so that a teammate could also score. At the time, rather amazingly, an umpire was left entirely to his own devices in such a predicament because there was as yet no rule addressing a situation in which a player who had scored, and was therefore by definition no longer a baserunner, interfered with a fielder. Nevertheless, the arbiter that day, one Wesley Curry, worked out what seemed to him a logical solution, and in the process set a precedent that eventually triggered a new rule.

Curry's handling of the situation will be found in the section on the rules pertaining to umpires, but unfortunately not all of the fascinating incidents that led to rule changes can be tackled in a single book. In the years ahead, as interest in the game's continuous evolution continues to spread rapidly—from scholars to baseball buffs—there will doubtless be many more efforts to help us draw a better bead on the whys and wherefores of baseball's rules. Meanwhile, this author hopes you have as much fun with this book as he did putting it together.

Introduction to the 2020 Edition of
The Official Rules of Baseball Illustrated

For a number of years after the original version of this book appeared in 1994, the lone revision in the playing rules occurred in 1995, when the lower level of the strike zone became a line at the hollow beneath the batter's kneecap rather than a line at the top of his knees. However, in the past decade alone, not only have we had a welter of new rules appear (pertaining to runner interference, home plate collisions, pitching changes, and other less momentous on-field events) but the entire rule book has also been reorganized to a degree that makes its antecedents hopelessly outdated, as the game itself has changed significantly.

As early as the mid-1990s, largely due to the use of performance-enhancing drugs (PEDs), the complexion of baseball irretrievably transformed—particularly those features of it that required fans to trust in the legitimacy of statistical achievements produced by marquee players. Too, there began to be incidents almost every season where video replay demonstrated that umpires' decisions were often enough mistaken in crucial situations that baseball had to follow the lead of other major sports and introduce video replay to overturn decisions that were clearly faulty. Moreover, team officials, players, and managers alike have increasingly come to rely on analytics and Statcast metrics like WAR, launch angle, and average exit velocity rather than traditional statistics such as batting average, fielding average, and ERA to measure a player's worth. Some of these metrics are so arcane that they are nearly unintelligible to the average fan. Others seem designed only to promote the invention of new and even more attenuated metrics.

But all this leads to the observation that the game has evolved into an unparelleled pursuit of power, whether it be at the plate or on the mound.

It is now conceivable that a batter will face a different pitcher in every plate appearance in the course of a game, with each one not only fresher but throwing harder than his forerunner. It is also now the norm that practically every batter will be swinging to hit a game-winning home run in the late innings of a tie game, no matter who the pitcher is or what the defensive alignment he faces. In 2018, for the first time in major-league history, there were more strikeouts than base hits (and it occurred again in 2019). Yet, on the positive side, the 2018 season also brought the longest extra-inning game in World Series history, the first player since Babe Ruth to pitch more than 50 innings and hit more than 20 home runs in the same season (Shohei Ohtani), and a starting pitcher—Jacob deGrom of the New York Mets—that deservedly bagged the National League Cy Young Award despite winning only 10 games. On another front, contrarily innovative of late in their surreptitiously successful approach to the game have been the Tampa Bay Rays, so reliant on their bullpen that they arrived at the All-Star break in 2019 without having produced a complete game from their pitching staff since 2016, and in Ryne Stanek featured the first hurler ever to start as many as 25 games in a season while logging fewer than 50 innings pitched. In all, the Rays used 33 different pitchers in 2019 while squirming their way to an LDS appearance. Equally innovative are the Houston Astros who totally abandoned issuing intentional walks in 2019 because batters are hitting fewer ground balls, which create the double plays that intentional walks are meant to induce. Rather, batters are launching home runs at a record rate (6,671 in 2019, 671 more than the previous MLB mark of 6,105 set in 2017) turning the intentional walk into an invitation to surrender even more runs via the long ball. After hitting a record 260 homers as a team in 2018, the New York Yankees tacked on 36 more dingers in 2019 but nonetheless lost their team record when the Minnesota Twins outhomered them, 307 to 306.

This completely updated and expanded edition of *The Official Rules of Baseball Illustrated* explores many such far-reaching developments in the game's never-ending evolution, including some, like umpire Joe West's contentious ruling on Jose Altuve's drive that landed in the right-field stands in Game Three of the 2018 ALCS, which demonstrated that all the technological advances in the world cannot completely eliminate the human element in the decision-making process. In addition, earlier controversial moments in the game's long and rich history, such as the Merkle incident in 1908, the notorious "Pine Tar" game, and the bizarre circumstances surrounding the first batter not to be credited with the run that scored on his own home run are examined in greater depth as new information has emerged. With its new layout, altered rules, and many added anecdotes, *The Official Rules of Baseball Illustrated* is a book no baseball lover should be without.

1.00: Objectives of the Game

Seemingly, it would be safe to presume that the winner of a baseball game has always been the team that scored the most runs at the end of nine innings. However, the 1857 season (which introduced many critical changes to the playing rules), was the first time in which a game was required to go nine innings, with five full innings constituting an official contest, if play were halted for whatever reason. Prior to 1857, the objective was to score 21 runs (or aces). A game thus could end after a single inning or finish without a winner if neither team was able to tally 21 aces before darkness came. Why the teams that gathered at the landmark 1857 convention to solidify the rules of the game changed its length to nine innings rather than seven or eight—or even 10—is unknown. As good an explanation as any may be that many vital features of the game and its beloved statistics and milestones exist in threes or multiples of three: three strikes, three outs, nine men on a team, 300 wins, 3,000 hits, and .300 hitters. So why not nine innings unless, of course, the score was tied after the ninth frame, in which event, additional innings needed to be played to determine a winner. This has always been the case in tie games except in three seasons—1869, 1870, and 1871—when, if both team captains agreed after the ninth inning, the game was considered a draw. The most famous instance in which captains did not agree came on June 14, 1870, when the Brooklyn Atlantics snapped the fabled Cincinnati Red Stockings' all-time record winning streak of 81 games in 11 innings by a score of 8–7 after Cincinnati captain Harry Wright obstinately refused Atlantics captain Bob Ferguson's offer of a 7–7 draw at the completion of nine full innings.

The first game played by the Cartwright rules—devised to an unknown degree by Alexander Cartwright, who is widely recognized for having merged the best features of several bat-and-ball games of his time to create the game we know as baseball—took place at the Elysian Fields in Hoboken, New Jersey, on June 19, 1846, between the New York Nine and Cartwright's club, the New York Knickerbockers. The contest lasted only four innings as the Nine tallied their 21st run in the top of the fourth, added two more scores for safe measure, and then blanked the Knicks in their last turn at bat to prevail, 23–1.

Note that even though he is still considered by many historians to have been instrumental in drawing up the first set of playing rules—with the aid of club president Duncan Curry and others—it has long been is a matter of hot debate whether Cartwright is deservingly regarded as the true "father" of baseball. Much stronger cases can now be mounted for several other baseball pioneers active in the mid-1800s, most prominently Daniel "Doc" Adams who, unlike Cartwright, was also a skillful player and organizer. In addition, Major League Baseball's official historian, John Thorn, convincingly posits that the Gothams—not the Knickerbockers— were in truth the first organized baseball club. Supporting Thorn is an 1887 interview with William Rufus Wheaton in the *San Francisco Daily Examiner* indicating that Wheaton's team, the Gothams, had a set of written rules as early as 1837 and Wheaton laid claim to writing at least some of them. However, since Adams may be an unknown figure to many readers and fewer still will have heard of Curry and Wheaton, this author will streamline the controversy by referring throughout this book to the original set of written rules as the Cartwright rules with the understanding that Cartwright didn't singlehandedly do all the baseball activities he's credited with and perhaps never even participated at all in some of them. Cartwright, in other words, is simply the most well-known representative at the moment of the rules creation groundwork that may have been done in greater part by others.

2.00: The Playing Field

A t first appearance, all the rules pertaining to the shape and size of the playing field have changed appreciably since Cartwright's day, except for one: The bases are still 90 feet apart. Nothing was actually said about the distance between bases in the first formal code of playing rules that Cartwright drafted in 1845; the sole stipulation was that the stretch of ground from home to second base and from first to third base should be the same 42 paces. Since a pace for an athletic man walking briskly is roughly a yard, that worked out to be about 126 feet, or only a foot and a third short of the present distance between home and second base.

Historian Frederick Ivor-Campbell speculated that Cartwright chose paces for the sake of simplicity. An empty stretch of ground can be converted into a ball diamond in a few seconds if the distances between home and second and between first and third are stepped off, whereas using a yardstick or a tape measure takes considerably longer. Ivor-Campbell also theorized that Cartwright might have preferred 42 paces to 42 yards because it produced bases for players at a distance fit for their legs. As a result, children or women pacing out a diamond will naturally come up with shorter basepaths than adult men, resulting in a game more closely suited to their physical dimensions.

No one really knows the thinking of the game's early designers—the bases could as easily have been 80 or 100 feet apart and still would have allowed the playing field to retain its diamond shape—but sportswriter Red Smith once said, "Ninety feet between bases is the nearest to perfection that man has yet achieved." In addition, others have pointed out that while every other significant feature of the geometry of the playing field has changed since Cartwright's day, the 90-foot distance has remained a constant. In truth, however, the distances today between bases are *less* than 90 feet. The way the bases are situated now, the distance from the edge of home plate to the edge of first base is about 88 feet; from first to second and second to third, 88½ feet; and from third to home, 88 feet. Prior to 1900, when the shape of the plate changed, the distances were different still, depending on alterations in the size and positioning of bases.

> Rule 2.01 (a) Any Playing Field constructed by a professional club after June 1, 1958, shall provide a minimum distance of 325 feet from home base to the nearest fence, stand or other obstruction on the right and left field foul lines, and a minimum distance of 400 feet to the center field fence. (b) No existing playing field shall be remodeled after June 1, 1958, in such manner as to reduce the distance from home base to the foul poles and to the center field fence below the minimum specified in paragraph (a) above.

For many years after Union Grounds—the first enclosed baseball field—was constructed in May 1862 in Brooklyn so that admission could be charged, there was no minimum distance an outside-the-park home run had to travel. The Chicago White Stockings, for instance, played in Lakefront Park in the early 1880s, with a left-field power alley only 280 feet from the plate and a right-field barrier just 196 feet down the line. The park rule called for all balls hit over the short fences to be ground-rule doubles in every season except 1884, when they were designated home runs. That season the bandbox park helped the White Stockings to hit 142 home runs and the club's third sacker Ned Williamson to collect 27 dingers. These specious marks stood as team and individual major-league season records until the arrival of Babe Ruth. In 1885, the National League mandated that all balls hit over fences in parks that were less than 210 feet from the plate were ground-rule doubles . . . so the White Stockings unveiled a new park, West Side Park, which was more classically shaped for its time

By the 1890s, fences in major-league parks were required to be at least 235 feet from the plate. In 1892, the National League deemed that any ball hit over a barrier less than 235 feet from home was a ground-rule double. The minimum distance for an automatic home run was lengthened in 1926 to 250 feet and remained at that figure until 1958 (when the relocated Dodgers franchise was forced to play in the quirky Los Angeles Coliseum, expressly designed for football, until

Ned Williamson's specious 27 home runs in 1884 helped produce a .554 slugging average, the highest season mark prior to 1923 by a qualifier with a sub-.300 batting average. Library of Congress

their new park in Chavez Ravine was ready), but clubs were urged, whenever the neighborhood surrounding the park made it possible, to erect their fences at least 300 feet away from the plate.

Several parks extant in 1926 barely met the 250-foot minimum. The Polo Grounds, home of the New York Giants (for a time the New York Yankees and later the New York Mets' first domicile), was a mere 257½ feet down the right-field line and just 279 feet to the left-field foul pole.

Baker Bowl, the Philadelphia Phillies' home until 1938, had a right-field fence only 280½ feet away. In contrast, Boston Braves hitters in 1926 were daunted by a left-field wall at Braves Field that was 403 feet from the plate at its shortest point. As could be expected, the Braves rapped just 16 circuit clouts that year, the fewest in the majors and 31 less than Babe Ruth hit all by himself.

Most followers of the game are aware that to promote it worldwide in recent years, official major-league contests on occasion are being played in parks smaller than required by the rules. In 2019, the Yankees and Red Sox played two regular-season games at London Stadium in London, England. The park has artifical turf and served up a feast for home run lovers. Measuring only 385 feet to dead center, the park yielded 50 runs in the two-game set and a total of 10 home runs.

2.02 Home Base

Home base shall be marked by a five-sided slab of whitened rubber. It shall be a 17-inch square with two of the corners removed so that one edge is 17 inches long, two adjacent sides are 8½ inches and the remaining two sides are 12 inches and set at an angle to make a point . . .

One might inquire why home base is called home plate. The reasonable assumption is that it must originally have been shaped like a dish, and this is borne out by history. In all the early forms of baseball, home base was round and in casual games was fashioned out of whatever circular device was handy—including a dish or even a player's cap. In 1869, the circular shape was abandoned and home base became a 12-inch square, usually made of white marble or stone. The square was set in the ground so that one corner pointed toward the pitcher's box and its opposite corner toward the catcher's customary station. The pitcher's and catcher's positions were thereupon called "the points." Not until 1877, however, was home plate permanently set entirely in fair territory. The previous two seasons—the last two in which fair-foul hits were legal—the plate was entirely in foul territory.

In 1885, to spare the possibility of injuries to runners sliding home, the American Association stipulated that home base could no longer be stone but rather made of white rubber. Two years later, the National League added the same proviso to its rule manual, but home base remained a square until 1900. The later change of converting the plate to a pentagonal shape made it easier for umpires to pinpoint the strike zone and also gave pitchers a huge boost. The larger, 17-inch five-sided plate, plus the adoption of the foul-strike rule in 1901 by the National League (with the American League following suit two years later), contributed heavily to the sharp decline in offense that gripped the game from the early part of the twentieth century to the end of World War I, causing it to be dubbed "The Deadball Era."

2.04 The Pitcher's Plate

The pitcher's plate shall be a rectangular slab of whitened rubber, 24 inches by 6 inches. It shall be set in the ground so that the distance between the pitcher's plate and home base (the rear point of home plate) shall be 60 feet, 6 inches.

The **feature** of the playing field that has undergone the most drastic change since the first game played by the Cartwright rules is the pitching station. As late as 1880, pitchers hurled from a rectangular box, the forward line of which was only 45 feet from home plate. A pitcher was required to release the ball either on or behind the forward line, and was not allowed to advance beyond it after the ball left his hand. After the National League loop batting average dipped to .245 in 1880, and the Chicago White Stockings ran away with the pennant—winning by a 15-game margin with a schedule that called for just 84 league games—the pitcher's box was moved back five feet to generate more offense. In 1881, though the White Stockings still romped to an easy repeat pennant, the league average jumped 15 points to .260.

> See **STRIKE ZONE** in the **DEFINITIONS OF TERMS** chapter for more on the evolution of pitching.

Eleven years later, despite a flock of rule changes in 1887 that lengthened the pitching distance by half a foot and compelled many pitchers to radically alter their deliveries to conform to the prototype then in effect, the pendulum had swung the other way again and offense was back to its 1880 level. As such, another radical change was needed to restore a balance between hitters and pitchers as the NL average once again plummeted to .245, and stars such as Cap Anson (.272), Mike "King" Kelly (.189), and Jake Beckley (.236) all hit well below .300. With runs at a premium, the Rules Committee once more moved the pitching distance farther from the plate. One faux tale is that the present 60-feet, 6-inch distance resulted from an error made by a surveyor who misread the 60-feet written on the blueprint as 60-feet, 6 inches, and laid out the first pitcher's plates accordingly before the 1893 season. In truth, the Rules Committee carefully calculated the new pitching distance. Although required to release the ball at a point 60-feet, 6 inches from the plate, the typical hurler, after taking the one forward step he was permitted, finished his delivery with his front foot about 55 feet from home base or only five feet farther away from the batter than the forward line had been in 1892. Hence the pitching distance actually increased only about five feet rather than 10½ feet, as it must otherwise seem.

Once the 50-foot pitching distance went the way of the one-bounce out and the fair-foul rule in 1893, many pitchers who fashioned outstanding stats before the distance was increased were immediately impacted when they had to add "legs" to their sharp-breaking curves and keep their back foot anchored to a rubber plate as they released the ball. But probably none was made more miserable than Charles Leander Jones, known as "Bumpus." After winning 27 games in the minors earlier in the year, Bumpus Jones was purchased by the Cincinnati Reds in time to hurl the closing contest of the 1892 season. His first game in the majors coincided with the final day that pitchers threw from a rectangular box just 50 feet from the plate. On October 15, 1892, Bumpus Jones, in the process of launching his career, ushered out the old pitching distance with a feat that has never been duplicated. He twirled a complete game no-hitter in his initial major-league contest, beating Pittsburgh Pirates, 7–1.

Still aglow, Jones reported for spring training with the Reds in 1893, only to find that he would now have to fasten his pivot foot to a rubber plate 60-feet-6-inches from the plate. The transition was beyond him. Seven appearances into the 1893 season, Jones toted a 10.19 ERA, prompting his release. He was never again seen by a major-league audience.

In sharp contrast to the following diagram showing the current layout of the pitching mound are drawings and photographs of the playing field prior to 1893. The pitcher's boxes are flat in all of them but were in actuality elevated, if only just slightly, even by then in most parks.

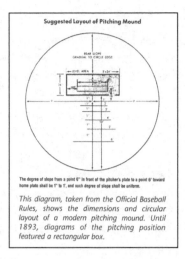

The degree of slope from a point 6" in front of the pitcher's plate to a point 6' toward home plate shall be 1" to 1', and such degree of slope shall be uniform.

This diagram, taken from the Official Baseball Rules, shows the dimensions and circular layout of a modern pitching mound. Until 1893, diagrams of the pitching position featured a rectangular box.

2.05 Benches

The home club shall furnish players' benches, one each for the home and visiting teams. Such benches shall not be less than 25 feet from the base lines. They shall be roofed and shall be enclosed at the back and ends.

The National League rule book first addressed uniformity in players' benches prior to the 1882 season, requiring the home club to place two benches 12 feet long and fastened to the ground on either side of the field outside the playing lines. Adjacent to each bench had to be a bat rack, big enough to hold at least twenty bats.

Remarkably, the term "dugout" did not first appear in the manuals until 1950, when the entire rule book was recodified and many features of the game that had slipped into existence without being given due recognition finally received formal acknowledgement. Dugouts had existed since 1909, when the first all concrete and steel stadiums were constructed in Pittsburgh and Philadelphia; previously players sat at field level on benches that were enclosed in canvas to sequester them from spectators—although it did not shield spectators from hearing players rant and rave. Only the disingenuous brought their wives, mothers, or girlfriends to a game and chose seats within shouting distance of a team bench.

As late as 1895, reigning heavyweight champion Jim Corbett sat through a doubleheader on the Washington bench as a celebrity guest watching his brother Joe play shortstop and pitch for the National League Senators club. Beginning in 1896, only players in uniform, the manager, and the club president were allowed to occupy their team's players' bench during the course of a game. This is now been expanded to include coaches, of course, along with other personnel authorized by the league.

The new concrete and steel stadiums also contained the first dressing rooms for visiting teams. Before 1909, visiting clubs had changed at their hotels and then traveled by carriages to the ballpark in full uniform. Prior to 1889, exceptions were often made, allowing a visiting player to change clothes and shower in a home team's dressing room if he happened to be from a city where his team was playing and staying at his family home rather than his team's hotel. This commonplace courtesy ended abruptly on April 9, 1889, when Cleveland Spiders outfielder Bob Gilks, a Cincinnati native, traveled to the Queen City for a preseason exhibition game. Rather than dress at his home, he brought his uniform and spikes to the Reds' park, as he was not traveling to the park with his Spiders teammates in the team carriage. Gilks was a gritty player—a master of the trap ball play but a weak batsman (as he was a sucker for wide curves that floated out of the strike zone). In the eighth inning of the game that afternoon, he reacted to brushback pitches from the Reds' Tony Mullane by complaining they were intentional, but the reality was that he had hung his head far out over plate so he could reach Mullane's wide sweeping curves. While changing in the clubhouse after the game, Gilks had more words with Mullane and came at him armed with a bat. The row dissolved into a savage fistfight between the two and resulted in severely curtailing the custom whereby players, who lived in a town their team was visiting, were allowed to dress in the home team's clubhouse.

3.00: Equipment and Uniforms

3.01 The Ball

The ball shall be a sphere formed by yarn wound around a small core of cork, rubber or similar material, covered by two stripes of white horsehide or cowhide, tightly stitched together. It shall weight not less than 5 nor more than 5¼ ounces avoirdupois and measure not less than 9 nor more than 9¼ inches in circumference.

This is one of the few rules in the manual that has changed little since the first rule books were written. In the 1840s, balls differed substantially in both size and weight, depending on which team provided the game ball and where that team's strength lay. A hard-hitting club was likely to furnish a tightly wound ball on the smaller side, whereas a nine that thrived on its defensive work, all of which at the time was performed barehanded, would select a heavier and softer ball.

In 1854, all organized clubs adopted the rule that balls must weigh between 5 and 5½ ounces and be between 2¾ and 3½ inches in diameter. The size and weight of ball changed twice more in the next thirteen years before the sphere settled on its present dimensions in 1868, as stipulated in Rule 1.09.

In 1879, the Spalding ball became the National League's official ball, but the American League chose the Spalding-made Reach ball at its inception in 1900. The discrepancy ended in 1977, when both leagues began using Rawlings balls. Other aspirant major leagues used brands of balls that in most cases have long since disappeared from the market.

The National Association, the National League's forerunner, used many different balls during its five-year run, from 1871 to 1875. When the American Association first surfaced in 1882 as a challenger to the National League, it chose as its official ball one made by the Mahn Sporting Goods Company of Boston. After using the Mahn ball for just one season, the AA abandoned it in favor of the Reach ball, which remained the official AA ball until the league ceased operation following the 1891 season.

In 1884, its sole year as a major league, the Union Association employed the Wright & Ditson ball, designed and manufactured by George Wright, the game's first great shortstop and part-owner of the Boston Unions franchise. The Reach and Spalding balls in 1884 were quite similar, but the Wright & Ditson ball was a "hitter's" ball, chosen in the expectation that fans would be drawn more to high-scoring games than a pitchers' duel.

The official sphere of the Players' League during the 1890 season, its lone campaign, was the Keefe ball, devised by Hall of Fame pitcher Tim Keefe, who hurled that year for the New York PL entry, and operated a sporting goods store in lower Manhattan in partnership with former teammate Buck Becannon. Like the Union Association's Wright & Ditson ball in 1884, the Keefe ball was considerably livelier than its counterparts and throughout the early 1890s leftover Keefe balls would occasionally be slipped into a National League game at key moments when the home team—which was responsible for furnishing the balls—had the meat part of its batting order due up.

In 1914–15, the Federal League—the last serious threat to the two established major-league circuits—utilized a ball made by the Victor Sporting Goods Company, who were at the time one of the leaders in the business after it formed in 1898. It later merged with Wright & Ditson.

Before we leave the rule on balls, we call attention to the phrase "white horsehide." Many readers will remember that in 1973, Oakland A's owner Charlie Finley had his defending world champions experiment with orange balls in spring training exhibition games. But unlike many of Finley's controversial innovations, this one died a quick death.

The last time a team played with balls that were a color other than white in a regulation major-league contest was in 1939, when Brooklyn Dodgers general manager Larry MacPhail tried dandelion yellow balls in two games, one against the St. Louis Cardinals and one against the

Chicago Cubs. The Dodgers first used MacPhail's yellow balls in the first game of a Tuesday doubleheader with the Cardinals on August 2, 1938, at Ebbets Field, but met resistance from the other National League teams, especially after they won, 6–2, behind pitcher Freddie Fitzsimmons (who threw a complete game).

3.02 The Bat

The bat shall be a smooth round stick not more than 2.161 inches in diameter at the thickest part and not more than 42 inches in length. The bat shall be one piece of solid wood.

Until 1893, bats were permitted which had one flat side, making it easier for hitters to execute "baby hits" (bunts) and also to deliberately slap pitches not to their liking foul. First adopted by the National League in 1885, the flat bat was incorporated by the American Association when both leagues began using the same rule book in 1887. Even after being deprived of this advantage, many hitters—especially Willie Keeler, a leading exponent of the flat-sided bat—flourished in 1893 when the pitching distance was lengthened. As was true that year for hurlers who now had to tailor their deliveries to the increased distance, some batsmen

JUDGE H. L. TAYLOR.
(Former Star of Baseball Diamond Now on the Bench.)

Harry Taylor.

were unable to adapt to bats that were entirely round and were soon out of the majors.

The major leagues have, on occasion, authorized bats that were not all of a piece. During the 1954 season, for instance, laminated bats were allowed on an experimental basis. Bats made of metal, in whole or in part, have never been permitted in the professional game. . . and pitchers can only pray they never will be.

During his relatively brief career, Harry Taylor used a bat that was one of a kind and employed it in ways the likes of which have not been seen since. Later a renowned jurist, Taylor was active in the majors only four years (1890–93), but at the turn of the twentieth century he served as chief counsel for the players in their first attempt to form a union. Amazingly versatile, he made his ML debut with the Louisville Colonels in 1890 (at second base) after leading the New York State League in batting the previous year while playing shortstop for Elmira. When he left the majors after spending the 1893 season with the original Baltimore Orioles under Ned Hanlon, he was regarded as the best fielding first baseman in the game (and also had found time to catch, play the outfield, and serve in six games at third base). Offensively, Taylor had little power—as witness a career slugging average just 37 points higher than his .283 career batting average—but was an excellent baserunner and superb bunter with a technique that many tried to emulate but none ever mastered. Taylor used a bat made of soft wood, legal at the time, and would spin it at the last second as a pitch came plateward so that the ball would carom off the handle rather than the barrel and die just a few feet from the plate, forcing the surprised catcher to make the play rather than the charging pitcher or third baseman. But he also had another trick up his sleeve which exasperated pitchers nearly as much. Taylor was "double-jointed" and deluded umpires into calling pitches he swung at foul balls because his joints would "crackle on the swing," making a sound like a foul tip, which as yet was not a strike. Most importantly, he was a respected field leader.

3.02 (c)

The bat handle, for not more than 18 inches from its end, may be covered or treated with any material or substance to improve the grip. Any such material or substance, which extends past the 18 inch limitation, shall cause the bat to be removed from the game. Note: If the umpire discovers the bat does not conform to (c) above until a time during or after which the bat has been used in play it shall be grounds for declaring the batter out, or ejected from the game.

Beyond any doubt, the most famous violation in major-league history of Rule 3.02 (c) was the "Pine Tar Incident" in 1983, which began on July 24 at Yankee Stadium in a game between the New York Yankees and the Kansas City Royals, but echoed deep into the offseason and did not culminate until late that December when Commissioner Bowie Kuhn fined the Yankees $250,000 for "certain public statements" made by owner George Steinbrenner about the way American League president Lee MacPhail handled the situation.

The controversy was ignited by Kansas City third baseman George Brett's two-run homer off Yankees reliever Goose Gossage with two out in the ninth inning, putting the Royals ahead, 5–4. As Brett started for the dugout after circling the bases, Yankees manager Billy Martin asked the umpires to check Brett's bat for excessive pine tar. Like many players, Brett used pine tar on his bat handle to improve his grip and prevent blisters. But Martin, after being tipped off by third baseman Graig Nettles, contended the application extended beyond the allowed 18 inches from the end of the handle. Plate umpire Tim McClelland looked at the bat, then consulted with his three associates, and the onus fell on crew chief Joe Brinkman.

When Brinkman measured the pine tar on Brett's bat handle against the 17-inch width of home plate, he discovered the substance exceeded the 18-inch limit by an inch or so. Whereupon the umpires ruled Brett out for using an illegal bat, to nullifying his home run and ending the game with the score reverting to 4–3, New York. Livid with rage, Brett raced back onto the field and had to be physically restrained from taking on the entire umpiring crew. While the argument raged around home plate, Royals pitcher Gaylord Perry furtively snatched Brett's bat. Before he could make off with it, however, he was intercepted by a uniformed guard, who saw to it that the bat was taken to the umpires' dressing room.

The Royals lodged an official protest with commissioner MacPhail. Four days later, MacPhail announced he was upholding the protest, marking the first time in his ten years as American League president that he had overturned an umpire's decision. The commissioner contended the fault lay not with his umpires, however, but with the rule, which needed to be rewritten to make it clear that a bat coated with excessive pine tar was not the same as a doctored bat—one that had been altered to improve the distance factor or to cause an unusual reaction on a batted ball (a corked bat, for instance).

With the protest espoused, the score once again became 5–4, Royals, with two out in the top of the ninth. When MacPhail ruled the game had to be finished at Yankee Stadium on August 18, an open date for both teams, Steinbrenner at first said he'd rather forfeit. The completion of the game eventually took place as ordered by MacPhail in a near-empty ballpark, but not before there was attempt by Yankees fans to get a court injunction barring the game and a last-ditch effort by Billy Martin to have Brett declared out.

As soon as the two clubs took the field on August 18, Martin had his infielders try appeals at first and second base. When the umpires—not the same crew who had worked the original game—gave the safe sign, Martin filed a protest with crew chief Dave Phillips, contending that the four umpires could not know that Brett had touched all the bases on his home-run tour since none of them were in Yankee Stadium on July 24. But Martin's argument had been anticipated. Phillips whipped out a notarized letter signed by Brinkman's crew stating that Brett and U. L. Washington, the runner who had scored ahead of him, had both touched all the bases.

The game took only twelve minutes to complete, as the Yankees meekly went down in order in the bottom of the ninth to seal the 5–4 Royals victory. However, the various court actions that the Yankees launched to have the result quashed were only just beginning. In the end, none of them came to much, but over the winter the Official Playing Rules Committee clarified the so-called "pine tar rule" to stipulate, as per the note in Rule 1.10 (c), that, "a violation of the 18-inch limit shall call for the bat's ejection but not for nullification of any play that results from its use."

Ironically, the Yankees were themselves once victimized by Rule 3.02 (c) [formerly Rule 1.10 (c)] before it was rewritten in such a way as to avert incidents similar to the Brett debacle. In a 1975 game, on July 19 against the Minnesota Twins at Metropolitan Stadium, Yankees catcher Thurman Munson singled in the first inning to drive home a run, but was called out by plate umpire Art Frantz when an inspection of his bat, instigated by Twins manager Frank Quilici, disclosed that the pine tar on it overstepped the 18-inch limit. Billy Martin no doubt was aware of Frantz's ruling eight years earlier when he requested that Brett's bat be checked.

3.03: Player Uniforms

(a) All players on a team shall wear uniforms identical in color, trim and style and all players' uniforms shall include minimal six-inch numbers on their backs.

A question frequently asked by fans unfamiliar with the history of uniforms is: Why have the New York Yankees retired the numbers of all their immortals, such as Ruth, Gehrig, Mantle, and DiMaggio, whereas the Detroit Tigers have never retired Ty Cobb's number? The answer has nothing to do with Cobb's lack of popularity. Rather, it is that Cobb never wore a number during his playing days. Nor for that matter did Walter Johnson, Tris Speaker, Eddie Collins, Honus Wagner, or numerous other stars of Cobb's era.

Although major-league teams as far back as the 1880s wore numbered uniforms on occasion, the experiment always failed, in part because few players fancied bearing a number on their backs like convicts. Not until 1929, when the Cleveland Indians and New York Yankees both adopted wearing numbers on the backs of their uniform blouses, did a team put numbers on its uniforms and keep them there. On May 13, 1929, at Cleveland's League Park, fans were treated for the first time to the spectacle of every player wearing a numbered uniform, and received a further treat when the Indians won, 4–3, behind Willis Hudlin. Two

How, then, did fans go about telling players apart without them wearing numbered uniforms? In truth, they often didn't—not even with a scorecard that listed that particular day's lineups. Changes were oftentimes made at the last minute, and in the early days went unannounced to the general audience. New York Giants bleacher fans in the late 1890s had especial trouble telling Cy Seymour (left) and Mike Tiernan apart, and would often go through an entire game uncertain which one was playing left field, as both were left-handed, clean shaven, and roughly the same height and build.

years later, the American League made numbered uniforms mandatory, but the National League did not follow suit until a year later. Meanwhile, Ty Cobb retired in 1928 before the rule was put into place.

3.03 (c)

No player whose uniform does not conform to that of his teammates shall be permitted to participate in a game.

It has always been customary for all the players on a professional team to wear identical uniforms, but not until 1899 was there a rule that every player on a team's bench had to wear a uniform that exactly matched those of his teammates in both color and style. Prior to then, it had been an unwritten rule that many clubs violated—particularly when on the road and forced to pick up a last-minute substitute. To curtail expenses, teams sometimes took to the road with as few as ten players—the minimum a club could dress at the time—and then hired local amateurs from the city they were visiting when disabling injuries occurred. Often these major-league "temps" were outfitted with makeshift uniforms. In some instances a temp was even allowed to wear the uniform of his amateur club, supplemented by the cap of his major-league team for the day, and on at least one occasion a substitute played in street clothes. In an American Association game at St. Louis on May 10, 1885, John Coleman, a pitcher-outfielder who had not suited up that day, left the bench to replace Bobby Mathews in right field for the Philadelphia Athletics. Mathews had begun the game in the box but switched to right when he hurt his hand. Coleman replaced him in the sixth inning after Browns manager Charlie Comiskey acceded to the A's request for an injury substitution.

In 1882, its first season as a rival major league, the American Association violated the uniform dress code custom for a very different reason, and the National League quickly followed suit. AA teams strove to be as gaudy in their attire as possible. At the opening of the inaugural season, clubs wore silk uniform blouses in as many different colors as there were positions on the diamond. The champion Cincinnati Red Stockings infield dressed as follows: First baseman Dan Stearns wore a candy-striped blouse, Hick Carpenter at third chose all white, and the two keystoners—second sacker Bid McPhee and shortstop Chick Fulmer—showcased purple and yellow-striped and maroon blouses, respectively. The National League, fearing that this innovation, bizarre as it seemed, might be received positively by the public, also voted to adopt color-coded uniforms at its annual meeting on December 9. 1881. The uniform experiment ended swiftly in both leagues after a string of comical on-field incidents made it apparent that fans and players alike were too often confused as to who was friend and who was foe.

The rule that all players must be wearing uniforms of exactly the same color harmed the Cleveland Indians in a 1949 game against the Boston Red Sox on September 20 at Fenway Park. Tribe ace Bob Lemon had a no-hitter going midway through the contest. It was a hot day, and before each pitch Lemon fell into the pattern of tweaking the red bill of his cap to rub the perspiration off his fingers. Observing that Lemon's gestures were causing the bill's color to fade as the game progressed, Red Sox manager Joe McCarthy claimed that it was no longer the same color as the cap bills worn by the rest of the Indians and therefore was not regulation. To avoid a rhubarb that would only further break his rhythm, as was McCarthy's intention, Lemon obligingly changed caps, but the damage was already done. The Red Sox proceeded to knock him out of the box with five runs in the sixth inning. The following day Lemon, ever able to find humor in the game, appeared on the field in pregame practice wearing a fedora.

In the 2005 ALCS, fans had occasion to note that the strictures implied in stipulation (c) of Rule 3.03, as in stipulation (d) of 3.03 (see below), have been relaxed in recent years. Though the TV broadcasting crew made much of the fact that, in Game Two, Los Angeles Angels lefty Jarrod Washburn wore an undershirt with a red left sleeve and the right sleeve cut off at the armpit, an apparent violation of Rule 3.03 (c), White Sox manager Ozzie Guillen never lodged a protest. Since then the rules on uniform uniformity have grown even more permissive. In Game Three of the ALDS at Cleveland between the Astros and Indians on October 9, 2018, Indians third baseman Josh Donaldson wore the sleeve of a polka dot undergarment on his left arm the entire game without provoking comment from anyone. Earlier that season, in a July 4 game at Chavez Ravine, several members of the Pirates (but not all) wore polka dot undergarments, but no Dodgers took issue with it. In fact, polka dot undergarments have become commonplace with some teams. Similarly, players have begun stepping up their demands to wear shoes and cleats in the colors and designs of their choice.

3.03 (d)

A league may provide that each team shall wear a distinctive uniform at all times, or that each team shall have two sets of uniforms, white for home games and a different color for road games.

Another long-standing custom that for many years was not formalized into a rule implored a team to possess two different uniforms; one to wear at home and the other while on the road. This practice first became an actual rule in 1904. Prior to then, it had been customary since the early 1880s for the home team to dress in white and the visitors in gray (or some other darker hue). Not until 1911 did it become mandatory, however, for the home team to wear white uniforms and the visitors dark uniforms as a way for fans, players, and umpires alike to distinguish more easily the players on one club from the other.

In recent years, "may" has become the operative word in Rule 3.03 (d). Many major-league teams in the mid-1990s began wearing dark uniform tops at home, and some of the teams using dark tops at home also wore them on the road. The result is that, on occasion, the easiest way for a fan quickly to distinguish between the home and road team today, when both are wearing nearly identical dark tops (usually black), is to observe the uniform pants, which remain white for home teams and gray for road teams. The socks can also be a distinguishing feature—but not in all cases, since many players now, rather than the traditional knickers style, wear long uniform pants that cover their socks.

Putting a player's name on the back of his uniform jersey has been

Special dispensation has to be granted from the commissioner's office for a player to wear any name other than his surname on his jersey. The most recent player to be granted this privilege was Ichiro Suzuki, seen above.

part of baseball for over half a century. It originated in 1960 by Bill Veeck while he owned the White Sox as a way of creating extra revenue by selling replica jerseys. Many of the smaller market teams still do it—especially when playing at home—but some of the wealthier clubs do not, although they encourage their souvenir shops to peddle jerseys with the names of their players on them. The Yankees are currently the only club that refuses to put names on both their home and road jerseys (though if you go to a store you can easily purchase a shirt or jersey with a player's name, both past and present).

3.03 (e)

Sleeve lengths may vary for individual players, but the sleeves of each individual player shall be approximately the same length, and no player shall wear ragged, frayed or slit sleeves.

Rule 3.03 (e) is comparatively new to the manual and was formerly Rule 1.11 (c). When the entire rule book was rewritten prior to the 1950 season, it was spelled out for the first time that a pitcher could not wear a garment with ragged, frayed, or slit sleeves, but long before then umpires had begun making pitchers shed offending garments, albeit on an arbitrary basis. One who escaped punishment for many years was Dazzy Vance, whose blazing fastball was rendered all the more effective by the tattered right undershirt sleeve he flourished over the vehement protests of rival batsmen.

Cleveland Indians hurler Johnny Allen was not so fortunate. Long known for his monumental temper tantrums, Allen faced the Boston Red Sox in Fenway Park on June 7, 1938, with umpire Bill McGowan behind the plate. Allen and McGowan had crossed swords before, so the stage was set for sparks to fly as soon as Allen began to complain about McGowan's decisions on pitches.

In the second inning, McGowan stopped play, strolled out to the mound, and told Allen he would have to cut off the part of his sweatshirt sleeve where he had cut diamond-shaped holes for ventilation, which made the sleeve wave whenever he delivered a pitch, a distraction to the batter. Allen refused to either remove the shirt or shorten the offending sleeve, and when he was confronted again in the top of the third inning, he stalked off the mound and vanished into the Cleveland clubhouse. Indians manager Ozzie Vitt promptly took him out of the game and fined him $250.

The offending shirt became a *cause célèbre*. When Cleveland owner Alva Bradley learned of the incident, he bought the shirt from Allen for $250—in effect paying the fine for his pitcher—and had it mounted in a glass showcase of the Higbee Company, a Cleveland department store. Bradley contended that the Higbee Company, and not he, had purchased the shirt, which may technically have been true. Bradley's brother, Chuck, was the president of the Higbee Company at the time. By then the entire country knew the tale of Allen's frayed temper and tattered sleeve. His shirt was eventually placed in the Hall of Fame as a reminder of one of the game's wooliest episodes.

3.03 (i)

No player shall attach anything to the heel or toe of his shoe other than the ordinary shoe plate or toe plate. Shoes with pointed spikes similar to golf or track shoes shall not be worn.

In the early days it was recommended but not mandatory that a player wear spikes attached to his shoes. Interestingly, most players then wore shoes of the same high-top design that is now the rage in baseball gear. Later all clubs made wearing spikes mandatory. The last player on record to be fined for not wearing spikes on his shoes was Pete Browning when he was with the Pittsburgh Pirates in 1891. Browning hated to slide and lived in fear of having his spikes catch when he did so. He nonetheless stole his share of bases.

Players have never been permitted to wear golf or track spikes for obvious reasons: No second baseman or shortstop would ever have stood in to take a throw at the keystone sack on a steal attempt if a Ty Cobb or a Rickey Henderson had come into the bag with track spikes flying.

During the 1976 season, several players—including Dan Ford of the Minnesota Twins and Matt Alexander of the Oakland As—briefly wore spikes similar to those on golf shoes before a rival manager spotted the violation and protested to umpires, forcing the offending players to change to shoes with regulation spikes.

3.03 (j)

No part of the uniform shall include patches or designs relating to commercial advertisements.

Without the comparatively recent addition of this rule addendum, one can readily imagine that the uniform jerseys of some of today's players would resemble the uniform blouses of five-star generals. Rule 3.09 similarly applies to all playing equipment including gloves, bats, the bases, the pitching rubber, and both the pitcher's toe plate and home plate.

3.04 Catcher's Mitt

The catcher may wear a leather mitt not more than 38 inches in circumference, nor more than 15½ inches from top to bottom. Such limits shall include all lacing and any leather band or facing attached to the outer edge of the mitt. The space between the thumb section and the finger section of the mitt shall not exceed six inches at the top of the mitt and four inches at the base of the thumb crotch. The web shall measure not more than seven inches across the top or more than six inches from its top to the base of the thumb crotch . . .

In a sense, it was Hoyt Wilhelm—and other knuckleballers of his ilk— who generated a rule limiting the size of a catcher's mitt. To help Gus Triandos and his other catchers handle Wilhelm while he was with the Orioles from 1958 to 1962, Baltimore manager Paul Richards had an elephantine mitt constructed that resembled the gigantic mockery of the catcher's mitt that Al Schacht, the Clown Prince of baseball during the 1920s and 1930s, utilized in his comedy act. Even with the oversized mitt, Triandos still set all sorts of modern records for passed balls. On May 4, 1960, he became the first backstop in American League history to let three pitches get by him in a single inning. Less than a week later, Triandos's backup receiver with the Orioles, Joe Ginsberg, tied his record. In 1962, another Baltimore catcher, Charlie Lau, fell victim three times in a single inning to the butterfly pitch.

After the 1964 season, the rules committee limited the size of a catcher's mitt—not that the lack of a restriction had ever seemed to offer much help to Triandos and the other receivers who had to cope with Wilhelm. In 1965, the first year the new rule was in effect, Wilhelm, by then with the White Sox, contributed heavily to the 33 passed balls Sox catcher J. C. Martin committed to set a post-1900 major-league season record. But Martin is only tied for 221st on the all-time list. In the nineteenth century, until the pitching distance was increased in 1893, the 1891 season was the only one in which no catcher had at least 50 passed balls.

3.05: First Baseman's Glove

The first baseman may wear a leather glove or mitt not more than thirteen inches long from top to bottom and not more than eight inches wide across the palm, measured from the base of the thumb crotch to the outer edge of the mitt. The space between the thumb section and the finger section of the mitt shall not exceed four inches at the top of the mitt and three and one-half inches at the base of the thumb crotch. The mitt shall be constructed so that this space is permanently fixed and cannot be enlarged, extended, widened, or deepened by the use of any materials or process whatsoever. The web of the mitt shall measure not more than five inches from its top to the base of the thumb crotch . . .

The 1895 season was the first that addressed gloves. As late as 1938, first basemen could still use a glove of any size or shape they wished. Detroit first baseman Hank Greenberg brought this custom to a halt when he concocted a glove with a web that looked like a fishing net. Prior to the 1939 season, a rule was inserted that a first baseman's glove could no longer be more than 12 inches from top to bottom and no more than eight inches across the palm and connected by leather lacing of no more than four inches from thumb to palm. The "Trapper" model, which first appeared in

Michael "Doc" Kennedy was the last known professional player other than a pitcher to play barehanded. He began his career as a catcher with a Memphis club in 1876, spent a short time in the majors, and finished in 1901 at age forty-seven as a gloveless minor-league first baseman with Buffalo of the Eastern League, although he may have worn a glove that season in the few games he caught.

1941 and quickly became the standard glove for the first base position, was circumspectly designed to conform to the new rule.

3.06 Fielding Gloves

Each fielder, other than the catcher, may use or wear a leather glove. The measurements covering size of glove shall be made by measuring front side or ball receiving side of glove. The tool or measuring tape shall be placed to contact the surface or feature of item being measured and follow all contours in the process. The glove shall not measure more than 13 inches from the tip of any one of the four fingers, through the ball pocket to the bottom edge or heel of glove. The glove shall not measure more than 7¾ inches wide, measured from the inside seam at base of first finger, along base of other fingers, to the outside edge of little finger edge of glove. The space or area between the thumb and first finger, called crotch, may be filled with leather webbing or back stop . . .

Prior to 1895, the rules said nothing about the size and shape of fielders' gloves for the simple reason that for many years no self-respecting player would stoop to wearing a glove in the field. By the mid-1870s many catchers had begun using protective mittens while behind the bat and a few players, such as Al Spalding, also sported gloves that were employed more to protect their hands than to aid in catching the ball. However, gloves did not become a standard item of equipment until the late 1880s—even then a number of players disdained fielding a ball with anything but their bare flesh. The last two bare-handed major leaguers of note

Bid McPhee, the best second baseman in Cincinnati Reds history prior to Joe Morgan and the last documented major leaguer to play without a glove. Largely because he spent a significant portion of his career in the rebel American Association, McPhee was forced to wait until 2000 before being selected for the Hall of Fame.

were second baseman Bid McPhee and third sacker Jerry Denny. Both balked at the notion of using a glove until the 1890s. Indeed, McPhee did not first wear a glove in the field until April 18, 1895, in an Opening Day game against the Cleveland Spiders.

Meanwhile, other players had long since recognized the advantages a glove could provide. When some began designing contraptions the size of manhole covers, a rule was devised in 1895 limiting fielders to gloves that could not be over 10 ounces in weight or more than 14 inches in circumference around the palm of the hand. Catchers and first basemen were exempted from any restrictions on the size or weight of their gloves, but were made to switch to a smaller glove if they played another position. For years afterward, however, it was still common practice for a former catcher like Lave Cross to use a modified catcher's mitt to play the infield—especially third base—as long as his mitt did not exceed the proscribed 10-ounce weight and 14 inches in circumference.

3.08: Helmets

A Professional League shall adopt the following rule pertaining to the use of helmets:

Of the six appendices regarding helmet requirements and usage, several were long overdue when they were added—tragically long overdue. Among them is 3.08 (e) requiring all base coaches to wear protective helmets. It followed the stunning death of Tulsa Drillers first-base coach Mike Coolbaugh on July 22, 2007, after being struck while in his coach's box by a line drive off the bat of Drillers catcher Tino Sanchez in the ninth inning of a Texas League game against the Arkansas Travelers. Sanchez's blow struck Coolbaugh in the neck and destroyed his left vertabral artery, causing so severe a brain hemorrhage that he was virtually killed on impact. It is uncertain that even a standard protective helmet would have served as an adequate preventative measure in this instance.

The 1971 season was the first when it became mandatory for batters to wear protective helmets, but most had adopted them long before then. In 1941, the Brooklyn Dodgers became the first team to wear plastic headguards after Pete Reiser, Joe Medwick, and several of the team's other stars were beaned. By 1957, the American League had recognized the need for protective headgear and made it obligatory. Batters had the option, though, of using plastic wafers in their caps, which offered less protection than a helmet—particularly one with ear flaps—but were more comfortable. The 1971 rule contained a codicil that permitted veteran players who preferred plastic wafers to helmets to use wafers for the remainder of their careers. Former catcher Bob Montgomery (1970–79) was among those who declined to wear a helmet, and has claimed that he was the last to bat in a major-league game without one.

Game photos from the 1960s reflect that some batters began wearing helmets on the bases even before the mandatory rule to wear them while batting was instigated. But curiously, the mandatory rule to wear them on the bases was not adopted until 2010.

3.10: Equipment On The Field

(a) Members of the offensive team shall carry all gloves and other equipment off the field and to the dugout while their team is at bat. No equipment shall be left lying on the field, either in fair or foul territory.

Only someone under the age of seventy could ask if there is any truth to the tale that players in the old days were permitted to leave their gloves on the playing field while their team was at bat. But then many who are not yet senior citizens might consider 1953 the old days. That was the final season in which players on all levels could leave their gloves in the field when they came in to bat. The last players permitted to do so were the eight members of the New York Yankees who discarded them before they came to bat in the bottom of the ninth inning in Game Six of the 1953 World Series. The game at that point was tied 3–3, and saw the Yankees score the run that gave them the game, 4–3, and clinched the Series over Brooklyn, four games to two. Among the eight were seven of the usual suspects on the 1953 Yankees such as Mickey Mantle, Phil Rizzuto, and Gil McDougald, plus the one name that is guaranteed to win you a bar bet against even the most rabid Yankees' fan you are likely to meet in your lifetime: first baseman Don Bollweg.

The popular custom was for outfielders to deposit their gloves near their positions, infielders to spread theirs around the edge of the outfield grass, pitchers to disgard theirs in foul territory, and catchers to haul their fielding tools into the dugout. Many players also left their sunglasses in the field, folded inside their gloves.

A thrown or batted ball that struck a glove left on the field was in play, and if a fielder tripped on a glove while chasing a hit, it was considered an occupational hazard. Everyone wondered how an umpire would rule if a fielder, while diving for a line drive, caught it with an opponent's glove after somehow getting his bare hand entangled in it. But this unlikely event never happened (at least to our knowledge). What often *did* happen was that teammates or opponents of squeamish players would tuck rubber snakes and such in their gloves while they were left unattended and then wait for their owners to shriek when the repellent discovery was made.

Probably no one alive today ever witnessed a major-league game in which a batted ball or a player was affected by a glove lying on the field. Some fifty years earlier, however, on September 28, 1905, in a game that was instrumental in deciding the American League pennant, the Philadelphia A's edged the Chicago White Sox, 3–2, when Topsy Hartsel scored the winning run from second base after Harry Davis's single to short left field struck Hartsel's glove, which he had left on the outfield grass when he came in to bat.

Rule 3.10 (originally Rule 3.14) was implemented in part for general safety, as by the mid-1950s improvements in design had created gloves with deeper pockets and fortified with webbing so intricate as to be a potential menace to fielders. No actual incidents were cited for this sudden change. After the new rule was adopted, some players, out of habit, continued to leave their gloves on the field until an umpire admonished them. Once in a while, before a glove was ordered removed, it would be allowed to remain on the field for a time, perhaps as a lorn reminder of a vestigial custom of the game whose passing most did not even know to mourn until long after the fact.

3.10 (b)

The use of any markers on the field that create a tangible reference system on the field is prohibited.

This rule was devised prior to the 2017 season after the New York Mets challenged the Dodgers' use of a laser system to aid in positioning their outfielders in a game at the Mets' Citi Field. The Dodgers argued that they had routinely made physical markings in the Dodger Stadium outfield and had offered opposing teams the same courtesy. Mets manager Terry Collins complained, "You just don't go paint somebody else's field." Note that the new rule bans the use of physical markings but does not explicitly ban the use of lasers.

The illegal use of electronic devices in baseball suddenly became front-page news in January 2020 when the Houston Astros were punished for using a video camera positioned in center field of their home park during the 2017 season—their lone championship to date—to steal catchers' signs. Team personnel, led by skipper A. J. Hinch and bench coach Alex Cora, watched the feed in a hallway between the clubhouse and dugout and then relayed what kind of pitch was coming by hitting a trash can with a bat. Houston's proscribed use of electronics to steal catchers' signs, though suspected, was not exposed in all its glory until former Astros hurler Mike Fiers told his Oakland teammates about it in 2019.

The investigation into the charge resulted in the Astros being heavily fined and stripped of their first- and second-round draft choices in 2020 and 2021. In addition, Houston general manager Jeff Luhnow and manager A. J. Hinch were suspended from baseball for a year and later fired by the club. Cora was also suspended for a year, and then bounced from his managerial post with the Red Sox; while Carlos Beltran, a key member of the 2017 Astros' sign-stealing crew who retired after the season and had signed to manage the Mets in 2020, agreed with the club to part ways soon after the scandal broke. No active players were penalized because investigators and the MLB Players Association struck a bargain early in the process that granted immunity in exchange for honest testimony. It was widely believed that MLB was quick to make such a generous offer largely because it did not think it could win subsequent grievances with any players it attempted to discipline.

Whether the Astros profited significantly from their crime against the game is debatable. In both 2017 and 2018, their offensive numbers and won-lost records were better on the road than at home. Although they did better at home than on the road in 2019, the club dropped the seven-game World Series to the Washington Nationals after losing all four in their home park while winning each of their three road games by lopsided margins.

Sign stealing in baseball is as old as the first team to be detected giving its players "secret" signals. It is perfectly legal—except when it utilizes systems or techniques that MLB has formally banned. Few pundits imagine the Astros have been alone in recent years in working to gain an illegal edge, just as few believe that none of the current plaque owners in the Hall of Fame used PEDs. Rogers Hornsby once acknowledged that he'd cheated, or somebody on his team had cheated in almost every single game he'd been in, and other great players have made similar admissions. So, then, why were the Astros dealt with so harshly? One school of thought is the dark cloud that currently looms over their entire organization first started forming in the early 2010s when they were believed to be tanking year after year to gather top draft picks and accrue added money to spend on signing amateur free agents who were not part of the draft. True or not, they are at present the face of modern technology's advantageous usage in sports at its worst.

4.00: Game Preliminaries

4.01 Umpire Duties

Before the game begins the umpire shall:

(a) Require strict observance of all rules governing implements of play and equipment of players;

(b) Be sure that all playing lines (heavy lines on Appendices No. 1 and No.2) are marked with lime, chalk or other white material easily distinguishable from the ground or grass;

(c) Receive from the home club a supply of regulation baseballs, the number and make to be certified to the home club by the League President. The umpire shall inspect the baseballs and ensure they are regulation baseballs and that they are properly rubbed so that the gloss is removed. The umpire shall be the sole judge of the fitness of the balls to be used in the game;

As per 4.01 (c), it was originally the challenging team's duty to provide the game ball. If, say, the Pittsburgh Pirates were to challenge the Philadelphia Phillies for bragging rights in the State of Pennsylvania, the rules in 1858 would have bade the Pirates to spring for the sphere regardless of where the game was played.

When teams began to meet for more than a single contest, the policy was for the visiting nine to furnish the balls if a series of games was played, and the home side to do so if the match called for only one game. In either case, at the close of each game the ball became the property of the victorious club. Even after the job of supplying the balls fell to the home team, this custom was retained. In 1887, when the National League and American Association first agreed to be governed by the same rules, both circuits stipulated that the last ball in play belonged to the winning team, and custom further dictated that the fielder who registered the last out fell heir to the ball. Challenges to this custom were few prior to 2004, when the ball that Boston first baseman Doug Mientkiewicz caught to register the final out in the World Series and thereupon end the Red Sox' eighty-six-year championship drought became a highly coveted trophy. Twelve years later, the ball that first baseman Anthony Rizzo caught to end the Cubs' 108-year championship drought was equally treasured.

4.01 (d)

Be assured by the home club that at least one dozen regulation reserve balls are immediately available for use if required;

Rule 4.01 (d) has come a long way. As late as 1887, the home team in both major leagues had to furnish the umpire with just two new balls; to be given him prior to a game and enclosed in a paper box that was secured with a seal of the secretary of either the National League or American Association. Upon receiving the sealed boxes, the umpire would call "Play" and then break open both of them in the presence of the two rival team captains. If either of the two game balls was lost or damaged to an extent that it could no longer be used, the home team was required to replace it with another new ball so that an umpire would always have an extra ball on his person. Balls were so reluctantly replaced for good reason; they were handmade and much more expensive than they are now. Consequently, prior to 1887, teams would often try to introduce worn balls into the game that had previously been used for batting or infield practice.

In the early years of professional play, the home team had to furnish the umpire with just one new ball and there was no rule that it had to be given in a sealed box. Frugal teams would remove a new ball from play after it had been served up to the required leadoff batter of the game and substitute a used ball. If the leadoff batter was luckless enough to make out on the first pitch, the new ball would only be in play for that one at-bat. This practice encouraged pitchers on the clubs that utilized it to lay the first pitch in there, hoping to retire the leadoff batter as speedily as possible and so preserve the team's new ball. Oftentimes the so-called "new" ball would be used in this manner for several games before an opponent or an umpire refused to accept it as new any longer.

4.01 (e)

Have in his possession at least two alternate balls and shall require replenishment of such supply of alternate balls as needed throughout the game. Such alternate balls shall be put in play when:

(1) A ball has been batted out of the playing field or into the spectator area;

(2) A ball has become discolored or unfit for further use;

(3) The pitcher requests such alternate ball.

Until fairly deep into the twentieth century, spectators were expected—and in some parks mandated—to return all balls hit into the stands, whether fair or foul, which were often put back into play. As late as the 1930s in some major-league parks, any fan that attempted to keep a ball he snared invited a struggle with the ballpark security force for possession of it.

In 1916, Cubs owner Charles Weeghman brought an end to the warfare in Wrigley Field (then called Weeghman Park) between park policemen and fans seeking souvenir balls when he opted to cede all balls hit into the stands. But other teams were loath to be so generous. In 1923, a Phillies fan, eleven-year-old Robert Cotter, was arrested and housed for several hours in the slammer for refusing to relinquish a ball hit into the Baker Bowl bleachers during a Phils game. Fourteen years later, ushers assaulted a New York fan when he tried to retrieve a foul ball that had become lodged in the home-plate screen at Yankee Stadium. His suit against the Yankees in 1937, which the club ultimately settled for $7,500, resulted in an unofficial truce between fans and major league teams on the issue.

Likewise, balls hit out of the park were customarily returned to the playing field—at least until the tail end of the nineteenth century. Most teams stationed guards and, sometimes, even substitute players outside the park to wrestle with passersby for balls fouled out of its confines and home runs that cleared the outfield barriers.

Prior to 1886, an umpire was required to wait five minutes before declaring a ball hit out of the playing field lost and putting a new ball in play. Even after 1886, teams continued to chase down balls hit out of the park and return them to play (depending on their condition). Whether a ball was still playable was often the subject of a furious debate. In a Union Association game between the Washington Nationals and St. Louis Maroons at St. Louis on October 11, 1884, St. Louis won by forfeit when Washington refused to continue after arguing in vain that a ball fouled out of the park in the fourth inning by Maroons pitcher Henry Boyle was too lopsided to be kept in play by the time it was returned.

Some four years later, American Association umpire Herman Doscher levied more than $300 in fines during a dispute midway through a game on July 6, 1888, between Cincinnati and Philadelphia. Doscher contended that a ball knocked over the outfield fence was useless when it came back covered with mud, and threw it out of play, overriding the protests of Athletics pitcher Gus Weyhing. After Doscher broke out a new ball, A's center fielder Curt Welch snatched it and heaved it out of the Cincinnati park, prompting Doscher to tender his resignation after the game and aver that "he would not again pass through such a scene." Under prodding, he nonetheless finished out the season before quitting for good. By 1890, Doscher had succumbed to the itch to get back into the game and umpired again in the American Association, but when he quit this time after facing the same magnitude of player belligerence, it really was for keeps.

Rarely was a ball taken out of play in the nineteenth century or, for that matter, in the early part of the twentieth century merely because it was heavily stained by grass or mud or tobacco juice or any combination thereof. No one worried whether the ball remained white and easily visible, only that it remained reasonably round and was not bursting at the seams.

By the early 1920s, however, umpires were encouraged to remove balls that were discolored or difficult for players to see. The one incident that more than any other forced both major leagues to stop economizing on the price of balls occurred at the Polo Grounds on August 16, 1920. That afternoon the New York Yankees entertained the first-place Cleveland

Indians on the home site they shared at the time with the New York Giants. Pitching for the Yankees was Carl Mays, who delivered the ball with an underhand sweep that was a challenge for batters to follow even when visibility was good, and conditions that afternoon were execrable. By the top of the fifth inning, when shortstop Ray Chapman led off for the Indians, a light drizzle was falling. The ball Mays held was damp and mudstained. Down he dipped and swung his arm. His submarine delivery shot out of bleachers in the deep background of the Polo Grounds.

The following day, the *Cleveland Press* reported, "Mays tossed an inshoot that seemed to hypnotize Chapman, or else he miscalculated it and believed the ball would sail by. Anyhow, it struck him on the temple, fracturing his skull, and paralyzing the nerve chords, making it impossible for him to talk."

After the beaning, Chapman underwent a delicate brain operation that evening and then lingered for several hours before passing away during the night. Mays was at first accused of deliberately throwing at Chapman, and there was a push—particularly in Cleveland—to charge him with manslaughter before he was exonerated of any wrongdoing. But in any event, Chapman's death, the only confirmed fatality resulting directly from an injury suffered in a major-league game, hastened long-overdue legislation to remove balls from play as soon as they become scuffed or discolored.

Balls were taken out of play long before the Chapman incident, however, if they were severely damaged. In 1882, the National League introduced a rule to allow an umpire, at the request of either team captain, to call for a new ball at the end of any completed inning if the old ball was badly ripped to expose its yarn or otherwise cut or misshapen. The American Association adopted the same rule, but authorized an umpire to replace a ball even if neither captain appealed to him. A year later, the NL permitted an umpire to replace a ball "at once" if in his judgment it was no longer fit for play, but the AA continued to direct its umpires to wait for the close of an inning until the two adopted the same rule book in 1887. Seldom, though, was a ball declared unfit for play unless it was clearly damaged. Typical of the time was a National League game between the Philadelphia Quakers (now the NL's Phillies) and Cleveland Blues on September 13, 1883. Played at Cleveland's Recreation Park after a heavy rain, the contest pitted Philadelphia's John Coleman against Hugh "One

Arm" Daily of the Blues. Coleman, loser in 1883 of a major-league record 48 games, was virtually unhittable that afternoon, but Daily was *literally* unhittable. Despite a boyhood accident that deprived him of his left forearm and obliged him to play with a pad attached to the stump of his amputated limb as an aid to fielding his position, Daily set the Phils down without a safety in a 1–0 win. Phillies followers met his hitless gem with contempt, though. One account of the game said the rain had rendered the field in a "wretchedly soggy condition and this soon made the ball so mushy it was impossible to hit if effectively."

No umpire in 1883 would have considered replacing the ball Daily hurled in his no-hitter solely because it was waterlogged. In fact, if a ball was not lost or visibly damaged, it could remain in play for the entire game. On August 4, 1908, the St. Louis Cardinals and Brooklyn Dodgers played a full nine innings at Brooklyn's Washington Park III using just one ball. That is not to say this was the last game of its kind, only that there was a documented instance of one as late as 1908. The contest lasted an hour and 25 minutes, with Brooklyn winning, 3–0.

Some historians have mistakenly attributed Ray Chapman's fatal beaning partly to the fact that pitchers in 1920 could still legally throw spitballs and also apply almost any foreign substance imaginable to a ball, in addition to hurling scuffed and discolored balls. But actually, the rule abolishing the spitball, the shine ball, the emery ball, the licorice ball, and all other deliveries that licensed a hurler to soil, deface, or in any way mar the texture of a ball was instituted on February 9, 1920, some six months before Chapman was beaned. A "grandfather clause" provision allowed each team to designate a maximum of two spitball pitchers for the 1920 season at least ten days prior to April 14, 1920, or the opening day of the campaign, and stated that thereafter none would be allowed. Mays was not among the seventeen grandfathered pitchers.

Though the spitball had ostensibly been banned by the time of the Chapman incident, there were several spitball pitchers still legally plying their trade. Most were hurlers who relied so heavily on the spitball that depriving them of it would have severely impaired their chances of continuing to earn a living at the major-league level.

Following the 1920 season, eight National League and nine American League pitchers were granted special dispensation to permanently continue to throw spitballs for the rest of their careers. Three of them—Stan

Coveleski, Red Faber, and Burleigh Grimes—went on to fashion careers that were subsequently deemed worthy of the Hall of Fame. Had the spitball been removed from their arsenal, all of them might have instead suffered the fate of the many skilled practitioners of the spitball in the late teens that had not yet advanced to the major leagues. Since they were not on the exempted "grandfather" list, these pitchers were forbidden from throwing a spitter in the event they reached the majors, though they were permitted to continue using the spitball in the minors. A few, like Hal Carlson, nevertheless worked their way up to the majors after developing other pitches to replace the spitter, but most languished in the minors for the remainder of their careers. Among them were Frank Shellenback and Paul Wachtel, both of whom had pitched in the majors prior to the spitball abolition, but not enough to be included on the exempted list. Subsequent to 1920, Shellenback won a record 295 games in the Pacific Coast League and Wachtel dominated the Texas League, collecting a record 233 wins in that circuit.

4.01 (f)

Ensure that an official rosin bag is placed on the ground behind the pitcher's plate prior to the start of each game.

Rosin Bags were first introduced before the 1926 season, when it was finally acknowledged that pitchers had been operating at an enormous handicap ever since the spitball and other freak deliveries were abolished in 1920. Since no one wanted to encourage hurlers to spit on their hands to get a better grip on the ball, small, finely meshed sealed bags containing rosin were provided by both major leagues for the umpires to hand out to pitchers. Since pitchers today are permitted to moisten their pitching hand and then wipe it dry as long as they are off the rubber, some will never seek a rosin bag for their entire careers.

4.02 Field Manager

(a) The club shall designate the manager to the League President or the umpire-in-chief not less than thirty minutes before the scheduled starting time of the game.

In the early professional game, the individual on a team who performed the same functions as a manager does today was generally called a field captain and was drawn from the ranks of the team's active players. A prime example was Adrian Anson, who was dubbed "Cap" when he assumed the captaincy of the Chicago White Stockings in 1879. Working in conjunction with the field captain on most teams was a manager, responsible for making travel arrangements, paying players, enforcing fines, etc. On some teams both roles were handled by one man, who sometimes also was the majority club owner. Charlie Byrne was the archetypal owner-manager who consulted with and answered only to himself when he ran the Brooklyn Bridegrooms in the mid-1880s. The last owner-manager to borrow Byrne's playbook was Judge Fuchs, who occupied the Boston Braves dugout for the entire 1929 season (although Ted Turner tried it with his Atlanta Braves for one best-forgotten game in 1977, and Connie Mack owned a piece of the Philadelphia Athletics during most of his long sojourn with the team).

Even by Byrne's time, few owners were still so egocentric as to act at the field helms of their clubs, and most teams now called the individual who filled this role as the manager. Playing managers remained common, but the two best teams during the 1890s, the Boston Beaneaters and the Baltimore Orioles, were skippered by Frank Selee and Ned Hanlon—men who were exclusively bench pilots during their pennant-winning seasons. By then the duties that the manager had formerly executed were in most cases the province of another club official, often the secretary.

4.02 (b)

The manager may advise the umpire-in-chief that he has delegated specific duties prescribed by the rules to a player or coach, and any action of such designated representative shall be official. The manager shall always be responsible for his team's conduct, observance of the official rules, and deference to the umpires.

It was common in the nineteenth century for non-playing managers such as Jim Mutrie and Frank Selee to sit on their team's bench in street clothes (at that time consisting of a tie and sometimes hat) and leave all on-field responsibilities to one of their players. In Selee's case, soon after he took the reins of the Boston National League club, he rarely left the Boston bench and handed over the team's leadership to third baseman Billy Nash. On some days Selee did not appear at the park at all but spent the afternoon scouting a prospective player at a minor-league or amateur game near where his Beaneaters were playing. What was never seen in the nineteenth century was a non-playing manager sitting day after day on his team's bench in full uniform. To this day, no one knows for certain what manager initiated this custom, but John McGraw is the most likely candidate.

4.02 (c)

If a manager leaves the field, he shall designate a player or coach as his substitute, and such substitute manager shall have the duties, rights and responsibilities of the manager. If the manager fails or refuses to designate his substitute before leaving, the umpire-in-chief shall designate a team member as substitute manager.

Many managers over the years have continued to manage their clubs from the deep recesses of the dugout, or even from a spot in the stands after being ejected from a game. Before there were dugouts or sheltered stands, let alone cellphones and such, ejected managers had to be particularly resourceful. In 1884, Ted Sullivan, the player-manager of the Union Association's Kansas City Cowboys, had on his squad a pitcher named William Walter "Peak-A-Boo" Veach. There are two stories as to how Veach acquired his nickname. It was sometimes said that he was named after "Peak-A-Boo," a popular song written by the actor-comedian W. J. Scanlan for his Irish comedy *Myles Aroon*. The version Veach preferred was that he got the nickname with Kansas City in 1884 because he was so poor at watching the bases that Sullivan would sit on the bench and tip him when to throw to first to catch a runner off base. During games in which Sullivan was ejected while Veach was pitching, he would hide behind a pole and hold out a stick to signal Veach. The stance Veach took in the box so as to watch Sullivan without making it apparent where his ejected manager was hiding made him look as if he were peeking over his shoulder at something. Eventually teammates shortened the nickname to "Peekie," but Veach continued to sign his letters "Walter Willie Veach" or

"Peak-A-Boo Veach," and there were many of them, almost all of which were eagerly printed by the newspapers to which they were mailed. As but one example, in 1901, Veach wrote to *The Sporting News*: "I have just received an offer to coach the Blind Asylum team. That will be a job out of sight. However, I will consider it carefully as I don't want to go at anything blindly."

4.03 Exchange of Lineup Cards

Unless the home club shall have given previous notice that the game has been postponed or will be delayed in starting, the umpire, or umpires, shall enter the playing field five minutes before the hour set for the game to begin and proceed directly to home base where they shall be met by the managers of the opposing teams. In sequence:

(e) As soon as the home team's batting order is handed to the umpire-in-chief the umpires are in charge of the playing field and from that moment the umpire-in-chief shall have sole authority to determine when a game shall be called, suspended or resumed on account of weather or the condition of the playing field. The umpire-in-chief shall not call the game until at least 30 minutes after he has suspended play. The umpire-in-chief may continue the suspension so long as he believes there is any chance to resume play. Nothing in this Rule is intended to affect a Club's ability to suspend or resume any game pursuant to a policy governing severe weather, significant weather threats, and lightning safety that has been filed with the league office prior to the championship season.

Prior to the 1896 season, it was left to the judgment of the home team captain whether the field was fit to continue after play had been stopped. Naturally, this had high potential for abuse. A home side trailing, 10–0, before a game had gone the required five innings to become an official contest was unlikely to want to continue to play if there was a single drop of water on the field that could be cited as a possible hazard. Conversely, the home captain was apt to wait until dark before calling a game if his team happened to be down a run in the late innings when the heavens opened.

The first upheld American League forfeit fell under the post-1896 rule change. It came in Chicago on May 2, 1901, barely a week after the rival major league first opened its gates for regular season play. With a steady rain falling and the skies ever darkening, the home team, behind the pitching of team captain Clark Griffith, held a 5–2 lead over Detroit in the ninth inning with two out when third baseman Fred Hartman made a wild throw to first. Within minutes, Detroit had raced to a 6–5 lead. Griffith at that point began pressuring umpire Tommy Connolly to stop the game due to the intensifying rain, expecting that darkness would fall soon thereafter and force the score to revert to the previous inning. But Connolly refused to halt play and issued repeated warnings to Griffith for stalling. Griffith proceeded to walk Tigers second baseman Kid Gleason and attempted to do the same with right fielder Ducky Holmes, but Holmes doubled, plating Gleason and giving Detroit a 7–5 lead. Holmes then ran illegally from second to home, begging to be declared out so the top half of the inning could end—but Connolly had seen enough and forfeited the game to Detroit. Had Griffith managed to hold off the umpire for just a minute or two longer, he would have gotten his wish for a rain stoppage that under the old rule would have allowed him as field manager to call the game on account of darkness with Chicago winning, 5–2. The skies burst into a torrential downpour almost immediately after Connolly's forfeit proclamation, but the deluge did not stop the crowd from rushing the field, attempting to get at the umpire. One fan reportedly took a swing at him before he could escape to a dugout. Chicago president and former player Charlie Comiskey hurried down to the field from his grandstand box and was able to scatter the angry fans.

Because Detroit had taken the lead before the forfeit was declared, the Tigers' Emil Frisk received credit for the win and player-manager Griffith, who was as responsible as anyone for his team's stalling tactics, took the loss. After the series between the two teams, which was clogged with kicking and bickering, *Sporting Life* observed, "Connolly will have to get up more nerve if he expects to succeed in the American League."

Kid Gleason would later be the manager of Chicago during the 1919–20 Black Sox scandal. In 1953, despite his extremely rocky and at times spineless start at officiating in the majors, Connolly shared the honor with Bill Klem of being the first two umpires voted into the Hall of Fame.

4.05 Special Ground Rules

The manager of the home team shall present to the umpire-in-chief and the opposing manager any ground rules he thinks necessary covering the overflow of spectators upon the playing field, batted or thrown balls into such overflow, or any other contingencies. If these rules are acceptable to the opposing manager they shall be legal. If these rules are unacceptable to the opposing manager, the umpire-in-chief shall make and enforce any special ground rules he thinks are made necessary by ground conditions, which shall not conflict with the official playing rules.

A prime example of a special ground rule of the type depicted in this rule occurred in the very first modern World Series in 1903 between the Pittsburgh Pirates and Boston Americans. The two clubs played to overflow crowds in several games at both Boston's Huntington Park and Pittsburgh's Exposition Park, located in Allegheny, Pennsylvania. When the Series moved from Boston to Exposition Park in Game Four, the two managers—Fred Clarke of the Pirates and Jimmy Collins of the Americans—agreed to call any ball that rolled under a rope holding back the overflow crowd in fair territory a ground-rule triple. As a result, a Series-record 17 triples were hit in the four games in Pittsburgh alone, and Tommy Leach of the Pirates set an individual Series mark with four three-baggers. Boston ultimately won the fray, five games to three.

Twelve years later, the Boston club, known by then as the Red Sox, was again the beneficiary of another overflow-crowd ground rule in a World Series. Facing the Philadelphia Phillies in 1915, the Sox played to a sellout crowd in Philadelphia's Baker Bowl on October 13, 1915, in what turned out to be the final game of the Series when Boston outfielder Harry Hooper homered in the top of the ninth to give his club a 5–4 win over future Hall of Famer Eppa Rixey. It was Hooper's second home run of the contest and both were fly balls that bounced into temporary seats in right field that had been installed to accommodate the overflow crowds and declared, by mutual agreement, territory for a ground-ruled four-base hit. At the time, batted balls that ended up in the stands in fair territory, whether it be on the bounce or on the fly, were home runs.

Rule 4.05 (formerly Rule 3.13) is now all but an anachronism on the major-league level, since big-league teams no longer allow overflow crowds that infringe on the regular playing field, but there are still parks in which special ground rules apply.

4.06 No Fraternization

Players in uniform shall not address or mingle with spectators, nor sit in the stands before, during, or after a game. No manager, coach or player shall address any spectator before or during a game. Players of opposing teams shall not fraternize at any time while in uniform.

For a long time, it was left up to each individual team to monitor its own players when it came to fraternizing with opponents, but the early rule books clearly stated that players in uniform were not permitted to sit among spectators. They also forbade umpires, managers, captains, or players from addressing the crowd during a game, but added the stipulation "except in case of necessary explanation." It was not unusual in the 1870s and 1880s for an umpire to stop play while he explained a ruling to the audience or for a team captain to appeal to spectators for help when an umpire's decision did not go his way. Similarly, umpires in the early years on occasion would call upon members of the crowd for help on plays where their vision was blocked or they otherwise felt incapable of rendering a decision without impartial aid.

The fraternization rule, in no matter whose hands its enforcement is placed, has always been abused with near impunity. Anyone fortunate enough to go to a major-league game at a park where they still let fans in early enough to watch batting practice will see players and coaches on both teams mingling freely around the batting cage. Rules against players, coaches, and managers chatting during a game with opponents and even spectators have been likewise ignored. Prior to the 1883 season, the management of the Philadelphia Athletics team in the American Association handed down a list of club rules that included the following: "No member of the team while dressed in his uniform shall be permitted to flirt with or 'mash' any female or lady." This edict had about as much chance of being obeyed as did another club rule that said: "While away from home every player must report at the hotel to the Manager before 11:30 p.m. and retire to his room for the night. No player shall lie abed after eight o'clock in the morning while on a trip unless he is sick or disabled."

4.07 Security

(a) No person shall be allowed on the playing field during a game except players and coaches in uniform, managers, news photographers authorized by the home team, umpires, officers of the law in uniform and watchmen or other employees of the home club.

(b) The home team shall provide police protection sufficient to preserve order. If a person, or persons, enter the playing field during a game and interfere in any way with the play, the visiting team may refuse to play until the field is cleared.

PENALTY: If the field is not cleared in a reasonable length of time, which shall in no case be less than 15 minutes after the visiting team's refusal to play, the umpire in-chief may forfeit the game to the visiting team.

The 2020 season marks the 46th anniversary of the last occasion when a visiting team won by forfeit after spectators invaded the field while a game was in progress and the home team was unable to stifle the havoc. To bolster sagging attendance in a city riddled by inflation and rampant unemployment, the Cleveland Indians designated their June 4, 1974, night contest with the Texas Rangers a special "10-Cent Beer Night." The affair brought in a crowd of 25,134, but at a high cost when it proved to be perhaps the most embarrassingly inept promotional scheme in MLB history. Cleveland failed to added extra security for the contest, despite the fact that the same two clubs had brawled on the field in Arlington the week before. There is no record of the number of cups of beer that were sold—one estimate was between 60,000 and 65,000 10-ounce cups of Stroh's—but it was definitely astronomical and, in any event, was instrumental in the sale of beer and other alcoholic beverages at major league parks eventually being halted after the seventh inning.

With the score tied, 5–5, in the bottom of the ninth and the winning Cleveland run perched on third base with two out, Tribe fans in various stages of inebriation poured out of the right-field stands and began tussling with Texas outfielder Jeff Burroughs. Burroughs fought back, but when more fans surrounded him, players from both teams rushed to his aid, some armed with bats. Order was eventually restored, but the peace was short-lived. After umpire Nestor Chylak suffered a lacerated hand when a fan threw a chair at him to start another melee, the game was forfeited to Texas. Nine fans were arrested after the incident; seven more were hospitalized and Texas manager Billy Martin summed up the evening, declaring, "That's probably the closest we'll come to seeing someone get killed in the game of baseball."

Ironically, the Rangers franchise had also been involved in the last previous forfeit that was triggered by a crowd-related incident while a game was in progress. On September 30, 1971, the Rangers franchise was still based in the nation's capital and about to conclude its last game as the Washington Senators, a night contest against the New York Yankees at RFK Stadium. The game meant nothing in the standings to Washington, which was buried deep in fifth place in the American League East Division, but New York stood at 81–80, needing a win to finish above .500.

Behind, 7–5 with two out in the top of the ninth, the Yankees were suddenly given an unexpected gift as Horace Clarke strolled to the plate to face Washington reliever Joe Grzenda. Outraged at owner Bob Short's decision a few days earlier to move the club to the Dallas area, thus bringing an end to major-league baseball in a city that had had a team for the past seventy-one years, the bulk of the Washington crowd of 14,460 swarmed onto the field and began ripping up home plate, the bases, and the pitching rubber. Realizing the chances of completing the game were nil, the umpires had no choice but to award the Yankees a 9–0 forfeit victory, thereby assuring them of a winning season.

5.00: Playing the Game

Rule 5.01 (a) says, in effect, that the home team must bat last—but that has not always been the case. In fact, the opposite was true in 1877, when a new rule required the home club to take first raps. The National League reverted to the pre-1877 custom the following season, which called for the two captains to determine which club first took its turn at bat. The usual method was a coin flip, with the visitors accorded the honor of making the call and the winner of the flip then given the option of batting first or last.

In 1885, the American Association allowed the home captain to choose which club batted first, and the National League adopted the same policy in 1887, when the two circuits agreed to be governed by one rule book. It remained more an ingrained tradition than a rule that the home team would bat last until 1950, when Rule 4.02, an ancestor of Rule 5:01 (a), was added to the manual. By the early part of the twentieth century, having your last raps was viewed as an advantage. Previously, though, teams had often preferred to bat first, largely because it gave them first crack at the game ball, which often was the only new ball put into play that day.

In the very first World Series played to completion between two rival major leagues, the best-of-three 1884 matchup between the National League champion Providence Grays and the American Association champion New York Metropolitans, the Mets batted first in the opening game despite being the home club in all three matches. Six years later, in the last World Series between the two loops, the home side batted last in all seven contests, but there were still occasions in 1890 when the home boys elected to bat first. One came in a Players' League contest on June 21 between the Chicago Pirates and the Brooklyn Ward's Wonders, played at Chicago's South Side Park. Chicago manager Charlie Comiskey opted to put his club up first and his decision deprived his pitcher that day, Silver King, of an opportunity to achieve the only no-hitter in Players' League competition. The lone run of the game was tallied by Brooklyn's George Van Haltren in the bottom of the seventh inning after he reached second base on a double error by Dell Darling, a catcher filling in that afternoon at shortstop. Because Brooklyn did not have to bat in the ninth after Chicago sealed the 1–0 verdict by going scoreless in the top of the frame, King did not work the necessary nine innings that a pitcher as per present rules must do to gain credit for a no-hitter even though he was credited with a complete game.

5.02 Fielding Positions

When the ball is put in play at the start of, or during a game, all fielders other than the catcher shall be on fair territory.
(a) The catcher shall station himself directly back of the plate. He may leave his position at any time to catch a pitch or make a play except that when the batter is being given an intentional base on balls, the catcher must stand with both feet within the lines of the catcher's box until the ball leaves the pitcher's hand.
PENALTY: Balk.

Note that the rule regarding a catcher's positioning when an intentional walk is being issued no longer applied as of 2017—at least not while experimentation with intentional walks being issued simply by a manager or his surrogate signaling for one is underway in one of the multitude of endeavors to shorten the time it presently takes to play an average major-league game. This rule change, which by now appears to be permanent, is regarded by many pundits as an unfortunate one. Requiring a catcher to remain within the confines of the catcher's box until the ball leaves the pitcher's hand makes issuing an intentional walk more of a challenge.

Until a half century or so ago, there were frequent occasions when a batter would spoil an intentional walk attempt. In the heat of the 1948 AL pennant race, Cleveland Indians player-manager Lou Boudreau foiled an effort to purposely pass him by throwing his bat at a wide pitch and sailing the ball into right field for a single. Don Mueller, known as "Mandrake the Magician" because of his dexterity with a bat, also is well remembered by New York Giants fans during the 1950s for thwarting efforts to walk him. Boudreau's and Mueller's legerdemain was a rarity only in that it was successful. Batters in the pre-expansion era commonly fought against accepting intentional walks and were ready to lash out if a pitcher slipped and delivered a ball close enough to the plate that it could be ripped.

Prior to the rule change, in recent years either pitchers had become more skilled or batters less audacious. Wild pitches and passed balls still occurred during an attempt to walk a batter intentionally, but ploys like Boudreau's and Mueller's were almost extinct. An extreme rarity occurred on June 22, 2006, at Camden Yards when Florida's Miguel Cabrera spoiled an attempt to intentionally walk him by lacing Orioles reliever Todd Williams's lazy looping first pitch up the middle for a single to bring home the go-ahead run in the 10th inning of the Marlins' 8–5 win.

Lost now as well to fans are situations in which a catcher rose to pretend an intentional walk was imminent on a 3-and-2 count against a heavy hitter and his pitcher then fired a third strike right down the pipe, to the batter's astonishment. Perhaps the most memorable example came in Game Three of the 1972 World Series at Oakland on October 18. With Cincinnati batting with two men on base in the top of the eighth inning and a 3-and-2 count on Johnny Bench, the Reds' hard-hitting catcher, after first visiting the mound for a conference with his battery men, Athletics manager Dick Williams quietly returned to the dugout. Back behind the plate, catcher Gene Tenace rose and held out his throwing hand, seemingly following Williams's order given while he was visiting the mound to walk Bench intentionally as reliever Rollie Fingers came to the set position. But then, as per the prearranged plan, Fingers brought

A's fans to their feet when he shocked Bench by throwing a slider for strike three. The Reds nonetheless won the game, 1–0.

But suddenly with us are situations fringing on ludicrous where relief pitchers can enter a game and depart without throwing a single pitch even though they are credited with facing a batter. The first to do so was Cleveland Indians reliever Oliver Perez on June 29, 2018, at Oakland. In the bottom of the seventh inning, with the Indians trailing the A's, 2–1, Cleveland manager Terry Francona brought in the southpaw Perez to relieve starter Trevor Bauer and gain the platoon advantage with lefty hitter Dustin Fowler due up. As soon as Perez's name was announced, A's skipper Bob Melvin countered by sending righty hitter Mark Canha up to pinch-hit for Fowler. Francona then opted to intentionally walk Canha with lefty Matt Joyce slated to bat next. But Melvin again countered the platoon advantage by pinch-hitting righty Chad Pinder for Joyce. Francona's answer was to remove Perez before he had thrown a single warm-up pitch with right-hander Zach McAllister. McAllister fanned Pinder to end the inning without any damage being done, and thereupon avoided the embarrassment of having Perez charged not only with a walk but with an earned run despite never actually participating in the game.

Note that the Perez episode may never occur again if a radical new rule, introduced in 2020, proves effective. In an effort to reduce the number of pitching changes, MLB will institute a rule that requires pitchers to either face a minimum of three batters per appearance or pitch to the end of a half-inning, with exceptions for injuries and illnesses.

5.02 (b)

The pitcher, while in the act of delivering the ball to the batter, shall take his legal position;

In the nineteenth century, the rule regarding a pitcher's legal position changed almost every season and balks were called when he failed to comply with the new restrictions. Today a balk is an infrequently seen event.

See **BALKS** in the **DEFINITIONS OF TERMS** chapter for more on the nature of balks throughout history.

5.02 (c)

Except the pitcher and the catcher, any fielder may station himself anywhere in fair territory.

Since no team in its right mind would station its players anywhere but in fair territory nowadays, Rule 5.02 (c) (formerly Rule 4.03) on the surface might seem superfluous. The rule was put in partly to keep any team or player from making a travesty of the game. Rube Waddell reputedly would call all his infielders and outfielders to the sidelines sometimes in exhibition games and then strike out the side while working with just his catcher. No one cared to see a pitcher try this in a regulation game.

There was a time, however, when players not only could legally be stationed in foul territory but it behooved them to do so. In 1876, the National League's first season of operation, it was still a rule that any batted ball that struck earth initially in fair territory was fair regardless of where it ended up. Many players, headed by Ross Barnes—the 1876 National League batting champ—mastered the fair-foul hit, which involved chopping down on the ball in such a way that it hit in front of the plate and then immediately spun off into foul territory. To protect against these batsmen, teams were compelled to position their first and third basemen outside the foul-line boundaries.

Speaking of foul-line boundaries, initially they were only chalk lines drawn between home plate and first and third bases. The two foul lines beyond the bases were generally made by digging furrows with a plow; but by the early 1860s, in most parks used by teams that took the game seriously—were extensions of the chalk lines that theoretically could, in cases where there were no outfield fences, go on as far as the eye could see (although they seldom did). Many parks, beginning in the 1860s, did install foul posts extended to the length of the field, however, and beginning in 1878 foul lines often were extended to the length of the foul posts as well. The posts varied in size and were sometimes topped by a flag, but it was doubtful that any were taller than a few feet.

Note that 5.02 (c) says, "Except for the pitcher and catcher, any fielder may station himself anywhere in fair territory." This wording can create a situation that will confound the best umpires in the game. One such time happened on June 14, 1958, at Wrigley Field. Facing a sacrifice situation in the second inning, Cincinnati Reds manager Birdie Tebbetts had second baseman Johnny Temple and first baseman George Crowe switch positions. Crowe, however, continued to wear his first baseman's mitt. Temple charged the plate on Bob Purkey's pitch, caught pitcher Johnny Briggs's pop bunt with the runners on the move, and fired to Crowe, who was covering first, for a double play. Cubs manager Bob Scheffing protested the game, but it was withdrawn when the Cubs won, 4–3. Nevertheless, NL president Warren Giles later ruled that a first basemen switching to another position must discard his mitt in favor of a glove. But Giles's adjudication may have been meaningless since nothing in the rules defines what a first basemen is or where he must play other that he must have both feet in fair territory when he is stationed on the first base bag to await a pickoff throw with a runner on first. It would seem therefore that one of the seven non-pitchers in fair territory, regardless of where he chooses to station himself, is entitled to wear a first basemen's mitt. To further complicate the matter for rules gurus, Crowe, a lefty, was credited in the box score of the game with having played both first base and second base and registering put outs at each position.

George Crowe, among the few lefties to play second base, did it for all of one batter but was credited with a putout at that position.

Tebbetts, an exceptionally heady former catcher in the Paul Richards mold, employed an equally imaginative defensive alignment in his rookie year as a manager with the Reds. On May 22, 1954, at Busch Stadium I, the Reds led St. Louis, 4–2, with two out in the bottom of the eighth behind Art Fowler. But after Red Schoendienst singled, bringing up Stan Musial, Tebbetts replaced Roy McMillan at shortstop with Nino Escalera, a rookie left-handed outfielder. The Reds then played minus a shortstop and deployed Escalera in deep right-center. The ploy worked when Musial fanned to end the inning. Tebbetts then removed Escalera in the bottom of the ninth in favor of utility infielder Rocky Bridges and escaped with a 4–2 win while Escalera was credited with his only major-league game at shortstop. Tebbetts went on to deploy four-man outfields several more times during his managerial career.

5.03 Base Coaches

(a) The team at bat shall station two base coaches on the field during its time at bat, one near first base and one near third base.

Base coaches have been with us ever since it was recognized that a baserunner could not both keep track of the ball and make time on the bases. To assist runners, teams in the early days customarily stationed two players outside the first-base and third-base foul lines. These players were called "coachers." Once the realization evolved that a coacher could do more than just stand and wait for a runner to come his way, a new breed of base coach developed.

5.03 (b)

Base coaches shall be limited to two in number and shall be in team uniform.

In amateur and sandlot games, teams often use people as base coaches who are not in uniform. This first became illegal on the major-league level in 1957. Until then a Connie Mack or a Burt Shotton—to name but two of the managers who have piloted their teams while wearing street clothes—was free to coach third or first any time the mood struck him.

5.03 (c)

Base coaches must remain within the coach's box consistent with this Rule, except that a coach who has a play at his base may leave the coach's box to signal the player to slide, advance or return to a base if the coach does not interfere with the play in any manner. Other than exchanging equipment, all base coaches shall refrain from physically touching base runners, especially when signs are being given.

A form of this rule first appeared in 1914, with embellishments to it coming in 1920 and 1949. Not until the latter year, however, was a runner who was touched or physically assisted in any manner by a coach declared out even if no play was made on him. Before 1914, a coach was licensed to tackle a runner if need be to keep him from making what seemed to the coach a foolhardy bid to score. Nowadays, it is considered coach's interference even if a runner racing for a base runs past it and accidently collides with a coach.

5.03 (c) PENALTY:

If a coach has positioned himself closer to home plate than the coach's box or closer to fair territory than the coach's box before a batted ball passes the coach, the umpire shall, upon complaint by the opposing manager, strictly enforce the rule. The umpire shall warn the coach and instruct him to return to the box. If the coach does not return to the box he shall be removed from the game. In addition, coaches who violate this Rule may be subject to discipline by the League President.

Base coaches are indeed occasionally ejected from games for ignoring repeated warnings to stay in their boxes and for straying onto the playing field—even if only accidentally—while time is in. Boxes for base coaches were first established in 1887. Before then, the only restriction on coaches was that they could not come within 15 feet of the foul lines to coach baserunners. The 15-foot restraining lines were first required to be drawn on all professional fields in 1877, and they appear in many game photos between that year and 1886. The 1887 rule also stipulated that all team members not at bat or on the bases had to stay at least 50 feet outside of the foul lines except for the two base coaches.

The coaches' boxes began 75 feet from the catcher's lines when they were first established in 1887. According to the new rule, coaches had to stay in their boxes at all times when the ball was in play and were restricted to only coaching runners. If a coach left his box, he could be fined $5 by an umpire unless he was also the team captain and ventured outside the box to appeal a decision that involved a misinterpretation of the rules.

How much money did the National League and the American Association collect in 1887 from coaches who were fined for leaving their boxes? The answer is about as much as they got earlier in that decade from pitchers who were fined for deliberately hitting batters. With all the minds there were in the nineteenth century working on refining the rules, until 1898 there was still usually only one umpire on the field to act as their enforcer. The newly designed coaches' boxes no more kept coaches within their confines than the many interference rules on the books stopped fielders from tripping base runners. Until the early part of the twentieth century, base coaches were even free to deceive enemy fielders—as did Ned Hanlon in a National League game on May 9, 1883, between the Detroit Wolverines and the Chicago White Stockings.

Though only in his fourth major-league season, Hanlon, an outfielder, had already displayed the ingenuity that would make him one of the game's greatest managers a decade later when he took over the reins of the moribund Baltimore Orioles.

Never more than an average player, Ned Hanlon quickly grew into a venerated manager once his playing days ended. But after he won five pennants in a seven-year span, he spent most of the rest of his career wallowing in the second division.

As a result, Wolves manager Jack Chapman frequently used Hanlon to coach third base. He was there on that May afternoon with runners at the corners. When the runner on first attempted to steal second, White Stockings catcher Silver Flint rifled the ball to shortstop Tom Burns, who had moved over to cover the bag. Burns was among the better shortstops in the game at the time, yet managed to fall victim to Hanlon. Upon seeing that his teammate would be out at second, Hanlon faked a dash down the third-base line as if he were the runner on third trying to score. Decoyed by the move, Burns held the ball, allowing the runner to slide into second safely.

Even though the game was at Chicago, Hanlon was applauded by the crowd for his fast thinking, but it was not uncommon for a baseball audience in that period to see a base coach act similarly to deceive a fielder. In 1904, a rule was finally introduced to declare a runner at third base out if the third base coach, with less than two out, broke toward the plate on a ground ball to draw an unnecessary throw. Ten years later, an addendum also made this true for a fly ball, and the rule has since been refined to make it interference any time a third-base coach leaves his box in an attempt to deke an opponent.

An eerie example of Rule 5.03 (c) in action took place in a Georgia-Florida League game on June 21, 1953, between Fitzgerald and Tifton. Nursing an 8–7 lead in the bottom of the ninth with the bases jammed and two out, Tifton's Bob Badour went to a 3-and-0 count on Don Stoyle. Badour then threw the next pitch wide, and for a moment it seemed that Stoyle had walked to force in the tying run. But the plate umpire noted that Fitzgerald catcher Tony Fabbio, coaching at third, had faked that he was stealing home on the pitch and properly called the runner on third out to end the game. Along with depriving Stoyle of the game-tying RBI, the decision took away what ought to have been his 100th ribby of the season; he finished with 99.

Fabbio's fabricated theft of home occurred in a lower minor-league game well over sixty years ago, but current major-league coaches can also blunder. On September 5, 2010, the Texas Rangers trailed the Minnesota Twins, 6–3, in the top of the ninth at Target Field, but rallied and were down, 6–4, with runners on second and third with two outs against beleaguered reliever Matt Capps. Designated hitter Vladimir Guerrero then hit a grounder up the middle that Twins second baseman Orlando Hudson gloved, but realized he would be unable to catch Guerrero at first as the runner on third scored. Instead, Hudson threw late to third in an attempt to trap the trailing runner, Michael Young. But Young, in rounding third, made contact with third-base coach Dave Anderson's extended arm and was immediately ruled out on coach's interference by third-base umpire Alfonso Marquez, ending the game forthwith with the final score 6–5, Twins.

The problem of base coaches who unduly taunt umpires or badger opposing players was first addressed by the rule book as far back as 1887, though umpires usually tried to ignore the offender unless he became inordinately loud or profane. All the rules prohibiting it notwithstanding, heckling a thin-skinned opponent or arbiter has always been part of a base coach's job. Pitchers in particular are considered fair game.

In almost every case, it is now against the rules for a base coach to distract a pitcher while he is in the midst of his delivery. It is not illegal, however, for a base coach to try to disrupt a pitcher's rhythm or to hoodwink him. One nugget, now forbidden, that was worked on unwary pitchers—particularly during the era when pitchers clandestinely doctored the ball—involved a base coach, ideally with a runner on third, calling to a pitcher that he was certain the pitcher was illegally doctoring the ball and demand to be shown it. If the unsuspecting pitcher was so foolish as to toss the coach the ball for an examination, the coach stepped aside and let the throw go by him while the runner waltzed home. On August 7, 1915, at Robison Field, the St. Louis Cardinals pilfered a run from the Brooklyn Robins when St. Louis player-manager Miller Huggins, coaching at third, pulled this trick on rookie hurler Ed Appleton and Dots Miller trotted home with what proved to be the winning run in the Cards' 6–4 victory.

By the mid-1880s, teams like the St. Louis Browns were utilizing their most vociferous players as coachers and licensing them to jeer opponents and umpires along with encouraging their teammates. The Browns' leading coacher was third baseman Arlie Latham, a relentless heckler and an ace sign stealer. So vaunted did Latham become at the job that he carved a new niche in the game after his playing days were over. In 1900, Cincinnati Reds owner John Brush, at the behest of his manager, Bob Allen, hired Latham to do nothing more than coach runners, making him the first contracted base coach.

5.04 Batting

(a) Batting Order
(1) Each player of the offensive team shall bat in the order that his name appears in his team's batting order.
(2) The batting order shall be followed throughout the game unless a player is substituted for another. In that case the substitute shall take the place of the replaced player in the batting order.

Here, in (2), we discover that in the event the order is not correctly followed, a player can be declared out and charged with a time at bat even though he never steps up to the plate. This deprivation has happened many times, and to some of the game's greatest stars. In a game against the Philadelphia Phillies on July 24, 1953, St. Louis Cardinals immortal Stan Musial was ruled out in the following manner for violating then-Rule 6.07.

Cards player-manager Eddie Stanky turned in a lineup card showing shortstop Solly Hemus leading off, himself batting second, and Musial up third. After Hemus followed Stanky and singled, Phils skipper Steve O'Neill bolted from the dugout to appeal. Hemus's hit was nullified and Musial was declared out because he, rather than Hemus, had been slated to follow Stanky according to the lineup card. The unemployed time at bat cost Musial a point on his batting average. He finished the season at .337 but would have had a .338 mark were it not for Stanky's oversight.

Big Steve Bilko once came to bat twice in succession in the same inning. A rule violation negated his first at bat, but in his second appearance he homered.

Ironically, less than a month after he saddled Musial with an empty time at bat, Stanky was involved in another batting order boo-boo that saw his team profit from having a player hit out of turn, even though the mistake was caught. In a game against Cincinnati on August 21, 1953, first baseman Steve Bilko led off the Cardinals' half of the second inning by grounding out. As rookie third baseman Ray Jablonski strolled to the plate, Stanky, suddenly realizing that Jablonski—not Bilko—had been scheduled to lead off the frame, sprinted up to home plate umpire Bill Stewart and notified him of the mixup. Stewart ruled Jablonski out for missing his turn, and Bilko was sent back to the plate since he was due up after Jablonski. Given a second opportunity, Bilko homered off Harry Perkowski for the game's first run, and the Cardinals went on to win, 4–0.

The incident, though stemming from a seemingly honest mistake by a manager (though with Stanky you could never be sure), purportedly raised a thought-provoking issue that Baltimore manager Paul Richards seized upon in a 1960 game against Detroit. The story goes that Richards, knowing full well that his pitcher, Gordon Jones, was due up, instead sent leadoff hitter Jerry Adair to the plate. The story then has Richards later saying he purposely had Adair bat out of turn hoping he would work the count to 3-and-0 and Jones could then be rushed to the plate to finish the at-bat and get a walk before the Tigers appealed Adair's batting

Many Clevelanders in the 1950s believed the Indians picked the wrong former major-league catcher to manage the Tribe after Lou Boudreau was fired when they went with Al Lopez. Had they instead gone with Paul Richards (right), the Indians and not the Yankees might have dominated the decade of the 1950s and then some. One more thing we will never know.

out of order. But Adair spoiled his skipper's plan by hitting a two-run single that was nullified when Tigers pilot Jimmy Dykes brought the violation to the umpire's attention.

Nifty idea by Richards, right? Actually not. The tale, though widely circulated for many years (perhaps starting with Richards himself), is apocrophal from beginning to end. Adair wasn't even on the team in 1960—let alone its leadoff hitter—until he was called up at the tail end of the season for a grand total of five at-bats. Nevertheless, as the rule presently stands, a manager—particularly in the National League where there is no DH for the pitcher—can still send up his leadoff batter with a weak-hitting pitcher due at the plate. Even if the leadoff batter reaches base and the opposing manager appeals—as he almost certainly will if he's paying attention—little is lost since the pitcher is an almost certain out anyway. Meanwhile, the leadoff hitter has gotten an extra look at the pitcher that he may be able to turn to his advantage, as did Bilko.

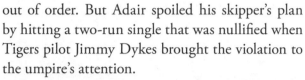

5.04 (a) (3)

The first batter in each inning after the first inning shall be the player whose name follows that of the last player who legally completed his time at bat in the preceding inning.

In the early days of the game, this was not the case. In the first inning, teams were free to shuffle their batting orders at will depending on developments. After that, the batting orders were locked in for the rest of the game, but the first batter in each inning was not always the next batter in the order. Rather, he was the batter that followed the man who had made the last *out* in the previous inning. As an example, Smith is on first base with two outs and Jones is up; Jones singles Smith to second base. Brown, the next batter, rifles a single to center field but Smith is thrown out at the plate trying to score. Since Smith made the last out, Jones leads off the next inning with Brown to follow him. This process as a result often led to players deep in the order receiving more turns at bat than those near the top of the order.

Subsequent to the 1878 season, a form of the present rule was first introduced: "After the first inning the first batsman of subsequent innings shall be the striker who follows the last batter to complete a time at bat." Its essence has remained a rule ever since.

5.04 (b) The Batter's Box

The batter shall take his position in the batter's box promptly when it is his time at bat.

Early rule books had no equivalent to Rule 5.04 (b) (formerly 6.02 (c)). In its absence an umpire, for the lack of an alternative, would simply rule a player out for "refusing to bat" if he did not come up to the plate for whatever reason. In a National League game against the Philadelphia Phillies on August 22, 1891, New York Giants hurler Amos Rusie was declared out in this fashion by umpire Tim Hurst. The following notation appeared in the box score of the game to explain why the Phillies registered only 26 putouts: "Rusie declared out for refusing to bat." Adding to the puzzle is the fact that Rusie was on the losing end of the game, 9–5.

Whatever reason Rusie had for declining to take his cuts, it was not that he was a poor hitter. In 10 seasons he had a .247 career batting average, well above the norm for a moundsman in his time.

Tim Hurst defended his profession as an umpire by saying, "The pay is good, and you can't beat the hours—three to five." The pay was decent but nothing extraordinary, around $1,500, and Hurst would actually rather have been a player or a manager. Yet, for a small, hot-tempered Irishman from a coal mining family who was quick-witted and fast with his fists it was the ideal venue in the 1890s.

5.04 (b) (3)

If the batter refuses to take his position in the batter's box during his time at bat, the umpire shall call a strike on the batter. The ball is dead, and no runners may advance. After the penalty, the batter may take his proper position and the regular ball and strike count shall continue. If the batter does not take his proper position before three strikes have been called, the batter shall be declared out.

But if the rules in 1891 on batters who were loath to bat were open-ended, there is still considerable leeway in how they are enforced. For instance, the amount of time a batter has to return to the batter's box after being warned to do so depends heavily on the situation and the umpire. At the beginning of the 1993 season, with umpires under pressure to speed up games, there was an illustrative incident on April 16 in the Atlanta Braves' first visit of the campaign to San Francisco's Candlestick Park. In a game already studded with several heated disputes involving home-plate umpire Mark Hirshbeck, the Braves trailed the host Giants, 1–0, in the top of the ninth with two out, the potential tying run on second base, and Ron Gant at bat.

With the count at 1-and-0, Gant looked at a pitch from Giants reliever Rod Beck that he thought was ball two. Hearing it called a strike, Gant stepped out of the box and swatted the air with his bat—the traditional way for a batter silently to voice his disagreement with a call. Hirshbeck ordered Gant back into the box, and when he dallied, Hirshbeck signaled Beck to throw and then called the pitch a strike. Braves manager Bobby Cox flew out of the dugout to protest and was speedily ejected. Behind now in the count 1-and-2, Gant flied to right on the next pitch to end the game.

Afterward, Gant said of Hirshbeck's decision, "It was worse than anything I've seen in Little League. What a joke." Crew chief Bruce Froemming contended that Hirshbeck was merely following what was then Rule 6.02 (c) that had been on the books for a while, albeit seldom invoked until umpires were told to enforce it conscientiously to help speed up games. One San Francisco reporter chortled that the pitch to Gant while he was out of the box had looked low and outside but, given Hirshbeck's wrath toward the Braves by that point, he probably would have called the delivery a strike even if Beck had heaved it into the stands.

The reporter was apparently unaware that once Hirshbeck set the machinery of Rule 6.02 (c) into motion, he was obliged to call Beck's pitch a strike regardless of where it was delivered.

5.04 (b) (4) The Batter's Box Rule

(A) The batter shall keep at least one foot in the batter's box throughout the batter's time at bat, unless one of the following exceptions applies, in which case the batter may leave the batter's box but not the dirt area surrounding home plate:

There are eight exceptions to the above rule, but this historic moment of action was not one of them. In a 1965 game against the St. Louis Cardinals on August 18 at Sportsman's Park, none other than Hank Aaron had a home run rescinded when he left the batter's box in his hunger to tackle a Curt Simmons changeup. In the eighth inning, the Milwaukee Braves slugger rocketed the ball onto the right-field roof, but even before Aaron could start his tour of the bases, plate umpire Chris Pelekoudas signaled him out and soon afterward ejected Braves manager Bobby Bragan for protesting the decision. The Braves nonetheless won the game, 5–3.

"Aaron was running up on the pitch," Pelekoudas said later in defense of his call. "His left foot was at least three feet out when he swung." The lost four-bagger deprived Aaron of a home run that would have hiked his career total to 756. However, almost every other great slugger, including Babe Ruth, Jimmie Foxx and Lou Gehrig, also lost at least one home run during his career to a rule technicality or violation.

5.05 When the Batter Becomes a Runner

(a) The batter becomes a runner when:
  (1) He hits a fair ball;

This rule seems so self-evident at first look as to be unnecessary. Surely a batter has always become a baserunner the moment he hits a fair ball. On the evidence, however, the rules were originally silent on the point. As a result, in 1874, a rule was introduced saying that when a batter has fairly struck a fair ball, he shall vacate his position and be considered a baserunner until he is put out or scores a run. This seemed clear enough, until some players began to test the rule in ways that its originators had not considered.

On June 30, 1883, in a National League game between the Providence Grays and Boston Red Stockings, Boston scored the winning run in its 3–2 victory over Charley Radbourn through an imaginative bit of baserunning—or more accurately, non-baserunning—by Red Stockings left fielder Joe Hornung. With teammates Ezra Sutton on second base and Sam Wise on first, Hornung hit a routine groundball to Providence second baseman Jack Farrell. Sensing an easy double play in the making, Hornung stood fast in the batter's box rather than running to first base. Since Hornung refused to try to make his base, in umpire Stewart Decker's judgment he kept Sutton and Wise from being forced to vacate theirs, although both had started running as soon as the ball was hit. No longer subject to being forced out at second base, Wise had to be tagged in a rundown play between first and

Ezra Sutton, a valued member of the Boston National League team for more than a decade and one of its seven ironmen in 1878 that played in all 60 official league games. The club's other two regulars— shortstop George Wright and pitcher Tommy Bond— participated in 59 games.

second involving Farrell and Providence first sacker Joe Start while Sutton whipped around third and scurried home safely.

On the evidence available, Decker was wrong in his judgment even at the time. Nevertheless, Hornung's maneuver induced rule makers to tighten the 1883 equivalent to the present rule and apprise both umpires and the defensive team that even if a batter refused to leave the batter's box, it could no longer be a sanctuary once he put the ball in play.

5.05 (a) (2)

The third strike called by the umpire is not caught, providing (1) first base is unoccupied, or (2) first base is occupied with two out;

Why is it important that first base not be occupied with less than two out in order for a batter to be entitled to run if a third strike is muffed by the catcher enabling a batter to make first base and the runner on first to move up at least one base or perhaps even more? Well, because it protects the team at bat from falling victim to an intentionally dropped third strike that can result in a double play or, quite possibly, even a triple play. Not until fairly late in the nineteenth century did a version of the current rule first appear in rule books. Before that time, a catcher could almost routinely orchestrate a double or triple play under the right circumstances. For example, with the bases loaded a catcher could deliberately muff a third strike, pick up the ball, and touch the plate, forcing out the runner on third, then throw to the third baseman for a second force out, at which point the third sacker had his choice to throw to either second or first base and complete the triple play.

With the umpire having no recourse to prevent it, this exact scenario occurred on a several occasions before the rule was changed. Interestingly, on at least one occasion, an umpire stymied a triple play in the making under what were the ideal circumstances for one to occur at the time. Until the mid-1880s when season schedules were lengthened to well over 100 games, major-league teams frequently played exhibition games against minor-league and independent clubs on their off days for the extra revenue. Often these games took place at their rival's park, and there was precious little reportage, if any, on them. In an exhibition game at Indianapolis of the League Alliance on May 18, 1877, the visiting National League Boston Red Stockings faced the minor-league Hoosier club's ace, "The Only" Nolan, and trailed, 2–1, heading into the seventh inning. At that point Boston loaded the bases with none out, a tailor-made situation for a possible triple play if the Red Stockings' batter, catcher Blower Brown, struck out. When he did, the Hoosiers' catcher, Silver Flint, later a fine defensive backstop with the National League Chicago White Stockings, purposely dropped the third strike and then initiated a quick triple play, tagging home base before firing the ball to third baseman Fred Warner for a force out there. Warner then routed the ball to second baseman Joe Quest to seemingly complete the triple play, but umpire D. T. Titus wasn't buying it. According to the *Boston Globe*, to Indianapolis's dismay, Titus "decided" only the striker, Brown, was out, "and after a wrangle of half an hour play was resumed." When Nolan retired the next two batters on a foul out and a strikeout, Indianapolis escaped the inning still holding a narrow 2–1 lead, which was the score when the game ended.

All that is known of Titus is that he was a "foreigner" from New Jersey, and his umpiring was judged by the writer at the game, presumably an Indianapolis rooter, to be "as foreign as his residence." Probably no one will ever know the extent of Titus's umpiring career or if he even had one. Nor will it ever be known if he was familiar with the rules at the time and simply chose to ignore them because he didn't fancy allowing such an easy triple play on his watch or instead was unfamiliar with many of their intricacies and made the call that just seemed to him the most sensible under the circumstances. It is also conceivable that he was cowed into a wrongheaded decision by the eventual 1877 National League champion Red Stockings and their venerated manager Harry Wright.

Whatever the case, we would not be reading about Titus now if it were not for this one decision he made on May 18, 1877, in the seventh inning at Indianapolis. For, in the eventual scheme of things, his call a few years later, rather than a subject of ridicule, became the norm.

5.05 (a) (5)

A fair ball passes over a fence or into the stands at a distance from home base of 250 feet or more. Such hit entitles the batter to a home run when he shall have touched all bases legally . . .

This rule makes it clear that a batter must make a complete tour of the bases after hitting an outside-the-park home run unless he is so severely disabled that he cannot, in which case a pinch runner has to finish the base tour and Rule 5.12 (b) (3) (a) applies. One of the more painfully amusing examples of the extremes to which umpires once had go in order to enforce this rule was seen by Brooklyn fans on August 5, 1926. Hall of Famer Zack Wheat, then in his 18th season with the Robins, pasted a home run over the wall off Jesse Haines in the bottom of the 10th inning of an 11–9 loss to the Cardinals at Ebbets Field. But by the time Wheat reached second base, he had twisted an ankle so badly he couldn't walk, forcing him to sit down on the bag while he tried to massage his leg into allowing him to continue. When five minutes had elapsed and Wheat was still in too much agony to cover the final 180 feet, Robins manager

Wilbert Robinson requested permission to have a courtesy runner complete the home run journey. Wheat begged for more time, however, and eventually was able to crawl to his feet and limp the rest of the way home. The trip was worth the effort, though Wheat could not have known that then. The home run was the last he would ever hit at Ebbets Field, for he was released after the 1926 season.

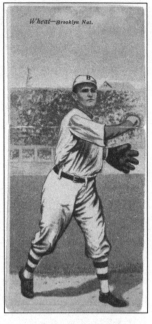

Incidentally, the phrase "entitles the batter" is of significance. There is still no rule that a batter is required to touch them all when he swats a ball out of the park. In today's homer-happy climate, it is unimaginable that any batter would not. But while unusual, it was not unheard of for a batter to smack a ball out of the yard and stop at third base in the nineteenth century. One such instance occurred in a National League game at New York on April 25, 1889, between the Giants and Boston. Since New York opted to bat first, Boston came up in the bottom of the ninth trailing the Giants' Cannonball Titcomb, 11–9. Here is what the next day's *New York Times* had to say about the finale: "The Giants held the lead from start to finish. With the exception of the last inning the on-lookers never felt fearful of the result. At that stage, however, with two men out, Hardy Richardson hit over the left-field fence for a home run, but preferred to remain at third base so as to make Catcher [Will] Brown get close to the batter [Billy Nash]. The latter, however, did not bite at his bait. He paid no attention to Richardson, but retired the batsman after the occupant of third base had walked home."

At the close of the 1919 season, his 11th in the majors, Zack Wheat owned a .299 career batting average. With the coming of the Lively Ball Era in 1920, his career mark jumped 18 points to .317 in his final eight seasons. What are we to make of that beyond the obvious: that Wheat had a long career? Whatever we care to.

What exactly did Brown not bite on by refusing to move closer to the plate? Richardson's threat to steal home! Brown would of course had to have been an idiot to take the bait, for Richardson's run on a steal would only duplicate the relatively meaningless one he already could have tallied on his home run. But to Richardson it was worth a try. That was how little home runs meant 130 years ago.

Until the early part of the twentieth century, a ball hit out of the park was not necessarily a home run—even if that was the batter's desire. What could prevent it? A blocked ball, which was defined as "a batted or thrown ball that is touched stopped, or handled by any person not engaged in the game. Whenever a Block occurs, the umpire shall declare it and the base runners may run the bases without being put out until the ball is returned to and held by the pitcher standing in his position."

Here is a blocked-ball home run from the 1890s that would never be more than a ground-rule double in every major league park today. On June 18, 1895, in a game at Brooklyn's Eastern Park, pitcher Gus Weyhing of the visiting Louisville Colonels looped a ball to right field that landed fair and then bounced foul into the right-field pavilion. The ball was hastily thrown back onto the field by a fan to Brooklyn right fielder George Treadway, who relayed the ball to first baseman Candy LaChance. LaChance then gunned it to catcher John Grim in time to catch Weyhing at the plate trying for an inside-the-park home run. Umpire Tim Keefe, the former Giants pitching great, called Weyhing safe, however, as per then Rule 35 that any blocked ball—one leaving the field of play and handled by someone other than a player—must be returned to and held by the pitcher, in this case Ed Stein, before it could be put back into play. Note that the fan in this case was not necessarily a Brooklyn rooter trying to assist his team; he was only doing what every law-abiding spectator did at that time: returning a ball.

Meanwhile, at Cincinnati's League Park II in the 1890s, the ground rules were a bit different. A ball making it into the center-field bleachers was an automatic home run, but a ball that landed in the left- or right-field bleachers (which often were nearly empty) was fair game for any outfielder fleet enough to climb into them, retrieve the ball, and heave it toward the pitcher to perhaps hold the batter to only a double or triple. Rather than rely on an umpire's judgment as to what section of the bleachers their balls landed in, savvy batsmen in the Reds' park ran all out from the moment they left the batter's box.

That was the way the game was played then.

5.05 (a) (6)

A fair ball, after touching the ground, bounds into the stands, or passes through, over or under a fence, or through or under a scoreboard, or through or under shrubbery, or vines on the fence, in which case the batter and the runners shall be entitled to advance two bases;

Until 1930 in the American League, a batted ball that got under, through, or over an outfield fence in fair territory in any manner whatsoever was a home run. The first pinch-hit grand slam homer in American League history by Cleveland's Marty Kavanagh on September 24, 1916, reportedly squirted through a hole in the fence at Cleveland's League Park. That same season, on May 6, second baseman George Cutshaw beat the Philadelphia Phillies and Erskine Mayer with a home run that mysteriously scaled the fence at Ebbets Field. With the score knotted, 2–2, in the bottom of the 11th, Cutshaw smacked a liner to right field that skipped to the fence. As Phillies right fielder Gavvy Cravath prepared to take the ball on the carom, Cutshaw's hit struck an embankment in front of the fence that gave it a weird spin. Instead of ricocheting off the fence, the ball began to climb it. Reaching the top of the barrier, the ball teetered there for an instant, and then toppled into the stands. Apart from his fluke homer, Cutshaw hit only one other four-bagger in 1916.

After the 1930 season, the National League imposed the same rule the AL had originated that year. Beginning in 1931 in both major leagues, all batted balls that stuck in or bounced through or over an outfield fence were ground-rule doubles unless the special ground rules of a park stated otherwise. In Brooklyn's Ebbets Field, a batted ball that went through the wire on the right-field fence was a home run, as was a ball that stuck in the wire if a fielder could not dig it out in time to keep a batter from circling the bases. Pee Wee Reese hit a famous home run in the sixth inning off Robin Roberts that lodged on a ledge in the right-field screen sector at Ebbets Field in the final game of the 1950 season on October 1 to tie the Dodgers with the Philadelphia Phillies at 1–1 and set up Dick Sisler's dramatic three-run homer in the 10th inning that brought the Phils their first flag since 1915.

5.05 (a) (8)

Any bounding fair ball is deflected by the fielder into the stands, or over or under a fence on fair or foul territory, in which case the batter and all runners shall be entitled to advance two bases;

If put to a guess, most fans will venture that this contingency has been a rule ever since the first professional League, the National Association, formed in 1871. Actually not. On July 26, 1889, in a National League game at Pittsburgh's Recreation Park, Cleveland Blues first baseman Jay Faatz's hot shot down the third-base line struck Alleghenys third sacker Deacon White on the foot and caromed under a row of seats adjacent to third base, giving him time to circle the bases for a historic three-run homer that never reached the outfield. Why was it a home run? Because the rule at that time required fielders to go into the stands, under benches, through accidently left open gates or wherever to retrieve overthrows or batted balls misdirected out of the field of play to prevent a batter or baserunner from touching them all.

Jay Faatz, a rare first baseman in his day who made his rep on stealing bases and getting hit by pitches.

5.05 (a) (9)

Any fair fly ball is deflected by the fielder into the stands, or over the fence into foul territory, in which case the batter shall be entitled to advance to second base; but if deflected into the stands or over the fence in fair territory, the batter shall be entitled to a home run. However, should such a fair fly be deflected at a point less than 250 feet from home plate, the batter shall be entitled to two bases only.

When Jose Canseco's skull got an assist on the homer Cleveland's Carlos Martinez hit off Kenny Rogers on May 26, 1993, at Cleveland Stadium, the Texas Rangers outfielder became perhaps the most celebrated player to be beaned by a long fly that evolved into a four-bagger. But many gardeners have suffered the ignominy of seeing a ball they mishandled disappear over the fence for a circuit clout. There are several ways in which it can happen. The most straightforward development is something on the order of what Western Carolina League fans saw on June 7, 1961, in a night game between Belmont and Newton-Conover. Belmont right fielder Eddie Montellanico tracked a towering fly ball hit by Newton-Conover player-manager Joe Abernathy back to the fence when he suddenly lost it in the lights. The ball struck Montellanico on top of the head, knocking him unconscious, and caromed over the fence for Abernathy's only home run of the season.

In his days as an outfielder, Jose Canseco was nearly kayoed by a ball that bounced off his head into the stands for a home run. But he was virtually the only player or former player that talked sensibly in the 2005 Congressional Hearing on steroids.

More controversial is the type of four-bagger that helped Denver's Bill Pinckard win the Western League home run crown and his Bears the loop flag in 1952. Facing Omaha in a scoreless pitcher's duel on August 9 at Denver, Pinckard socked a drive to deep left field. Omaha left fielder Dick Cordell leaped high for the ball as he crashed into the fence, but Pinckard's blow ticked his glove and hit the fence, then came back to clip Cordell in the forehead and ricochet over the retaining barrier. After a long argument with the managers of both teams, the umpires awarded Pinckard a home run. Cordell's testimony must have been ignored, for if Omaha could have established that the ball struck the fence before it caromed off Cordell's head and then went over the fence, the hit properly should have been called a ground-rule double because it became a bounding ball the instant it hit the fence rather than a ball in flight. In any case, Pinckard's homer proved to be the game's only run and enabled the Bears' Barney Schultz to win a 1–0 verdict over Omaha's Gary Blaylock.

When the Western League season ended a few weeks later, it developed that Pinckard's disputed round-tripper had spelled the difference in the pennant race. Had Omaha won the game, Denver, Omaha, and

Colorado Springs would have all tied for the flag with identical marks of 87–67.

Note that no mention is made in this rule about what happens when a batted ball that will clearly be a home run is short-circuited because it hits an object that is not a regular part of the playing field, say the roof of a domed stadium. In such an instance the number of bases awarded, if any, depends on the park ground rules.

No one has ever struck a low-flying plane in a major league game, but with two on and no one out in the top of the first inning, Mike Schmidt hit a blast off Astros starter Claude Osteen on June 10, 1974, that smacked into the public-address system hanging from Houston's Astrodome roof 326 feet from home plate and 117 feet above the playing field. Left unimpeded, Schmidt's shot would probably have traveled around 450 feet. In any event, it would have been a home run in every other park in the country. But according to Astrodome ground rules, the ball remained in play, and Schmidt had to settle for a single while the runners ahead of him, Dave Cash and Larry Bowa, moved up only one base.

In contrast, Larry Walker of the Expos hit a lazy fly ball on May 5, 1992, that struck one of the loudspeakers hanging 150 feet above the field at Montreal's Olympic Stadium. Even though the ball was descending when it hit the speaker and would likely have been an out, the existing ground rule in the Expos' park forced umpire Terry Tata to call it a home run. "It's the easiest out turned into a home run that I've ever had," Walker said after the game. "I like that ground rule."

5.04 (b)

The batter becomes a runner and is entitled to first base without liability to be put out (provided he advances to and touches first base) when:
   (1) Four "balls" have been called by the umpire;

Observe that a comment accompanies this rule. It implies that a batter must proceed directly to first base after the fourth called ball. There have been numerous instances in amateur games when a batter has been called out for detouring on his way to first to deposit his helmet or batting gloves on his team's bench and even some in major-league games. The rule's inception was sparked by an instance that occurred in an 1891 American

Association game at Columbus on August 2, when Baltimore outfielder George Van Haltren walked with the bases loaded in the bottom of the 10th to give the Orioles an apparent 3–2 victory, but controversy flared when Van Haltren followed his "walk-off" walk by heading toward the Baltimore bench rather than first base. At that point, Columbus manager Gus Schmelz shouted for umpire Jumbo Davis to declare Van Haltren out. Davis demurred, as did AA president Louis Kramer the following day when Schmelz protested the game, but Van Haltren's near blunder made it incumbent for future arbiters to declare a batter out if he detoured on his way to first base or neglected entirely to touch it.

5.05 (b) (2)

He is touched by a pitched ball which he is not attempting to hit unless (A) The ball is in the strike zone when it touches the batter, or (B) The batter makes no attempt to avoid being touched by the ball;

If the ball is in the strike zone when it touches the batter, it shall be called a strike, whether or not the batter tries to avoid the ball. If the ball is outside the strike zone when it touches the batter, it shall be called a ball if he makes no attempt to avoid being touched.

APPROVED RULING: When the batter is touched by a pitched ball which does not entitle him to first base, the ball is dead and no runner may advance.

Since players nowadays wear all manner of jewelry, in 2019 the following overdue codicil was added to Rule 5.02 (b) (2): *Comment: A batter shall not be considered touched by a pitched ball if the ball only touches any jewelry being worn by a player (e.g., necklaces, bracelets, etc.).*

As Alexander Cartwright made no mention in his playing rules of bases on balls, he also made no provisions for a batter who was hit by a pitch. The notion of awarding a batter his base for being hit by a pitch was not universally embraced by the rules until the game was nearly half a century old. As late as 1886, a full decade after the National League was founded, the senior league still refused to penalize pitchers—like Charley

Radbourn and John Clarkson—for throwing at enemy hitters to intimidate them.

As a consequence of the National League's sluggishness in addressing the hit batsman problem, situations like the following one often arose to confound umpires. In a game on July 29, 1884, between the Chicago White Stockings and Detroit Wolverines, with Stump Weidman of Detroit on first, rookie Wolves backstop Chief Zimmer was struck in the arm by a pitch as he flailed at it and missed. The ball then caromed off Zimmer and skipped past Silver Flint, the Chicago catcher, allowing Weidman to move to second base. Cap Anson, the White Stockings' first baseman-manager, heatedly protested that the ball should be ruled dead and Weidman made to return to first.

The lone umpire working the game, Stewart Decker, then had to decide whether to call the pitch a strike or to rule it no pitch and a dead ball. Rule 30 in 1884 defined a ball "striking the batsman's person while standing in his position, and without it being struck at" as a dead ball. Decker, feeling that the rule supported Anson's argument, sent Weidman back to first and deemed the delivery to Zimmer no pitch.

Detroit manager Jack Chapman contended in vain that Zimmer's act of swinging at the pitch precluded it being called a dead ball and that Zimmer should have been assessed a strike and Weidman allowed to advance. League officials later realized, however, that both Anson and Chapman had an equally valid argument and also foresaw that if Decker had sided with Chapman, as he well could have, there was nothing in the rules to deter a batter from deliberately allowing a pitch to hit him as he swung in the hope of providing runners with an opportunity to move up a base. Actually, in the pre-National Association era, for a long time the ball was not dead when it hit a batter. Shortstop Candy Nelson would even let a ball hit him in the head to gain a base for a runner.

But for all their recognition that a more comprehensive rule covering hit batsmen was long overdue, National League moguls still tarried for another two years before finally joining the American Association prior to the 1887 season, when both major leagues adopted a uniform rule book, in decreeing that a batter hit by a pitched ball was entitled to first base provided he had not first swung at the ball, in which case it was automatically dead.

Meanwhile, the American Association had adopted the hit batsman rule in 1884, largely to combat the tactics of two of its pitchers—Will White and John Schappert, both of whom were notorious for deliberately trying to plunk batters. Schappert was looked upon as so dangerous an intimidator that, after the 1882 season, other AA moguls persuaded St. Louis owner Chris von der Ahe not to renew his contract with the Browns. Released by St. Louis, Schappert hooked on with Harrisburg of the Interstate League in 1883. The campaign was barely a month old before his welcome was nearly worn out in that circuit, too. In the June 10, 1883, edition of *Sporting Life*, Schappert was accused of the "cowardly habit . . . in maliciously crippling men at the bat. . . The manager of the Columbus club, defeated by the Harrisburg team last week, attributed the defeat to Schappert's action, the Ohio men being afraid to stand up at the plate." White, meanwhile, saw his effectiveness decline sharply in 1884 after the hit batsman rule was implemented.

Before the hit batsman rule was adopted, an umpire had only one tool at his disposal to stop a potential beanball war if a pitcher like Schappert or White was working the points. In 1879, the National League authorized its arbiters to fine hurlers for deliberately hitting batters with pitches, the levy ranging from $10 to $50. Even a $10 fine could be painful in that era, since many players made less than $1,000 for the season. But umpires were reluctant to make pitchers dig into their pockets unless the offense was too brazen to pass unpunished. Part of the reason was because an umpire in the late 1870s could not afford to alienate a team if he wanted to keep his job. Umpires had to be approved by clubs in order to receive assignments to work games, and one of the surest ways to be denied approval was to anger a team's pitching ace by socking him in the pocket.

Even after National League umpires were first made salaried employees of the leagues in 1883, fines for hitting batters were few and far between. What usually deterred pitchers from throwing at rival batters was the fear of becoming clay pigeons themselves when they batted. Not only were pitchers required to hit in 1883, but many also played other positions on days when they were not in the box. Though the schedule that season called for just 98 games, Charley Radbourn collected 381 times at bat and another Hall of Fame twirler, Jim Galvin, took 322 official turns at the plate.

Since the National League batters who were hit by a pitch were not given their base until 1887, we must wonder now if Lee Richmond's perfect game on June 12, 1880, the first of its kind in big league history, was really a perfecto by today's rules. It is entirely possible, and even likely, that Richmond hit at least one Cleveland batter in the course of shutting down the Blues, 1–0.

It is also likely that without the hit batsman rule, Hooks Wiltse of the New York Giants would have logged a perfect game on July 4, 1908. Facing the Philadelphia Phillies that day with two out in the ninth of a 0–0 game, Wiltse got two quick strikes on his mound opponent, George McQuillan. One strike away from a perfecto, Wiltse then blazed a pitch that McQuillan took for what both Wiltse and his catcher Roger Bresnahan were certain would be called a third strike. But plate umpire Cy Rigler granted the Phillies pitcher a reprieve when he ruled it a ball. Disconcerted, Wiltse then hit McQuillan with his next delivery to give the Phils their first baserunner.

Roger Bresnahan was credited with many accomplishments in his career but never with catching a perfect game thanks (he later swore) to the plate umpire muffing a called third strike with two out in the ninth inning in Hooks Wiltse's 1908 near perfecto.

What was the pitcher doing up at bat with two out in the ninth inning of a potential perfect game? The score at the time was 0–0! Wiltse subdued the mild threat by retiring Phillies leadoff hitter Eddie Grant, continued to hold the Phils hitless in the 10th, and then got a run in the bottom of the frame to win 1–0 and receive credit for a no-hitter.

Hooks Wiltse, the only hurler to miss out on a perfect game when an errant pitch hit his mound opponent that day with two out in the ninth inning.

Remarkably, Wiltse might still have achieved a perfect game after hitting McQuillan had the National League not encountered rigorous opposition when it quixotically abolished the hit batsman rule prior to the 1901 season, along with instituting a rule calling for a strike on every foul hit ball with less than two strikes. Both rule changes were greeted with scorn. Connie Mack, the newly hired manager of the fledgling Philadelphia American League entry, in the March 16, 1901, issue of *Sporting Life*, remarked "Calling foul ball strikes is an awful 'doggy' rule, and the League in legalizing the pitcher to soak a batsman in the head whenever he wants to is going to cause no end of trouble during the season."

American League president Ban Johnson had already announced that his loop would disdain both of the NL's new rule changes. He relented on the foul strike rule two years later when the two leagues made peace, but long before then the NL had restored the abolished hit by pitch rule after early results in 1901 spring training games bore out Mack's prediction. On the eve of Opening Day, April 18, 1901, senior leader president Nick Young announced that NL owners had voted to rescind the rule revision and return to the old hit by a pitch rule, and so it has remained in both major leagues ever since.

An earlier effort by the NL to mitigate the hit batsman rule was likewise met with eventual disfavor. In 1892, when the National League and American Association merged, the hit batsman rule was revised to read that a batter became a baserunner "if, while he be a batsman without making an attempt to strike his person (excepting hands or forearm, which makes it a dead ball) or clothing be hit by a ball from the Pitcher, unless—in the opinion of the Umpire—he intentionally permits himself to be so hit."

The addendum in parentheses became known as "The Welch Amendment," although it was never officially called that, and emanated from what were considered cheap bases received, with fleet outfielder Curt Welch the leading culprit. Welch had set a new hit-by-pitch record in 1891 with 36, breaking his old mark of 34 set the year before. With catchers still wearing rudimentary protective gear and no catcher's box rule yet in place, catchers generally played several feet behind the batter without runners on base while the umpire was stationed behind them. Given that, Welch would often fake a bunt, bringing the catcher racing out from behind the plate to potentially field it and leaving the umpire completely exposed as the pitch came in. While the alarmed umpire was busy duck-ing the incoming ball, Welch would stick up his left hand and bat—he was a right-handed batter—and deliberately let the pitch graze either the bat or his hand, usually the former. The grateful umpire, often victim for the first time to Welch's chicanery, usually would give him the benefit of the doubt that he had been making a genuine effort to ward off the pitch when his team began clamoring he had been hit on the hand while the opposition claimed he had brought it on himself.

The present hit-by-pitch rule was not restored until 1897, although there were yearly disputes at NL meetings as to whether the new rule was a good one. The catalytic event occurred on May 12, 1896, at Louisville's Eclipse Park II when Brooklyn second baseman Tom Daly was hit on the wrist by a Chick Fraser pitch and had to convince Louisville hurler Bert Cunningham, who was umpiring the plate that day as a substitute official, that he was hit on the shoulder in order to get his base. After the game, it emerged that Daly's wrist had been broken by Fraser's pitch, an absurd development that led to an almost unanimous vote to rescind the Welch Amendment.

Another point to consider in tracing the history of the hit batsman rule is whether a batter has always been given his base, as he is now, if a pitch merely touches him. The hit batsman rule that the American Association introduced in 1884 read that if a batsman be *solidly* hit by a ball from the pitcher when he evidently cannot avoid the same, he shall be given his base by the umpire. What constituted a solid hit was left to an umpire's judgment. In a July 27, 1884, game at Cincinnati, rookie umpire Robert Ross delighted the home crowd when he was bullied into ruling that a pitch by Louisville's Guy Hecker nicked Cincinnati hurler Bill Mountjoy's uniform blouse and awarded Mountjoy his base to force home the tying run in the ninth inning. After Cincinnati tallied four runs off Hecker in the 11th to win the game, Mountjoy gleefully confessed to any who would listen that the pitch had never touched him, let alone hit him solidly.

It is also rewarding, and sometimes downright amusing, to examine how an umpire determines that a batter is not entitled to be given his base because he did not make sufficient effort to get out of the way of a pitch. Not being a mind reader, an umpire obviously can't be certain whether a batter deliberately let a pitch hit him. Experienced arbiters know that even a Phil Niekro knuckler can freeze a batter expecting a fastball and prevent him from dodging it. Umpires therefore almost always give a hit batsman his base unquestioningly, and a fan can go to a game every day for several seasons without seeing a batter denied a free trip to first after being hit by a pitch.

Those fans that were at Dodger Stadium, however, on May 31, 1968, witnessed the most renowned enforcement of stipulation (2B) to rule 5.05 (b). That night, after pitching four successive complete-game shutouts, Dodgers right-hander Don Drysdale was on the threshold of breaking Walter Johnson's fifty-five-year-old record for the most consecutive scoreless innings pitched (56) as he entered the ninth frame protecting a 3–0 lead over the San Francisco Giants. Drysdale then stumbled and loaded the bases with none out. With a 2-and-2 count on Giants catcher Dick Dietz, Drysdale hit him with his next pitch, apparently forcing home a run and ending his bid to shatter Johnson's mark. But plate umpire Harry Wendelstedt ruled that Dietz hadn't made a sincere effort to avoid the pitch and called it simply ball three.

With the count now full, Dietz skied out to left field, too shallow for the runner on third to tag up and score. Drysdale then retired the next two batters to tally his fifth straight shutout and preserve his scoreless skein, which ultimately reached 58 innings before it was halted.

After the game, the Dodgers claimed that Wendelstedt's call was both correct and courageous. Giants vice president Chub Feeney said it would have been courageous only if Wendelstedt had made it at San Francisco's Candlestick Park.

Dietz and Giants manager Herman Franks naturally argued their cause at the time the incident occurred, but it was in vain. Another argument pertaining to stipulation (2B) to rule 5.05 (b) that prior to the introduction of video review in 2014 was almost always a futile exercise for a batter, was contending that a pitch hit him when an umpire failed to see it. On rare occasions, however, the dispute hinged on evidence of his claim that a batter was unexpectedly able to produce. In Game Four of the 1957 World Series, Nippy Jones of the Milwaukee Braves won his case in the following manner.

With his team trailing the New York Yankees, 5–4, Jones led off the bottom of the 10th as a pinch hitter for Warren Spahn. Yankees southpaw Tommy Byrne fed Jones a wicked low and inside curveball in the dirt that scooted to the backstop in Milwaukee's County Stadium and then rebounded almost back to the plate. Already embroiled in an argument that the pitch had hit his foot, Jones stooped to retrieve the ball and located a black smudge on it. He then showed the mark to plate umpire Augie Donatelli; Jones contended the smudge was shoe polish while the Yankees said it had been caused by the ball hitting the backstop.

Donatelli sided with Jones and awarded him his base. Felix Mantilla ran for Jones and was sacrificed to second by Red Schoendienst. Johnny Logan followed with a double to tie the game, and then Eddie Mathews hit a two-run homer to win it for the Braves, 7–5. Whether Jones was right in his argument or simply lucky will forever be a topic for debate. In any event, his shoe was immortalized even if its owner was soon history. After the "Shoe Polish" incident, Jones never again reached base safely in a major-league game.

5.05 (b) (3)

The catcher or any fielder interferes with him. If a play follows the interference, the manager of the offense may advise the plate umpire that he elects to decline the interference penalty and accept the play. Such election shall be made immediately at the end of the play. However, if the batter reaches first base on a hit, an error, a base on balls, a hit batsman, or otherwise, and all other runners advance at least one base, the play proceeds without reference to the interference.

In the nineteenth century, when most games were under the auspices of only one umpire who often stood behind the pitcher with men on base, catchers would routinely impede an opponent's bat without being detected. Connie Mack reputedly was a master at hindering a batter's stroke. The rule book for the 1899 season was the first to stipulate that a batter became a baserunner if a catcher obstructed his swing. Not until twenty-one years later, however, did the manual specify that catcher's interference occurred even if a receiver merely tipped a hitter's bat. In amateur games, even though the catcher's interference with a batter rule is often invoked, for well over a century so few infractions were seen at the major-league level that it earned Baltimore receiver Clint Courtney a spot in the record book when he was cited twice on June 19, 1960, in a game against the Detroit Tigers. In the fourth inning, home-plate umpire Ed Hurley nailed Courtney for tipping Tigers outfielder Sandy Amoros's bat, and two frames later Hurley caught Courtney repeating the offense against first baseman Steve Bilko.

Courtney's record has since been tied several times, but the infraction still occurs relatively rarely in the majors, and only seven players have been the beneficiary twice in one game, for a total of eight instances: Ben Geraghty in 1936, Pat Corrales (himself a catcher) twice in 1965, Dan Meyer in 1977, Bob Stinson (also a catcher) in 1979, David Murphy (after a thirty-one-year lull) in 2010, Jacoby Ellsbury in 2015, and Tommy La Stella on June 7, 2018. Ellsbury also holds the single-season record for being the recipient of catcher's interference calls with 12 in 2016 as well as the career record, formerly held by Pete Rose. On September 11, 2017, he passed Rose with his 30th base received on catcher's interference in the fourth inning of a game moved from St. Petersburg to New York's Citi Field due to Hurricane Irma, when he victimized Tampa Bay Rays catcher Wilson Ramos. We say victimized because Ellsbury, in an otherwise uneven career, has made reaching his base via catcher's interference an art form. Ellsbury missed all of the 2018 and 2019 seasons with hip and foot injuries, but in the interim La Stella, now with the Angels, has emerged as his potential eventual successor. In his lone postseason appearance in 2018 in the National League Wild Card Game, La Stella,

then with the Cubs and serving as a pinch-hitter, reached base on catcher's interference for the fifth time that season, even though he had fewer than 200 plate appearances. In 2019, La Stella reached base on catcher's interference an American League–leading six times despite being sidelined by a broken leg for a large chunk of the season. On extremely rare occa-

Tommy La Stella, the present-day master at reaching base on catcher's interference calls.

sions a batter is called out for intentionally initiating the interference with a catcher, but it is an almost impossible call for an umpire since he can't be a mind reader.

5.05 (b) (4)

A fair ball touches an umpire or a runner on fair territory before touching a fielder. If a fair ball touches an umpire after having passed a fielder other than the pitcher, or having touched a fielder, including the pitcher, the ball is in play.

The first contingency of this rule can often penalize the team at bat, even though a hit is automatically awarded. On September 17, 2010, in a National League game at Philadelphia, after the Washington Nationals had scored a run in the top of the first inning, the Phillies threatened to break the game open in the bottom half. With three runs already home and only one out, the Phils had the bases loaded with shortstop Wilson Valdez at the plate. Valdez rocketed a groundball up the middle past Nats pitcher Jason Marquis before striking second-base umpire Tim Tschida and zipping into center field. Since the ball had passed the pitcher and no other fielder, Tschida properly called the ball dead immediately and gave Valdez first base on a single, allowing all three baserunners to move up only one base due to the force created by Valdez's single. In all likelihood, the Phils would have scored at least two runs on Valdez's hit, thus the penalty. But since they ended up tallying six runs in the first after knocking out Marquis and eventually handing Roy Oswalt an easy 9–1 win, in the end Tschida's unintentional interference made no difference.

Tschida was also involved not long afterward in a play where the second contingency of this rule applied. In a June 8, 2011, contest at San Diego's Petco Park, Rockies right fielder Seth Smith lined a shot off Padres pitcher Dustin Moseley's hand that then struck Tschida, again working at second base that day. Because the ball had already contacted a fielder before hitting an umpire, Smith had to leg out a single and Troy Tulowitzki, who was on first, had to make it safely to second on his own.

5.06 Running the Bases

(a) Occupying the Base

(1) A runner acquires the right to an unoccupied base when he touches it before he is out. He is then entitled to it until he is put out, or forced to vacate it for another runner legally entitled to that base.

Rule 5.06 (a) / 5.06 (c) Comment: If a runner legally acquires title to a base, and the pitcher assumes his pitching position, the runner may not return to a previously occupied base.

Supposedly, the comment attached to Rule 5.06 (a) and 5.06 (c) was triggered by Germany Schaefer, a zany infielder with several American League teams in the early part of the twentieth century. But here is another tale that may be more myth than fact. For one, there are at least two very different versions of the motivating incident.

In *The Glory of Their Times*, Davy Jones insisted it happened in a 1908 game between Detroit and Cleveland. Jones was on third base for the Tigers and Schaefer on first in the late innings of a tie game. Trying to manufacture a run, Schaefer lit out for second, hoping to draw a throw from Cleveland catcher Nig Clarke so that Jones could then score. But Clarke refused to bite. Safe at second with an uncontested stolen base,

Speedster Clyde Milan was the first player in American League history to play as many as 16 seasons, all with the same team, and never be on a pennant winner. A star outfielder with Washington between 1907 and 1922, he retired two years before the Senators won their first pennant. Milan also had the bad luck to overlap with Ty Cobb for his entire career and watch Cobb obliterate most of his otherwise extraordinary baserunning feats.

Schaefer reportedly shouted, "Let's try it again," and then raced back to first base. Clarke still did not throw. But when Schaefer again tried to pilfer second on the next pitch, Clarke finally succumbed and threw down to the bag. According to Jones, he took off for home as soon as Clarke let go of the ball, and both he and Schaefer were safe.

Another version had Schaefer on first base and Clyde Milan on third for the Washington Senators in the ninth inning of a 1911 game with the Chicago White Sox. The same sequence of events occurred that Jones reported in his memoirs, except that the Sox catcher steadfastly refused to let go of the ball as Schaefer went through his reverse steal routine and Milan failed to score.

Schaefer possibly pulled his stunt on more than one occasion, in which case both stories may be true. But it seems more likely that neither tale has much substance in fact, for a form of Rule 7.08 (i), prohibiting a runner from running the bases in reverse order to create havoc, was not devised until 1920. By then, roughly a decade had passed since Schaefer had reportedly turned the game on its ear with his reverse steal gimmick, far too much time if the rule makers were really as embarrassed as legend would have us believe.

> **5.06 (a) (2)**
>
> Two runners may not occupy a base, but if, while the ball is alive, two runners are touching a base, the following runner shall be out when tagged and the preceding runner is entitled to the base, unless Rule 5.06 (b) (2) applies.

Rule 5.06 (b) (2) deals with a runner forced to move up a base tagging that base before a preceding runner, also forced to move up a base has vacated it, in which case the preceding runner is out if either he or the base he was required to move up to are tagged. This rule is so rarely enforced that few fans even know it exists, but contingency (2) of the rule on occupying a base is another matter.

Even though there is no situation, however far-fetched, whereby two runners can legally occupy the same base, despite all the rules against it, a far-fetched situation once occurred in which *three* runners tried to occupy the same base. The bizarre development came at Brooklyn's Ebbets Field on August 15, 1926, with the Robins facing the Boston Braves in the opening game of a doubleheader. Trailing, 1–0, in the seventh inning against right-hander Johnny Wertz, Brooklyn tied the count when Johnny Butler led off with a single and came home on catcher Hank DeBerry's double into the left-field corner. After pitcher Dazzy Vance dribbled a single down the third-base line and leadoff batter Chick Fewster was hit by a pitch to load the bases, Braves manager Dave Bancroft lifted Wertz in favor of lefty George Mogridge.

Mogridge got Merwin Jacobson to hit a weak pop to the mound, and up came rookie first sacker Babe Herman with one out. Getting a pitch he liked, Herman belted a towering fly to deep right. DeBerry properly tagged at third base even though it seemed likely the ball would fall safely. Vance, at second, also held up, fearing it would be caught. Meanwhile, Fewster traveled nearly to second and waited on developments. Certain that the ball was out of right fielder Jimmy Welsh's reach, Herman put his head down as soon as he left the plate and ran at top speed.

The ball bounced off the fence, allowing DeBerry to score easily. But Vance, who had loitered near second until the ball dropped, was convinced after he rounded third that he would be a dead duck if he tried to score, and retreated to the bag . . . at the same time Fewster was reaching third. Seeing Vance returning there, Fewster headed back to second. But before he could get more than a few yards from third, Herman, who had run the whole way with his head down, roared past him and slid into the bag. Dumbfounded, Fewster decided that he too might as well add to the logjam at third. For a few seconds, Brooklyn had three runners on the same base.

Only Vance rightfully belonged there, and he was not about to budge. After getting the relay throw from catcher Oscar Siemer, Boston third sacker Eddie Taylor had no idea who belonged where, but he knew he had someone dead to rights. First he tagged Vance and then he slapped the ball on Herman, upon whom it was just dawning that he might not have hit a base-clearing triple. In fact, Taylor's tag was unnecessary; Herman was automatically out the moment he passed Fewster between second and third, though he would be credited with a double on the play.

Fewster, the lone Brooklyn runner who had done his job correctly thus far, set sail for second when he saw the clutter at third. Taylor rifled the ball to second baseman Doc Gautreau. Realizing he could not beat the throw,

Fewster left the basepath and veered into the outfield with Gautreau on his tail. After the tag was made on Fewster, the three umpires working the game, Beans Reardon, Charlie Moran, and Ernie Quigley, huddled and quickly came forth with the verdict that it was a twin killing, ending the inning. Herman thus had doubled into a double play. Almost lost in the turmoil was the fact that DeBerry had scored on the two-bagger, putting Brooklyn up, 2–1. When the Dodgers won, 4–1, Herman's blow became the game-winning hit, but that will never be how it is remembered.

An interesting footnote to the Herman *faux pas*: Not until 1907 did it become a rule that a baserunner was immediately out if he passed a team-mate on the basepaths. If the three-men-on-third incident had occurred before then, the Dodgers could have emerged successfully had Fewster somehow managed to scramble back safely to second base and Herman all the way to first.

Meanwhile, the decision as to who gets the putout on a play like the one in which Herman passed Fewster can flummox even members of baseball's inner circle. As an example, in the fourth inning of Game Three of the 1992 World Series, the Atlanta Braves had Terry Pendleton on first and Deion Sanders on second with no outs and David Justice at the plate. Justice walloped a pitch from Toronto Blue Jays right-hander Jose Guzman to deep center field, but Devon White made a sensational catch against the 400-foot marker.

Certain it would be an extra-base hit, Pendleton had rounded second base and passed Sanders. Not realizing the umpires had already called Pendleton out, the Blue Jays relayed the ball to first baseman John Olerud. Amid the chaos, Sanders headed for third base but was eventually chased back to second by Kelly Gruber, who narrowly missed tagging him out for what would have been the first World Series triple play since 1920.

When the dust had settled, TV announcer Sean McDonough informed the viewing audience: "If you're scoring, it's 8-4-3 as they dou-bled up Pendleton."

McDonough was wrong; Pendleton was out the moment he passed Sanders. The throws from White to Blue Jays second baseman Roberto Alomar to Olerud were superfluous. Pendleton's putout properly went to Toronto shortstop Manny Lee, the closest Blue Jay to Pendleton when he passed Sanders, and there was no assist on the play. But McDonough was not alone in his mistake. The morning after the game, several newspapers gave White an assist in their box scores and failed to credit Lee with the putout.

5.06 (b) Advancing Bases

5.06 (b) (4) Each runner including the batter-runner may, without liability to be put out, advance:

(A) To home base, scoring a run, if a fair ball goes out of the playing field in flight and he touched all bases legally; or if a fair ball which, in the umpire's judgment, would have gone out of the playing field in flight, is deflected by the act of a fielder in throwing his glove, cap, or any article of his apparel;

(B) Three bases, if a fielder deliberately touches a fair ball with his cap, mask or any part of his uniform detached from its proper place on his person. The ball is in play and the batter may advance to home base at his peril;

(C) Three bases, if a fielder deliberately throws his glove at and touches a fair ball. The ball is in play and the batter may advance to home base at his peril;

(D) Two bases, if a fielder deliberately touches a thrown ball with his cap, mask or any part of his uniform detached from its proper place on his person. The ball is in play;

(E) Two bases, if a fielder deliberately throws his glove at and touches a thrown ball. The ball is in play;

Rule 5.06 (b) (4) (B) through (E) Comment: In applying (B-C-D-E)the umpire must rule that the thrown glove or detached cap or mask has touched the ball. There is no penalty if the ball is not touched.

The history of *Rule 5.06 (b) (4)* and its many contingencies needs considerable additional research. Fielders in the pre-National Association era (1871–75) on occasion caught balls in their caps; some threw their caps at balls they could not reach. The 1873 season marked the first appearance of a rule that specifically addressed this misdeed. One base was awarded if a fielder stopped a ball with his hat or cap instead of a part of his body. No mention was made of a thrown glove, as the only gloves worn in the 1870s were catchers' protective shields that could not readily be peeled off or detached from the hand.

Beginning with the inception of the National League in 1876, base-runners were awarded two bases if a fielder used his cap or any other part of his attire to interfere with a batted ball. Still no mention was made in the rules of gloves until 1910, when it was decreed that if a fielder stopped or caught a batted ball with his cap, glove, or any part of his uniform, while it was detached from its proper place on his person, the batter and any base runners were entitled to three bases. In 1914, the rule was restructured to make the penalty three bases for a batted ball and two for a thrown ball. The three-base levy was imposed because most violations came when outfielders, despairing of reaching balls hit over their heads or in the gap, flung their gloves in the hope of knocking them down. Since these hits were almost certain doubles anyway, it was well worth a two-base penalty to throw a glove at them, if only to corral those that would otherwise go for triples or even inside-the-park home runs.

There is surprisingly little documentation as to what went on between the mid-1880s, when most players started using gloves, and 1910. With nothing in the rules to prevent it, one can imagine that fielders were quick to heave their gloves at balls they could not reach. However, if that had been done with any frequency, seemingly a preventive measure would have been drafted long before 1910.

Yet we know there were players who took advantage of the absence of a rule, just as players will always take advantage whenever they see an opening. In the mid-1890s, Baltimore Orioles groundskeeper Tom Murphy purportedly was instructed to let the outfield grass grow long in Orioles Park so that balls could be secreted in it. Rather than give chase when an opponent hit a gapper, Joe Kelley, Willie Keeler, Steve Brodie, and other Orioles outfielders would scoop up one of the hidden balls and fire it into second base, nailing the shocked runner who had been positive he had a stand-up double. Did Kelley, Keeler, and Brodie resort to tossing their gloves at hits they could not flag down in enemy parks, where the grass did not provide them with a better option? In all likelihood they did, but the proof of it has failed to survive. Observe that the word purportedly prefaces the description of this ploy, for it would seem that opposing outfielders would also have taken notice of the concealed balls and made an issue of them, thereby nipping the Orioles' tomfoolery in the bud.

Before we return to the manual, note that Rule 5.06 (b) (4) omits mention of any penalty if a fielder throws his glove at and touches a foul ball. This omission might seem insignificant. Why would a fielder hurl his glove at a ball that was going foul anyway? It has been done, however, and for good reason.

In the sixth inning of a game with the St. Louis Browns on July 27, 1947, Boston Red Sox first baseman Jake Jones topped a ball that slowly trickled outside the third base line toward St. Louis third sacker Bob Dillinger. Although the dribbler was foul, Browns pitcher Fred Sanford, realizing it might roll fair and Dillinger would be unable to throw Jones out, fired his glove at the ball and hit it. Umpire Cal Hubbard promptly awarded Jones a triple.

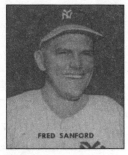

FRED SANFORD

Fred Sanford is remembered today mostly for throwing his glove at a foul ball to assure it stayed foul but was so highly coveted by the Yankees after he lost 21 games for the Browns in 1948 that they gave up three players, including future All-Star catcher Sherm Lollar and $100,000 for him. He finished his ML stay three years later with a 37–55 career record and a 4.55 ERA.

In 1954, the rule was changed to apply only to fair balls, making it possible now for a pitcher or an infielder to do as Sanford did with impunity as long as the ball—in the umpire's judgment—is clearly going to remain foul.

The crucial thing to remember in Rule 5.06 (b) (4) is that the ball, whether fair or foul, has to be touched by the glove or apparel thrown for a crime to have occurred. The act of throwing it will not, in and of itself, be cause for a penalty but nonetheless can be one for embarrassment, as Texas Rangers shortstop Elvis Andrus learned in a game against the Angels on July 25, 2015. Even though the Rangers came away with a 7–6 victory, Rangers manager Jeff Banister was steamed afterward. "It was a lapse of mental consciousness . . . not really understanding the three-base rule if you clip the ball. That's the second time I have seen it, and both times the guy didn't know the three-base rule."

While throwing a glove to knock a ball foul or keep it from rolling fair is explicitly covered in the rules, another form of obstruction is not—at least not explicitly. On May 27, 1981, in a game between Kansas City and Seattle at the Kingdome, Royals center fielder Amos Otis tapped a slow roller down the third-base line in the sixth inning. Mariners third baseman Lenny Randle dropped to his hands and knees and successfully blew the ball foul. The umpiring crew ruled it a foul ball until Royals skipper Jim Frey threatened to protest the game. They then changed their call to fair, crediting Otis with a single and Randle with illegal obstruction because he had altered the course of the ball even though he never touched it. The next batter, George Brett, was retired, ending the top half of the sixth. The play had no impact on the game—the Royals won, 7–4. But the jury is still out on whether their protest would have been upheld if the umpires had not backed down and the Mariners had won. The incident is so well known among veteran umpires, however, that the ruling today would almost certainly be the same.

5.06 Dead Balls

The Dead Ball rules have not been altered in some while, but in 2019 this addendum to the comment following Rule 5.06 (c) (7) first appeared in the rule book in paragraph four.

> If a ball is intentionally placed inside a player's uniform (e.g., a pants pocket) for the purpose of deceiving a base runner, the umpire shall call "Time." The umpire will place all runners at least one base (or more if warranted, in the umpire's judgment, in order to nullify the action of the ball being put out of play), from the base they originally occupied.

Previously, infielders—particularly left-handed first basemen—would fake a return throw to the pitcher after a failed pickoff attempt and slip the ball instead into a back pocket momentarily before surreptitiously removing it after showing the runner an empty left hand. Granting all runners a base in this situation appears to be another effort to abort a delay in play. Unhappily, the hidden ball trick itself may soon become a thing of the past. Bill Deane, the authority on HBTs, points out there has only been one since 2013. For the HBT to work, the fielder with the ball must alert an umpire it's in his possession while the pitcher paws the ground or engages in some such act aimlessly, all of which takes time, and saving time now is of the essence. How much time is saved here is highly debatable since an umpire has to stop play to make his call and the stoppage remains in effect until all runners have moved up one base or more.

5.07 Pitching

(a) Legal Pitching Delivery

There are two legal pitching positions, the Windup Position and the Set Position, and either position may be used at any time.

The legal pitching position in 1845 bore little similarity to what it is in 2020. Alexander Cartwright's rules called for a pitcher to stand on a line four yards long, 45 feet from home plate, and drawn at right angles to a line from home plate to second base.

In 1863, the pitching restriction became two lines instead of one, with the front line 45 feet from the plate and the back line 48 feet distant, forming an imaginary 12 x 3 foot box. At the moment he released the ball, a pitcher had to have both feet within the box's boundaries. The rear line of the box was moved back one foot in 1866. A year later, the length of both the back and front lines was shrunk to six feet, but the pitcher's station did not evolve into an actual rectangular box until 1874, with the box's dimensions constricted to 6 x 4. In 1879, the box's dimensions were changed to 4 x 6. Two years later, the front line of the box was moved back to 50 feet, but the box's size remained the same until 1886 when it was made 7 x 4. In 1887, the length was reduced to five and a half feet, although the width went unchanged.

In addition to having to learn to pitch from inside a box whose dimensions were constantly changing, a pitcher prior to 1893 faced several other restrictions. Most importantly, he had to alter his style of delivery frequently in order to keep pace with the rapidly changing rules. Until 1872, a hurler was required to deliver the ball with a straight arm swinging parallel to the body or in much the same manner as the delivery of a slow-pitch softball pitcher. In 1872, pitchers for the first time were permitted to deliver the ball with their elbows bent, enabling them to snap their wrists and, thus, throw curveballs as long as they kept their pitching hands below their hips at the point of release. The rule was modified in 1878, requiring pitchers to keep their hands below their waists. A year later, it was decreed that a pitcher had to face the batter when he took his position to deliver the ball, thereupon making it easier for an umpire—as well as a batter—to observe the release point, but this rule was often ignored depending on the umpire.

The 1883 season marked the next attempt to simplify an umpire's task, as pitchers now could hurl the ball from any angle or height below their shoulders. But when this modification still proved too difficult for arbiters to monitor, the National League threw up its hands in 1884 and allowed overhand pitching for the first time.

Spalding's Baseball Guide for the 1884 season commented: "The League simply allows what experience has taught them they could not effectively prevent." The surrender to exponents of overhand pitching was a concession that many observers feared would reduce the offensive quotient of the game to near zero. That dire prediction did not prove to be the case, but hitters suffered enough in the 1884 season to cause the National League to restore the ban on overhand pitching the following spring. The prohibition once again was so hard to enforce, though, that a month into the 1885 season the NL reverted to the previous year's rule. Within days, the American Association and the other professional circuits also grudgingly lifted all restrictions on the height from which a pitcher could deliver the ball.

But even though overhand pitching was now universally legal, Will White, Tim Keefe, and many more of the game's leading hurlers continued to throw with an underhand wrist snap, both because they felt it saved wear and tear on their arms and because they were too far along in their careers to change. By the early 1890s, overhand pitching became the norm as young phenoms such as Amos Rusie, Kid Nichols, and Cy Young appeared on the big-league scene. All were adolescents in 1885 when the overhand delivery was first legalized permanently, still in the formative stages of learning their craft, and so were quickly able to adapt when the last restriction was lifted on the style a pitcher could employ to deliver the ball to a batter.

Prior to 1887, which some authorities consider the true beginning of the so-called modern era, pitchers were free to assume any position they wanted before beginning their delivery. Even after the rule was tightened in 1878 so that the pitcher at least had to face the batter, pitchers were still permitted to utilize a running start, which might also include a series of hops, skips and, as in the case of "Jumping" Jack Jones, even a leap into the air before releasing the ball. Also prior to 1887, disputes as to whether pitchers exceeded the boundaries were rampant, but with only one arbiter on the scene to detect violations, the argument almost always went against the offensive team.

In July 1884, the Cincinnati Reds of the American Association, after complaining all season that Louisville's Guy Hecker strode beyond the front line of the box repeatedly when he delivered the ball, finally laid a row of smooth stones in front of the pitcher's box in Cincinnati's American Park so that Hecker would slip on them if he finished his delivery outside it. In retaliation, the Louisville club, after grumbling to no avail that Cincinnati ace Will White stood out of bounds when he started his delivery, planted a wall of stones along the right side of the pitcher's box in Eclipse Park.

In 1887, along with some idiosyncratic temporary rule changes like awarding a batter a hit for every walk he earned and requiring four strikes instead of three for a strikeout were several enduring revolutionary ones. Among them was a new rule eliminating a batter's liberty to signal for either a high or a low pitch, a privilege that had belonged to all batters ever since 1867. Of even more significance, the pitcher's box was reduced to a 4-foot by 5½-foot rectangle, and hurlers for the first time were required to anchor their front foot on or behind the front line of the box before delivering a pitch. Many pitchers saw their careers suffer from this change. Charlie Ferguson, one of the top pitchers in the National League in 1886, was transitioning to second base at the time of his tragic death after the 1887 season. Meanwhile, Ed Morris, arguably the game's first great southpaw, owned 114 wins after his first three seasons in the majors (1884–86), but won only 57 games thereafter. Most significantly, in 1886, the last year a running start was permitted, Baltimore Orioles rookie left-hander Matt Kilroy fanned an all-time record 513 batters, and another southpaw hurler with Louisville, Tom Ramsey, got 499 hitters to saw the air. The following year, with batters now given four strikes, Ramsey's whiff total fell to 355 and Kilroy collected just 217 Ks.

Other than lengthening the pitching distance to its present 60-feet, 6 inches from the plate, the pitching rules were, in essence, permanently established in 1887. It may even be said that as pitchers develop today, meaning from Little League to the major leagues, they only have to overcome a distance change. The rules for delivering the ball remain the same as they were in 1887.

Incidentally, a pitcher can still deliver a ball underhand like a slow-pitch softball hurler, as Pacific Coast League southpaw Chesty Johnson did on occasion in the early 1950s. But even though there is no limit on the height of a pitch's arc, underhand "moon" balls are eschewed because they would be crushed by major-league hitters. Cleverly disguised bloopers are another matter. Rip Sewell and Bobo Newsom in the 1930s and 1940s both developed excellent bloopers that were very effective when mixed in with their other deliveries. Sewell called his the "eephus" ball, after Pittsburgh Pirates teammate Maurice Van Robays said the pitch was eephus, which in baseball parlance at that time meant it was nothing. Sewell's blooper sometimes arced as high as 25 feet, and for years he was able to gloat that no one had ever hit a homer off it. In the 1946 All-Star Game at Boston's Fenway Park, Ted Williams ended Sewell's boast by sending one of his eephus balls into orbit in the eighth inning. It was Williams's second homer in the 12–0 AL rout.

5.07 (a)
Pitchers shall take signs from the catcher while in contact with the pitcher's plate.

This contingency of Rule 5.07 (a) presumes that signs are always given by the catcher. Even though they often originate from the dugout with a manager or a coach, the pitcher must nonetheless make a pretense of taking his stance on the pitcher's rubber and facing the catcher before commencing his delivery. There is no definitive evidence when catchers, for the most part, began signaling for pitches. No doubt the opposite often occurred in the early days, with pitchers signaling what they intended to throw. Tony Mullane, one of the most controversial figures in the game's history, acknowledged after he retired that in 1884, while with Toledo of the American Association, whenever he was caught by Moses Walker—a mixed-race catcher famous for being the first to overtly defy the unwritten color line in major-league baseball—he would ignore Walker's signals and throw whatever he wanted. Clark Griffith, especially after he became a pitcher-manager, reputedly did the same after signaling his catcher what the pitch would be.

5.07 (b) Warm-Up Pitches

When a pitcher takes his position at the beginning of each inning, or when he relieves another pitcher, he shall be permitted to pitch preparatory pitches to his catcher during which play shall be suspended. A league by its own action may limit the number of preparatory pitches and/or may limit the amount of time such preparatory pitches may consume. If a sudden emergency causes a pitcher to be summoned into the game without any opportunity to warm up, the umpire-in-chief shall allow him as many pitches as the umpire deems necessary.

As early as the aught years of the twentieth century, baseball moguls grew concerned about the increasing length of games, which had often begun lasting as long as two and a half hours. In an effort to shorten matters, both leagues adopted rules to reduce game length. American League president Ban Johnson went so far as to eliminate warmup pitches between innings, decreeing that a pitcher had to be ready as soon as the inning's opposition leadoff batter had raced in from the field, grabbed his bat, and stepped up to the plate. The new rule was short-lived, however, and pitchers were soon allowed the usual number of warmup pitches again.

An incident at Boston's Huntington Avenue Baseball Ground on June 27, 1911, played a decisive role in Johnson's shamefaced reversal of his own rule. With Philadelphia A's first baseman Stuffy McInnis due up in the top of the eighth inning, the Red Sox' Ed Karger, about to work his fifth frame in relief of Smoky Joe Wood, endeavored to lob a few quick warmup tosses to catcher Les Nunamaker. McInnis suddenly darted up to the plate, bat in hand, and smoked Karger's latest warmup toss deep into right field. Since Boston's outfielders had yet to take their positions, the ball scooted to the wall. Before anyone could track it down, McInnis

Stuffy McInnis, the owner of an inside-the-park home run during which not even the inkling of a play was made on his batted ball.

had crossed the plate with an inside-the-park home run, one of only 20 dingers he hit in his entire 19-year career.

Red Sox manager Patsy Donovan vehemently protested McInnis's gambit, but plate umpire Jack Egan only smiled at him. The game, by the way, took one hour and forty-seven minutes to complete, with Philadelphia winning, 7–3.

5.07 (c) Pitcher Delays

When the bases are unoccupied, the pitcher shall deliver the ball to the batter within 12 seconds after he receives the ball. Each time the pitcher delays the game by violating this rule, the umpire shall call "Ball." The 12-second timing starts when the pitcher is in possession of the ball and the batter is in the box, alert to the pitcher. The timing stops when the pitcher releases the ball.

Likewise, a batter can be assessed a strike if he fails to step into the batter's box within five seconds after an umpire calls that time is in. Since these are comparatively new rules, time will tell how strictly they are enforced. The results thus far are not promising. There was talk for a while about installing a 12-second clock (15-second clock when there is a runner or runners on base) in every major-league park so fans could excitedly watch the seconds tick away, but as yet it is no more than talk (although a 20-second clock with no runners on base was implemented in Triple-A leagues in 2015). In 2018, the clock time with no runners on base was shaved to 15 seconds.

5.07 (d) Throwing to the Bases

At any time during the pitcher's preliminary movements and until his natural pitching motion commits him to the pitch, he may throw to any base provided he steps directly toward such base before making the throw.

Comment: The pitcher shall step "ahead of the throw." A snap throw followed by the step directly toward the base is a balk.

For most of the nineteenth century, Rule 5.07 (d) did not exist—even in rudimentary form. Consequently, pitchers like the aforementioned Tony Mullane, who was ambidextrous and did not wear a glove unless he played another position, was thus able to start to deliver a pitch with his right arm and then abruptly shift the ball to his left hand and snap a pickoff throw to any base. Left-hander Matt Kilroy, the all-time single-season strikeout king, early in his career would stand facing the plate and then fire the ball to first base without either looking toward it or stepping in that direction, which was no longer permissible by the time he pitched his final ML innings in 1898. In a game between Louisville and the Philadelphia Athletics of the American Association, the A's light-hitting infielder Cub Stricker (.217 as a rookie in 1882) had what should have been a career day on August 29, 1883, when he went 4-for-4, but it was spoiled by the wiles of Louisville pitcher Guy Hecker, who duped Stricker into being picked off base a record three times in a single game. Hecker was among the numerous pitchers severely impacted by the elimination of hop, skip and jump deliveries. Stricker's unwanted record was later tied by Benny Kauff of the New York Giants on May 26, 1916, at the merciless hands of the Braves' Lefty Tyler.

5.07 (f) Ambidextrous Pitchers

A pitcher must indicate visually to the umpire-in-chief, the batter and any runners the hand with which he intends to pitch, which may be done by wearing his glove on the other hand while touching the pitcher's plate. The pitcher is not permitted to pitch with the other hand until the batter is retired, the batter becomes a runner, the inning ends, the batter is substituted for by a pinch-hitter or the pitcher incurs an injury. In the event a pitcher switches pitching hands during an at-bat because he has suffered an injury, the pitcher may not, for the remainder of the game, pitch with the hand from which he has switched. The pitcher shall not be given the opportunity to throw any preparatory pitches after switching pitching hands. Any change of pitching hands must be indicated clearly to the umpire-in-chief.

Known colloquially as the "Venditte Rule," this rule first appeared in its entirety when Pat Venditte, a switch-pitcher (capable of pitching proficiently with both arms), entered the professional ranks. After a successful career at Creighton University, Venditte was drafted in the 20th round by the New York Yankees in 2008. He labored seven years in the minors, mostly as a relief pitcher, before making his first major-league appearance in 2015 with the Oakland A's. Reasonably successful as a rookie, with a 1.19 WHIP in 22 games, all in relief, Venditte has since struggled. In 2018, after a good season with Lehigh Valley in the International League the previous year, Venditte was signed by the Dodgers. He lasted only 14 innings before being sent to Oklahoma City of the Pacific Coast League where he again shone, fashioning a 0.86 WHIP in 45 games. The 2019 season was a virtual repeat. In two appearances with the Giants, Venditte compiled a 16.20 ERA and then spent the rest of the campaign in Triple A. Now thirty-four, Venditte has proven over and over that his dual-armed talents work at the minor-league level but has yet to stick for a full season in the majors.

Preceding Venditte were several major-league hurlers who switch-pitched on one or two occasions, but none with anywhere near the proficiency of Tony Mullane, the winner of 284 games in the 1880s and early '90s. A one-year suspension in 1885 for contract jumping and suspicions that some of the games he lost might not have been on the level have thus far worked to deny him a spot in the Hall of Fame. Mullane was not only a frequent switch-thrower but also a switch-hitter and a fine all-around player. Early in the 1882 season, while playing for Louisville, in addition to hurling the first American Association no-hitter he became the first AA performer to steal second, third, and home in a single turn on the bases.

Tony Mullane was said to have two faces as well as the equal use of both arms on the ball field. The "Mr. Hyde" face engaged in contract jumping and was suspected at times of throwing games. The "Dr. Jekyll" face flat out belongs on a Hall of Fame plaque.

With Mullane's departure went a one-of-a-kind player, and the majors have not seen anything approaching his like since 1894. However, ambidextrous hurlers other than Venditte turn up now and again in the minors, usually just to provide box office appeal, although occasionally with a serious purpose. In an attempt to stifle Joe Bauman, a legendary left-handed slugger in the low minors who hit a minors-record 72 home runs in 1954, Audie Malone, normally a right hander, resorted to using his left arm when he squared off against Bauman, then with Artesia, in a Longhorn League game on July 4, 1952. Pitching for the Roswell Rockets, Malone got Bauman to fan on a slow curve in the first inning. But Bauman singled in his only other appearance against Malone, who was markedly unsuccessful against the rest of the Artesia lineup. He was pelted from the mound in the fourth inning and charged with a 12–8 loss. For the year, Malone posted a 12–16 record and a 5.45 ERA, whereas Bauman led the Texas circuit with 50 homers and 157 RBIs.

5.08 How a Team Scores

(a) One run shall be scored each time a runner legally advances to and touches first, second, third and home base before three men are put out to end the inning.
EXCEPTION: A run is not scored if the runner advances to home base during a play in which the third out is made (1) by the batter-runner before he touches first base; (2) by any runner being forced out; or (3) by a preceding runner who is declared out because he failed to touch one of the bases.

Note contingency (2) under the EXCEPTION clause. Its strict interpretation resulted in arguably the most controversial force out in major league history.

On September 23, 1908, in a game at the Polo Grounds against the Chicago Cubs with the NL pennant hinging on the outcome, New York Giants manager John McGraw chose Fred Merkle to replace regular first sacker Fred Tenney, who was idled by an ailing back. Then in just his second season with the Giants, Merkle rarely played but was privileged to sit on the bench beside McGraw, reputedly one of the keenest minds in the game.

With the score tied, 1–1, in the bottom of the ninth and two outs, the Giants had Moose McCormick on third and Merkle on first. Al Bridwell then shot a single to center, sending McCormick home with the apparent winning run. Upon seeing that Bridwell's hit would plate McCormick, Merkle started toward the Giants' clubhouse in center field, believing he had no further role in events. But when Cubs second baseman Johnny Evers began clamoring for the ball, Merkle got a sinking feeling that perhaps he had exited the stage prematurely.

What happened next will forever be contested. New York sportswriters at the Polo Grounds that afternoon swore that Merkle made for second base at that point and got there ahead of the throw to Evers, and even if he had not beaten it, the ball Evers was fed was not the one in play but another ball that was substituted. The game ball, according to some witnesses, somehow wound up in the possession of Giants pitcher Joe McGinnity, who flung it into the left-field bleachers. Chicago correspondents, on the other hand, swore that Rube Kroh, a seldom-used Cubs pitcher, wrestled the game ball away from McGinnity and flipped it to Evers long before Merkle arrived at the second-base bag. In any event, base umpire Bob Emslie claimed the crowd that had flooded onto the field after Bridwell's hit seemingly won the game blocked him from seeing the play at second, and the onus for making a decision fell on plate umpire Hank O'Day. After a lengthy delay, O'Day emerged from a conference with Emslie to rule that Merkle had been forced out at second and the game was still tied. Since it was impossible to clear the spectators off the field so the contest could continue, Cubs manager Frank Chance demanded a forfeit victory, but it went into the books as a 1–1 draw.

When the Giants and the Cubs finished the season deadlocked, the tie game had to be replayed. Three Finger Brown won the makeup contest for Chicago in relief of Jack Pfiester, outdueling Christy Mathewson, and the Cubs went on to best Detroit in the World Series and earn their last world championship prior to 2016.

Christy Mathewson logged 373 regular season wins but lost probably the most important game he ever pitched, the replay of the infamous Merkle game that decided the 1908 National League pennant.

Merkle's failure to touch second haunted him for the rest of his life, but the real goat should have been John McGraw. The nineteen-year-old Merkle was only following a slipshod custom—runners as late as 1908 often did not bother to touch the next base on a "sudden death" hit and some batters, most notoriously Boston's Chick Stahl, did not even bother to touch first base when a hit of his seemingly drove in the winning run. But on September 4, some three weeks before Merkle's boner, Johnny Evers had endeavored to have Warren Gill of the Pittsburgh Pirates called out by O'Day on a nearly identical play. O'Day demurred at the time but later that night, after debating the issue with Evers in a Pittsburgh hotel lobby, he realized that Evers had a valid argument. Since the Gill incident was widely reported, it ought to have been incumbent upon McGraw to remind his players of what Evers had tried to contrive against the Pirates, particularly when a repeat attempt was an imminent possibility with two out in the ninth and Giants runners at the corners.

Strangely, both the history of the problematical custom Merkle was following and documentation of successful attempts previous to Evers's to frustrate it have thus far eluded researchers. Though Evers today is considered to have been an ingenious groundbreaker, there were other efforts at the major-league level prior to the Gill incident to have a runner who neglected to touch a base as required by rule called out after an apparent sudden death hit. But for a parallel to events at the Polo Grounds on September 23, 1908, one must scour minor-league history to find a documented episode in which an umpire declared a runner on first forced out for failing to touch second after the supposed winning run crossed the plate. In a Western League game at Indianapolis on June 11, 1899, St. Paul pitcher Chauncey Fisher, after squandering an 11–5 lead, found himself trailing the Hoosiers, 12–11, in the bottom of the ninth inning. Facing Indianapolis's Doc Newton, Fisher singled to bring home teammate Frank Shugart with the tying run and move his catcher, Harry Spies, to third base. Eddie Burke then lined a single to George Hogriever in center field to plate Spies with the apparent winning run. Before running to second base, however, Fisher stopped to congratulate Burke for his hit, and Hogriever immediately sprinted to second and appealed to umpire Al Manassau. Manassau ruled Fisher forced out at second and disallowed the winning run, but not until the crowd had streamed onto the field and players from both teams had left the diamond, believing St. Paul had won the game. When Manassau could not clear the field, the final score was ruled to be 12–12. Manassau's decision was subsequently protested by St. Paul manager Charlie Comiskey, but one Briggs, *The Sporting News*'s St. Paul correspondent who witnessed the game, said Fisher's maneuver "was a chump play and I think there is no doubt but what the umpire's decision will be upheld." Given the fact that *The Sporting News* in that era was read from cover to cover weekly by players, managers, umpires, and fans at every level of the game, one can only marvel more than a century later how nine more years could have elapsed before a similar play and ruling occurred in a major-league contest.

Lest anyone believe the Merkle "boner" is so infamous that it can never be repeated in a major-league game, there is good reason to believe it can. In a game at Philadelphia on August 3, 2016, the Phillies had the bases jammed with the score tied, 4–4, and one out in the bottom of the 12th when Maikel Franco, facing San Francisco reliever Jake Peavy, singled to right-center to drive home Tommy Joseph with the apparent walk-off winning run. Giants center fielder Denard Span let the ball go past him, knowing that Joseph had scored. But while jogging toward the dugout, he noticed that Phillies runner Aaron Altherr, who had been on first, never touched second base. Although Altherr initially started toward second after Franco's hit, when he saw the ball make it to the outfield he peeled off to chase after Franco and congratulate him.

Seeing this, Span waved for right fielder Hunter Pence to retrieve the ball and get the force out on Altherr at second. Catcher Buster Posey, also observing the action, hastened to take Pence's throw at second. After considerable confusion, the official scorer, Mike Maconi, took a base hit away from Franco and recorded that he had hit into a force play at second. The game had been riddled with video replay challenges, but Giants skipper Bruce Bochy did not challenge here. We can only surmise that Bochy and the umpiring crew had been watching closely enough to verify that Cesar Hernandez, the runner on second, had made it to third. Had they not verified it, a successful video replay appeal at third would have meant that instead of a walk-off single, Franco would have been credited with hitting into an inning-ending double play. As it was, he stood to be deprived of his first career game-winning hit until MLB overruled Maconi and awarded him a single.

Evidence that Merkle's *faux pas* was already fading from memory came more than fifty years earlier on August 29, 1962, in a game at Dodger Stadium between the Dodgers and the Reds. In the bottom of the 13th inning, with the score deadlocked, 1–1, the Dodgers put runners on second and third with only one out. Duke Snider was then intentionally walked by Reds starter Joey Jay to load the bases and set up a possible double play, but catcher Johnny Roseboro spoiled it by looping a short fly to center that dropped in front of Vada Pinson. After Tommy Davis waltzed home from third to score the apparent winning run, Roseboro blundered by passing Snider—who hadn't bothered to run—between first and second and was called out.

Hall of Famer Duke Snider narrowly escaped committing the same base running blunder as Fred Merkle in a 1962 contest at Dodger Stadium.

Alarmed, Snider raced to second before the Reds realized what was occurring and barely avoided making the third out on a force play. Davis's run at that point became official, handing the Dodgers a 2–1 win that could have been foiled if Cincinnati had been more alert.

5.08 (b)

When the winning run is scored in the last half-inning of a regulation game, or in the last half of an extra inning, as the result of a base on balls, hit batter or any other play with the bases full which forces the batter and all other runners to advance without liability of being put out, the umpire shall not declare the game ended until the runner forced to advance from third has touched home base and the batter-runner has touched first base.

Rule 5.08 (b) Comment: An exception will be if fans rush onto the field and physically prevent the runner from touching home plate or the batter from touching first base. In such cases, theumpires shall award the runner the base because of the obstruction by the fans.

Probably the most famous instance of an umpire awarding a runner home plate because of fan obstruction was the wild ending on October 14, 1976, to the American League Championship Series that saw George Brett of the Kansas City Royals rifle a three-run homer into the seats at Yankee Stadium in the top of the eighth to tie the game, 6–6, only to have Yankees first baseman Chris Chambliss lead off the bottom half of the ninth inning by belting a solo dinger off reliever Mark Littell to clinch the pennant for the Yankees. In describing the pandemonium that ensued when Yankees fans began streaming onto the field almost the moment Chambliss's shot cleared the right-field barrier, Thurman Munson later said, "By the time Chambliss got to third base all hope of reaching the plate was gone. He never did make it."

Though Kansas City made no protest and the umpires seemed inclined to let Chambliss's interrupted journey around the bases pass without comment, hours later the Yankees' first baseman left the team's pennant celebration and crept out of the clubhouse, accompanied by two policemen, to touch home plate and make his flag-winning run official.

A similar play occurred on October 15 in Game Five of the 1999 NLCS, however, with a different result. With the bases loaded and the game tied, 3–3, in the bottom of the 15th inning, Mets third baseman Robin Ventura hammered a pitch from Atlanta reliever Kevin McGlinchy over the right-field fence in Shea Stadium for an apparent walk-off grand slam—the first such grand slam in postseason history. But Ventura was rightfully awarded only a single by the umpiring crew when he passed Todd Pratt, who had been on first base, when Pratt joined other teammates in mobbing Ventura before he could get to second base. Ventura's blow is now known instead as the "Grand Slam Single."

The honor of hitting the first walk-off postseason grand slam thus fell to Nelson Cruz of the Texas Rangers in Game Two of the 2011 ALCS at Rangers Ballpark in Arlington when his four-bagger off Detroit's Ryan Perry in the 11th inning made for a 7–3 final score—ironically what the final score would have been if Ventura's Mets teammates had allowed him to properly round the bases.

5.09 Making an Out

(a) Retiring the Batter
A batter is out when:
   (1) His fair or foul fly ball (other than a foul tip) is legally caught by a fielder;

Some playground forms of baseball still consider a batter out if his batted ball is caught either on the fly or the first bounce. Remarkably, the first-bounce rule was once in effect in all forms of baseball. Until 1865, any batted ball that was caught on the first bounce, whether it be a grounder to an infielder, a line drive to outfielder, a foul tip by a catcher, or a one-hopper to a pitcher, was an out; exceptions were balls that were bobbled and then scooped up on one bounce after they hit the ground.

Champions of the one-bounce-out rule felt that it saved injuries to players' hands, whereas its detractors contended that it not only made the game unmanly but there was nothing more frustrating to an admirer of good fielding than to see an outfielder nullify a hard-hit ball merely by stationing himself near enough to it to take it on the bound. When the proponents of a more "manly" game finally gained sway in 1865, however, the new rule in that year applied only to fair-hit balls. A foul ball snared on the first bounce remained an out as late as 1883 in the National League (after an experimental year in 1879 when it was not) and May of 1885 in the American Association. Upon the elimination of the first-bounce out on foul hits, *Spalding's Official Baseball Guide* for 1884 offered this accolade to National League moguls: "The continuance of the foul-bound catch would have been simply the retaining of a feature of the early period of base ball, in order to gratify the crowd and to help 'business,' and not the game."

A telling example of how heavily the foul-bounce-out rule could impact the outcome of a game occurred in an American Association contest between the New York Metropolitans and the Louisville Eclipse in Eclipse Park I on June 21, 1884. The AA, for reasons that are impossible to fathom now, had refused to follow the National League's lead in 1884 when the senior loop permanently eliminated the foul-bounce out, but the finale of the Mets-Eclipse game inspired a belated reassessment. After Jack Lynch of the Mets battled Eclipse ace Guy Hecker to a 2–2 draw at the end of regulation, New York solved Hecker for two runs in the second extra frame, but Louisville roared back in the bottom of the 11th, filling the bases with two out. Louisville catcher Dan Sullivan then sent a foul drive down the right field line that the Mets' Steve Brady speared on the first bounce to stifle the threat and end the game. Had Sullivan's hit landed fair instead of foul without being caught on the fly, rather than becoming the third out it would have resulted in at least a single, and in all likelihood would have sent home two runs and tied the game. What's more, the ball was conceivably catchable on the fly, but Brady may have chosen the easy way to corral it rather than risk muffing it after a long run. This sort of absurdity goaded AA officials to abolish the foul-bounce rule early in the 1885 season.

5.09 (a) (2)
A third strike is legally caught by the catcher

As a batter could be retired if his fly ball was caught on the first bounce, so at one time could he be put out when a catcher caught his third strike on the first bounce. In 1858, a rule was first introduced to allow a batter to run on a missed third strike. Until 1880, though, a batter was considered out if the catcher snagged his third strike either on the fly or the first bounce. The rule was so liberal largely because catchers wore little protective apparel in the early days, compelling them to play well back of the batter. Mitts and masks were rudimentary, chest protectors were skimpy, and shin guards did not really come into popular use until the early 1900s. Beginning in 1880, catchers had to move up close behind batters when the count reached two strikes. Before then it had been customary for a receiver to move up only with men on base and otherwise to play back and take balls on the first bounce, including third strikes. In 1901, it became mandatory in the National League for a catcher to play within 10 feet of home plate at all times; the American League adopted the same rule the following year.

If a foul tip is caught on what would otherwise be a third strike, the batter of course is out. That has always been the case. But prior to 1889, every foul-tipped ball that was cleanly caught by a catcher—either in his mitt or barehanded—was an out regardless of the strike count. In 1889, the rule was altered so that any foul hit not rising above a batter's head was deemed a foul tip and neither the batter nor any baserunners could be retired if it was caught. Moreover, it was just a foul ball, not even a strike. The rule was introduced to combat catchers such as Connie Mack and Wilbert Robinson, who were adept at making a clicking sound that imitated that of a foul tip closely enough to dupe umpires on what were otherwise merely swing-and-miss strikes.

5.09 (a) (4)
He bunts foul on third strike;

Rather remarkably, a foul bunt attempt was not universally deemed a strike until the 1894 campaign, and even then a batter was charged with a strike only if he bunted foul attempting to sacrifice. Heretofore, weak-hitting bat magicians such as Yank Robinson and Jack Crooks, as long as they were not too obvious about it, could tap pitches foul indefinitely without penalty until they finally drew a walk. Beginning in 1887, umpires were licensed to charge a batsman with a strike if they felt he was delaying the game by purposely fouling off pitches, but this rule was seldom invoked and often resulted in turmoil when an umpire did attempt to sanction an offender. An American Association game between St. Louis and Brooklyn on September 5, 1888, crumbled into mass confusion when umpire Fred Goldsmith, a star pitcher earlier in the decade with the Chicago White Stockings, instantly called a strike on Browns catcher Jack Boyle when he bunted a foul pop, deeming it a deliberate effort to hit foul, and then found himself obliged to void Brooklyn receiver Bob Clark's diving catch of the popup owing to his previous call of strike.

In 1895, the rules committee decreed that every foul bunt attempt, regardless of its intent, was a strike. That season was also the first in which a foul tip became a strike but only if the catcher caught it within the 10-foot lines of the catcher's box. Between the increased mound distance in 1893 and the impunity with which batters could foul off pitches at will—as long as the fouls were not palpable bunt attempts—it was small wonder that strikeout totals tumbled precipitously during the mid-1890s. In 1893, as an extreme example, the entire Louisville Colonels hill staff notched only 190 strikeouts in 114 games, and the New York Giants topped the National League with a mere 395 Ks, an average of about three and a half a game.

A prominent example of the impact the 1895 foul bunt rule change had on certain batters was Boston outfielder Hugh Duffy, who hit a record .440 in 1894. He was twenty-eight years old when the 1895 season commenced and was seemingly just coming into his prime. Nonetheless, his batting average plummeted 87 points in the season following his record-shattering year. In 1896, his average again dropped precipitously, all the way to an even .300, and although he rebounded in 1897 to hit .340, that season was his last that approached his peak years. Age, injury, lack of conditioning—none of the usual reasons accounted for his abrupt decline. Duffy had come to the majors a hunt-and-peck batter who deliberately poked pitches in the strike zone not to his liking foul in wait for exactly the one he wanted. In its April 14, 1900, issue, *The Sporting News* opined that the reason his batting had deteriorated so swiftly was the rule instituted in 1895 that assessed a strike on every failed bunt attempt. "As soon as the handicap was put on Duffy quit the bunting game and hit out, from which time his batting average grew beautifully smaller year after year." The *Chicago Times Herald* added that players usually slipped first in the field or in baserunning while "in the case of the captain [Duffy was first named Boston captain in 1896, replacing Billy Nash] he is still a grand fielder but a losing batsman."

We are obliged to observe that yet another MLB experiment now underway in lower leagues is giving a batter the equivalent of a fourth strike if he bunts foul on the third strike.

Presently, when a batter fouls off a two-strike bunt attempt it is almost always deemed strike three. But there are occasions when a batter squares to bunt and finds he has to dodge an inside pitch. If the batter yanks back the bat as he pulls away from the pitch, an umpire can rule it was not a bunt attempt even if the pitch touches the bat and rolls into foul territory; it is only a foul ball. Reds pitcher Michael Lorenzen benefitted enormously from such a ruling in a game against the Brewers at Great American Ball Park on August 29, 2018. With runners on first and second and no out in the bottom of the sixth, Lorenzen was nearly beaned after he squared to sacrifice with two strikes. The ball nonetheless struck his bat as he recoiled to escape being hit but was properly ruled foul, not strike three. On the next pitch, Lorenzen hit a three-run homer off Milwaukee's Taylor Williams.

5.09 (a) (5)
An Infield Fly is declared;

Strangely enough, the first version of an infield fly rule was adopted by a major league that lasted only one year—the ill-fated Players' League. Formed prior to the 1890 season, it also was the first circuit to employ two umpires in every game and move the front line of the pitcher's box back to 51 feet, a foot farther than its competitors—the National League and the American Association—in an effort to produce more hitting and scoring. Though all of its rule innovations produced the desired results— more offense, less rowdyism, and higher attendance than its two rival loops—the Players' League was outfoxed, largely by Chicago club president Al Spalding, and naively threw in the towel even while it had the two established circuits on the ropes. With its demise went all three of its newly devised rules.

The Players' League infield fly rule stated that if a baserunner was on first base and there were less than two outs and the batsman made a fair hit so that the ball would fall within the infield and the ball touches any fielder, whether held by him or not before it touches the ground, the batsman was out.

The term *infield fly* did not, however, first appear in the rule book used by the National League and American Association (which had combined forces in 1892) until 1894, a half century after Alexander Cartwright and his cohorts devised the first formal set of playing rules. As in the Players' League, it applied even if only first base was occupied. In 1895, it was modified to apply only if first and second base or all three bases were occupied with less than two out.

Prior to 1894, with the bases occupied, infielders (including pitchers and catchers) were free to drop infield pops or line drives on the gamble that they could then force out runners who had been frozen to their bases on the assumption the ball would be caught. Part of the reason it took so long for an infield fly rule to be adopted was that until the 1890s, when gloves became a fielding tool as well as a protective device, there was never assurance that a pop fly would be caught, let alone a line drive, and it seemed foolish for an umpire to call a batter automatically out and then sheepishly watch a fielder muff the ball. Initially, many infielders scorned the infield fly rule, feeling it deprived them of a defensive weapon. Brooklyn shortstop Tommy Corcoran demonstrated the most common form of disdain in a game against Baltimore on May 23, 1894, when he stood contemptuously still with a "hands-in-his-pockets" gesture with a man on base as a pop fly hit by John McGraw landed at his feet and umpire Tom Lynch perforce yelled something like, "Infield fly, if fair!" It is impossible now to ascertain the exact wording or signal given by an umpire on an infield fly in 1894, but today's rule is that once an umpire has signaled an air ball is an infield fly the batter is out only if it lands or is muffed in fair territory. An air ball drifting into foul territory before a play is made on it is no longer an infield fly, caught or not.

An extreme example of the way a quick-thinking fielder could take advantage of the absence of an infield fly rule was displayed in an American Association game at Cincinnati on June 22, 1882, between Cincinnati and the Pittsburgh Alleghenys. In the bottom of the 14th, with Cincinnati ahead, 5–2, Pittsburgh had Mike Mansell on second base and Ed Swartwood on first with none out when John Peters lifted an easy pop toward Cincinnati shortstop Chick Fulmer. After pretending to set himself for a catch, Fulmer let the ball drop and then scooped it up and fired to second baseman Bid McPhee. In swift order, McPhee tagged Mansell, who had remained on second base, and then touched the bag to force Swartwood. After McPhee returned the ball to pitcher Will White, White heeded a shout from his first baseman Henry Luff, directing his attention to Peters, who in disgust had not bothered to run out the popup, and fired to first to end the longest major-league game ever that culminated with a walk-off triple play (as Cincinnati, the home team, had batted first).

5.09 (a) (8)

After hitting or bunting a fair ball, his bat hits the ball a second time in fair territory. The ball is dead and no runners may advance. If the batter-runner drops his bat and the ball rolls against the bat in fair territory and, in the umpire's judgment, there was no intention to interfere with the course of the ball, the ball is alive and in play. If the batter is in a legal position in the batter's box, see Rule 5.04 (b) (5), and, in the umpire's judgment, there was no intention to interfere with the course of the ball, a batted ball that strikes the batter or his bat shall be ruled a foul ball;

Since the foul lines intersect the batter's box in such a way that the vast majority of it is in foul territory, the home plate umpire will almost always give the batter the benefit of the doubt if a ball hits his bat twice while he is still in the box. The same is generally true of balls that strike part of a batter's body after hitting his bat.

So rarely does an umpire rule a batter out in such a case that a protest is almost *de rigueur* when it happens. In a 1976 game on August 10 at Shea Stadium between the Mets and San Diego Padres, plate umpire John McSherry voided a sacrifice bunt attempt by Mets rookie Leon Brown in the bottom of the sixth inning and deemed it interference, claiming Brown's bat made contact with the ball twice. Mets manager Joe Frazier lodged the expected protest, but it was withdrawn when the Mets won the game, 5–4.

An example of a more commonly seen batter's interference call occurred in the bottom of the fourth at Arizona on August 2, 2019, between the Diamondbacks and Nationals. Leading off the frame against Washington's Joe Ross, Arizona outfielder Adam Jones hit a chopper near the plate that bounced up and hit him in the shoulder as he was heading toward first. Because, in plate umpire Bill Miller's judgment, he had completely left the batters' box and the ball hit him in fair territory, Jones was called out for interference. The play was scored as an unassisted putout by Washington catcher Yan Gomes. Far more memorable for most spectators than Jones's atypical out was that the Nationals used five pitchers in winning a combined 3–0 shutout.

Rule 5.09 (a) (8) Comment: If a bat breaks and part of it is in fair territory and is hit by a batted ball or part of it hits a runner or fielder, play shall continue and no interference called. If a batted ball hits part of a broken bat in foul territory, it is a foul ball.

Rule 5.09 (a) (8) **is complex**, and even then it does not cover every contingency. For instance, when a bat breaks and strikes a pitched ball not just once, not just twice, but three times, all seemingly in fair territory. Yes, it has actually happened. On October 22, 2012, at San Francisco's AT&T Park in Game Seven of the NLCS between the Giants and St. Louis Cardinals, Giants outfielder Hunter Pence, who had been struggling at the plate during the entire postseason, grounded a bases-loaded double to center field in the third inning off the Cardinals' Kyle Lohse that brought home all three runners (one on an error) and broke the game wide

open, with the Giants later winning, 9–0. Slow motion cameras and instant replay revealed that Pence's bat had broken on initial contact and it looked at first as if Pence would hit into a double play. But Cards shortstop Pete Kozma, after taking a step to his right, where the ball seemed headed, could not change course quickly enough when subsequent contact with Pence's shattered and crooked but still somehow intact bat pro-

Giants outfielder Hunter Pence's bases-loaded "broken" broken-bat double in Game Seven of the 2012 NLCS off the Cards' Kyle Lohse swiftly turned the affair into a 9-0 rout.

pelled it to Kozma's left side, where it trickled into center field, leading to three runs.

After the game, Cards outfielder Lance Berkman complained, "It hit the bat three times. It was actually an illegal hit, but there's no way you can expect an umpire to see that." But Berkman was wrong. Rule 5.09 (a) (8) demonstrates that even though he couldn't possibly have seen Pence's inadvertent bat machinations, plate umpire Gary Darling made the right call.

5.09 (a) (10)

After a third strike or after he hits a fair ball, he or first base is tagged before he touches first base;

Every fan has seen a batter try to pull away from or hold up on a pitch only to have it hit his bat and dribble into fair territory, rendering him an easy out. At one time balls that were hit unintentionally in this manner were not necessarily considered in play even if they went fair. Until 1892, whether a batter meant to hit a pitch that trickled off his bat was a matter for an umpire to judge. If it seemed the ball had been struck unintentionally, it was ruled dead and not counted as a pitch. Increasingly, however, during the late 1880s, umpires would rule the ball in play regardless of what they perceived the hitter's intent was, their logic being that no batter was about to let himself be deprived when a checked swing resulted in an accidental base hit.

But umpires in that era were particularly vulnerable to being talked out of their calls or influenced by the desire to appease such contentious players as Cap Anson or King Kelly, so a rule was inserted prior to the 1892 season clarifying that any fairly delivered ball that struck a batter's bat was in play if it went fair regardless of whether or not the batter intentionally meant to hit the ball.

5.09 (a) (11)

In running the last half of the distance from home base to first base, while the ball is being fielded to first base, he runs outside (to the right of) the three-foot line, or inside (to the left of) the foul line, and in the umpire's judgment in so doing interferes with the fielder taking the throw at first base, in which case the ball is dead; except that he may run outside (to the right of) the three-foot line or inside (to the left of) the foul line to avoid a fielder attempting to field a batted ball;

Rule 5.09 (a) (11) Comment: The lines marking the three-foot lane are a part of that lane and a batter-runner is required to have both feet within the three-foot lane or on the lines marking the lane. The batter-runner is permitted to exit the three-foot lane by means of a step, stride, reach or slide in the immediate vicinity of first base for the sole purpose of touching first

The three-foot boundary outside the first base foul line was first contained in the playing rules for 1858. In 1882, the National League mandated that the three-foot line had to be marked on the field in all its parks, but the American Association did not require it to be marked until three years later.

Normally, a batter is allowed to run either within the three-foot boundary or inside the first-base line, but there are notable exceptions. One is on a bunt fielded by the catcher or pitcher when a runner can impede the throw to first if he runs inside the line. In Game Four of the 1969 World Series on October 15 at Shea Stadium, with the score tied, 1–1, in the bottom of the 10th, New York Mets catcher J. C. Martin, who was pinch-hitting for pitcher Tom Seaver, dropped down a sacrifice bunt with runners on first and second. Baltimore pitcher Pete Richert fielded the ball and fired it to first baseman Boog Powell. But Richert's toss struck Martin on the wrist and bounded off into foul territory as pinch-runner Rod Gaspar raced home with the winning run. The Orioles screamed that Martin had run the last half of the distance to first illegally inside the foul line, but the umpires disagreed and the run stood. A videotape of the play made it appear that Baltimore had a valid case and that the run should have been nullified, with Martin ruled out. The 2–1 victory gave the Mets a formidable 3–1 Series lead and they won it the following day.

A less publicized but equally consequential violation that was disregarded occurred in Game Two of the American League Division Series between Cleveland and Baltimore at Camden Yards on October 2, 1996. In the bottom of the eighth inning of a 4–4 game, with the bases loaded and no outs, Orioles left fielder B. J. Surhoff hit a grounder up the middle that Indians reliever Paul Assenmacher speared and threw home to nail the lead runner. Tribe catcher Sandy Alomar then prepared to throw Surhoff out at first base for an easy double play, but had to take a side step to avoid hitting Surhoff, who was running inside the first-base line. Alomar then threw wildly to first baseman Jeff Kent, allowing Cal Ripken Jr. to score and the Orioles to install runners on second and third with only one out. Tribe manager Mike Hargrove protested the path Surhoff took to first base in vain, and Baltimore eventually won the game, 7–4, to take an insurmountable 2–0 lead. Afterward, analysts agreed that plate umpire Greg Kosc would almost surely have called

Surhoff out and the ball dead if Alomar had not tried to throw around Surhoff but simply drilled him in the back with the ball. If that were not irony enough, Cleveland's Kenny Lofton had been called out earlier in the game for runner interference on a play at second base.

The 2019 World Series featured a controversial run- ner interference call against Washington made by plate umpire Sam Holbrook in Game Six at Houston that fortunately proved inconsequential, as the Nats won the game, 7–2. In the top of the seventh inning, with none out and Yan Gomes on first base, Washington shortstop Trea Turner hit a chopper toward third base that was fielded by Astros reliever Brad Peacock. Even though replays showed that Turner ran a straight line to first and appeared to beat Peacock's throw to Yuli Gurriel, he was called out for interference when the throw hit him as he lunged for the bag and Gurriel's glove came off in the contact between the two. Holbrook's vehemently protested decision forced Gomes to return to first base with one

B. J. Surhoff. His controversial sprint from home to first base inside the foul line aided the Baltimore Orioles in taking a commanding 2–0 lead in games in their best-of-five ALDS against the Cleveland Indians in 1996.

out. Happily, Nats third baseman Anthony Rendon hit a two-run homer later in the inning to put the game out of reach and spare Holbrook the undying wrath of the Washington club. When Washington won again the following night, it marked the first World Series in which the road team won every game.

5.09 (a) (13)

A preceding runner shall, in the umpire's judgment, intentionally interfere with a fielder who is attempting to catch a thrown ball or to throw a ball in an attempt to complete any play;

   Rule 5.09 (a) (13) Comment: The objective of this rule is to penalize the offensive team for deliberate, unwarranted, unsportsmanlike action by the runner in leaving the baseline for the obvious purpose of crashing the pivot man on a double play, rather than trying to reach the base. Obviously this is an umpire's judgment play.

The most famous beneficiary of this rule was probably Orel Hershiser of the Los Angeles Dodgers. In 1988, Hershiser closed out the regular season with 59 straight scoreless innings to break the old record of 58, set in 1968 by another Dodgers pitching star, Don Drysdale. Like Drysdale, Hershiser needed a controversial umpire's decision to keep his streak alive and, also like Drysdale, the decision came in a game against the rival San Francisco Giants.

   On September 23, 1988, at San Francisco's Candlestick Park, Hershiser allowed Jose Uribe to reach third base and Brett Butler first with one out in the third inning. Ernest Riles then hit a potential double-play grounder but beat the relay to first from Dodgers shortstop Alfredo Griffin as Uribe scored. Hershiser himself was certain the steak had ended after 42 scoreless innings. But when he glanced toward second base, he saw umpire Paul Runge signaling interference on Butler for sliding out of the baseline to hamper Griffin's throw to first. The ruling meant that Riles and Butler were both out on an inning-ending twin killing that canceled Uribe's run.

   Hershiser went on to shut out the Giants, 3–0, running his skein to 49 consecutive scoreless innings. He then extended it to 59 against the San Diego Padres in his last start of the season on September 28, before being lifted for a reliever after the 10th of a 0–0 game that the Padres eventually won, 2–1, in 16 frames.

5.09 (b) Retiring a Runner

(3) He intentionally interferes with a thrown ball; or hinders a fielder attempting to make a play on a batted ball (see Rule 6.01 (j));

Violations of Rule 5.09 (b) (3) are common and usually arouse little controversy when they are called by an umpire. When they are not called, however, the controversy has the potential to loom enormous. In the National League Wild Card Game at Wrigley Field on October 2, 2018—eventually won by Colorado, 2–1, in 13 innings—no one can even begin to hazard what would have broken loose if the Cubs had won the game in the bottom of the 11th frame after Cubs shortstop Javier Baez, running from second to third, gathered up Colorado third baseman Nolan Arenado in a bear hug as Arenado put the tag on him several feet from the third-base bag on a potential double-play ball.

The interference seemingly went unaddressed because Arenado put up no struggle to try for an inning-ending double play at either second or first. In baseball terms, he failed to "sell the play." But Arenado's arms were bound to such a degree by Baez that he would have had to forcibly wriggle his right arm free just to create the impression he was trying to make a throw, by which time a double play would have been an impossibility. Meanwhile, Baez had sold the bear hug as a good-natured collision in which he made no effort to avoid the tag. Had the Cubs gone on to secure the winning run in the 11th inning, however, Colorado manager Bud Black might have had a difficult time explaining to critics why he didn't at least take issue with what would have instantly gone down in postseason history as "Baez's Bear Hug."

5.09 (b) (4)

He is tagged, when the ball is alive, while off his base.

APPROVED RULING: (A) If the impact of a runner breaks a base loose from its position, no play can be made on that runner at that base if he had reached the base safely.

APPROVED RULING: (B) If a base is dislodged from its position during a play, any following runner on the same play shall be considered as touching or occupying the base if, in the umpire's judgment, he touches or occupies the point marked by the dislodged bag.

The rule in the National Association, the first professional league, was quite the opposite with regard to a base bag that broke loose from its moorings; a runner had to hold on to the wayward cushion or else he was subject to being tagged out.

Beginning in 1868, the bag (and not the part to which it was fastened) was considered to be the base. When a base thief slid so hard he tore the bag out of its socket, he had to chase it down before a fielder got to him with the ball. Likewise, if a runner kicked the bag loose as he rounded it, any runners coming along behind him were obliged to touch the bag, not the spot where it had been. This rule prevailed during the five-year existence of the National Association, but was dropped in 1876 as the National League prepared to open play in favor of the pre-1868 edict, which was an ancestor of the current rule that establishes a base at the spot where it is located rather than the bag itself.

5.09 (b) (5)

He fails to retouch his base after a fair or foul ball is legally caught before he, or his base, is tagged by a fielder. He shall not be called out for failure to retouch his base after the first following pitch, or any play or attempted play. This is an appeal play;

In the 1880 season, for the first time a baserunner was out if he failed to return to his original base after a caught foul fly before he was either tagged out or the ball reached his original base ahead of him. Ever since 1876, runners had been allowed to return at their leisure on a foul ball without being subject to being put out but at the same time had been unable to tag up and advance if the foul was caught.

5.09 (b) (11)

He fails to return at once to first base after overrunning or oversliding that base. If he attempts to run to second he is out when tagged. If, after overrunning or oversliding first base he starts toward the dugout, or toward his position, and fails to return to first base at once, he is out, on appeal, when he or the base is tagged;

In 1871, a rule was first introduced stipulating a batter could overrun first base after touching it without being put out as long as he returned at once to the bag and made no attempt to try for second. This rule underwent many refinements over the years before it took on its present form. At the

amateur and high school level, runners are taught to be careful to turn to
their right whenever they overrun first so as not to leave their movements
to an umpire's judgment. In professional and college games, where the
officiating is of higher quality, the first-base umpire will generally overlook a runner turning to his left toward second base unless he makes a
distinctive move in that direction. Note that if a runner elects to slide,
though, in an effort to beat a throw to first, before 1940 he was out if he
slid past the bag and was tagged before he could return it.

5.09 (b) (12)

In running or sliding for home base, he fails to touch home base and
makes no attempt to return to the base, when a fielder holds the ball in
his hand, while touching home base, and appeals to the umpire for the
decision;

Rule 5.09 (b) (12) Comment: This rule applies only where runner
is on his way to the bench and the catcher would be required to chase
him. It does not apply to the ordinary play where the runner misses the
plate and then immediately makes an effort to touch the plate before
being tagged. In that case, runner must be tagged.

This comment bids us to inquire what an umpire should do if a player
carrying the game-winning run passes home plate without touching it
but the opposition fails to realize it. The answer is an umpire should do
absolutely nothing. He keeps his mouth shut, gives no signal of any sort as
to whether the runner was safe or out, waits for the players in the field to
vacate their positions, and then walks off the diamond himself.

That was precisely the manner in which way Game Five of the 1911
World Series ended. The Philadelphia A's and the New York Giants
were tied, 3–3, in the bottom of the 10th frame at the Polo Grounds on
October 25 when Fred Merkle of the Giants hit a potential sacrifice fly
along the right-field line with Fred Snodgrass on second and Larry Doyle
on third. Doyle tagged at third, waited for A's right fielder Danny Murphy
to make the catch, and then scooted home well ahead of the throw and
leaped into the arms of joyous teammates, none of whom noticed that
Doyle had skipped past the plate without touching it. When catcher Jack
Lapp and the rest of the A's also failed to spot Doyle's misstep, home plate

umpire Bill Klem just smiled to himself, though later he acknowledged to an Associated Press reporter that he would have ruled Doyle out if the A's had appealed. The gift victory extended the Series to a sixth game the following day at Philadelphia's Shibe Park, but when the A's won a 13–2 blowout, Doyle's phantom run became insignificant.

5.09 (c) Appeal Plays

(2) With the ball in play, while advancing or returning to a base, [the runner] fails to touch each base in order before he, or a missed base, is tagged;

Among the most hilarious illustrations of this rule in action occurred on June 17, 1962, at the Polo Grounds in the first game of a doubleheader between the Cubs and the fledgling New York Mets. After the Cubs scored four runs in the top of the first inning, aided by a fielding obstruction call against Mets first baseman Marv Throneberry, Throneberry came to the plate in the bottom half of the first with the bases loaded and no outs. Facing Cubs starter Glen Hobbie, Throneberry temporarily redeemed himself for his defensive bungle when he tripled to deep right-center, scoring all three runners. But, to add insult to injury. he was called out by umpire Dusty Boggess after Cubs first baseman Ernie Banks took a relay throw and stepped on second base while informing Boggess that Throneberry had missed the bag. Boggess agreed with Banks's appeal. When Mets manager Casey Stengel strolled out to argue the call, Boggess told him, "Don't bother arguing Casey, he missed first base, too." There are several versions of this story, but most agree that Stengel, after a pause, replied, "Well, I know he touched third base because

"Marvelous Marv" Throneberry epitomized the New York Mets' ineptness as a National League expansion team under Casey Stengel in the early 1960s. In the mid-1950s, however, he terrorized Triple-A pitchers as a Yankees farmhand, culminating in 1956 when he led the American Association in homers (42) and RBIs (145) in the second of his three consecutive seasons with Denver.

he's standing on it!" Throneberry's mistake proved costly, as the Cubs won the game, 8–7, but he nonetheless was credited with three RBIs on a single, a rarity.

Throneberry came to be known facetiously as "Marvelous Marv" after his gaffe, but he maintained a sense of humor about it. Later in life, he became one of the original spokesmen for Miller Lite beer, poking fun at himself in a series of TV commercials. His most famous line was: "If I do for Lite what I did for baseball, I'm afraid their sales will go down."

Throneberry's tale gives rise to the question what the ruling would have been if he had indeed missed first base but, because the appeal was made at second base, would he been credited with a single if his had been the Mets' only hit in the game? The answer is yes, absolutely yes, but no if the appeal had been at first base instead.

Before he died in 1959, Howard Ehmke was the leading specimen of how a pitcher could still be credited with a no-hitter if a rival batter stroked a clean hit but was subsequently declared out for missing first base. Pitching for the last-place Boston Red Sox on September 7, 1923, Ehmke twirled a 4–0 no-hitter against the A's at Philadelphia's Shibe Park that was nearly aborted early in the game when Ehmke's mound rival, Slim Harriss, cracked a liner over the shortstop that rolled all the way to the left field wall for an apparent double. But Sox first sacker Joe Harris, spotting that Harriss had missed first, called for the ball, thus preserving Ehmke's no-hit bid.

Red Sox pitcher Howard Ehmke (left) and Yankees hurler Bob Shawkey. The picture was probably taken at Yankee Stadium after the game of September 11, 1923, between the two teams in which Ehmke had lost his chance at a second consecutive no-hitter on a controversial scorer's decision.

Four days later, the breaks evened out for Ehmke when he lost his shot at becoming the first pitcher in major-league history to hurl two consecutive no-hitters. Working at Yankee Stadium, then in its first season, official scorer Fred Lieb ruled that a groundball Red Sox third baseman Howard Shanks mishandled on the Yankees' very first batter in the game, speedy center fielder Whitey Witt, rated a single. The tainted hit turned out to be the only one Ehmke surrendered in the game. One can only speculate today over what Lieb's ultimate ruling would have been if Witt's bobbled grounder had come in his final at-bat in the bottom of ninth inning rather than in the bottom of the first. As it was, in his autobiography, *Baseball As I Have Known It*, Lieb deemed his call that day "perhaps the saddest decision I ever made."

Many players in the early days lost inside-the-park homers for missing a base, and many in the years since have come away with less than a four-bagger when a teammate ahead of them on the bases either missed a base or mistakenly thought their hit was caught and peeled off toward their team's bench. In 1931, Lou Gehrig would have won the American League home run crown outright rather than sharing it with Babe Ruth if Yankees teammate Lyn Lary had not deprived him of a homer with a baserunning blooper in a game against Washington on April 26. Occupying second base in the top of the first inning when Gehrig rifled a ball off the Senators' Firpo Marberry into the center-field bleachers at Washington's Griffith Stadium, Lary left the basepaths after misinterpreting third-base coach Joe McCarthy's hand motion to slow down and trot home as a signal that the ball had been caught. Gehrig then passed Lary and was ruled out by umpire Bill McGowan. The Yankees ultimately lost the game, 9–7.

Similarly, Hank Aaron cost Milwaukee Braves teammate Joe Adcock a four bagger in one of the most famous games ever played, when he was guilty of mistakenly leaving the basepaths after Adcock hit an apparent game-winning home run.

Facing Pittsburgh southpaw Harvey Haddix on May 26, 1959, Aaron and the rest of his mates were set down in order for 12 straight innings. But when the Pirates were also unable to score off the Braves' Lew Burdette, Haddix was forced to take the hill again in the bottom of the 13th, even though he had already retired a single-game record 36 consecutive batters.

The Braves 37th batter, Felix Mantilla, led off the 13th by reaching first on a throwing error by Pirates third baseman Don Hoak, thereupon ending what was then considered the longest perfect game in MLB history. After Eddie Mathews bunted Mantilla to second, Aaron was purposely passed to set up a possible inning-ending double play. But Braves first baseman Joe Adcock laced Haddix's second pitch to him over the right center field barrier in Milwaukee's County Stadium for what seemed a game-winning three-run homer. However, Aaron thought the ball had landed in front of the fence. He touched second base and then headed toward the dugout. Adcock, who missed seeing Aaron leave the basepaths, was called out for passing Aaron by the time he reached third base, and the final score, instead of being 3–0, was 1–0, as only Mantilla's run counted. Haddix finished the night with a 13-inning one-hit loss and Adcock with the Braves' lone hit, though only a double instead of a home run. Note that first-base umpire Frank Dascoli initially determined the final score was 2–0 but was overruled by NL president Warren Giles, who rightfully pointed out that since the hit was only a double officially just one run actually scored.

Fortunately, Aaron touched second base before he deserted the base-paths. If there had been two outs at the time and Aaron had left the field without touching second, on an appeal play he would have been called out at that base for the third out, neither Adcock's hit nor Mantilla's run would have counted, the game might still be in progress, and Aaron would now be as infamous as Fred Merkle—and for much the same reason.

No pennant race or World Series has ever turned on a home run that was canceled when its striker missed a base, but all who were either in attendance or watching on TV when the Giants' Bobby Thomson hit his three-run "Shot Heard 'Round the World" that won the 1951 National League pennant still remember Jackie Robinson of the Dodgers holding his ground at second base and watching carefully to make sure Thomson touched them all before he finally bowed his head to the inevitable and left the field.

5.09 (c) (4)

He fails to touch home base and makes no attempt to return to that base, and home base is tagged.

We have already cited an example of this rule in action in a World Series game, but in the discussion of 5.09 (c) (4) the following appears for no clear reason in the fourth paragraph.

Appeal plays may require an umpire to recognize an apparent "fourth out." If the third out is made during a play in which an appeal play is sustained on another runner, the appeal play decision takes precedence in determining the out. If there is more than one appeal during a play that ends a half-inning, the defense may elect to take the out that gives it the advantage. For the purpose of this rule, the defensive team has "left the field" when the pitcher and all infielders have left fair territory on their way to the bench or clubhouse.

The paragraph pertaining to the possibility of an umpire having to recognize a "fourth out" first appeared in the 1958 manual in an effort to prevent further miscarriages, like one that occurred in an International League game on August 30, 1957. On that date, the Buffalo Bisons engaged in a tight struggle with the Toronto Maple Leafs for the IL pennant, hosted the lowly Montreal Royals, destined to finish in the cellar.

Montreal owned a 1–0 lead with one out in the bottom of the seventh, but Russ Sullivan, acquired only days before from Columbus, and all-league second sacker Lou Ortiz then proceeded to reach base for Buffalo. Third baseman Bill Serena followed with a long drive toward the center-field scoreboard. Thinking the blast was ticketed for extra bases, both Sullivan and Ortiz took off at full tilt. But Montreal center fielder Bobby Del Greco made a miraculous last-second grab and then wheeled and fired to first base, easily doubling Ortiz up for the third out. The sad problem for Montreal was that Sullivan crossed the plate before the third out was registered and the insoluble problem confronting umpire Harry Schwarts was that he had to rule Sullivan's run good even though Sullivan hadn't tagged up after Del Greco's catch and would have been subject to being doubled off second base if the Royals had not already recorded their third out of the inning by doubling up Ortiz.

Sullivan's tally knotted the score at 1–1 and Buffalo went on to win in 12 innings, 4–2. The Bisons ultimately fell a half game short of the IL pennant in 1957, but the controversy over Sullivan's tainted run and two other similar incidents during the 1957 season roused the rules committee to draft a revised section of the playing code stipulating that an umpire may be required to recognize an apparent "fourth out" when an appeal play on another runner is sustained subsequent to the third out.

The change in the rule meant that in a situation like the one in which Schwarts was forced to award Buffalo a run, the team in the field in the future would not be barred from making an appeal on a play more to its advantage solely because the side had already been retired. If today's rules had prevailed in 1957, Montreal would have been able to appeal Sullivan's run until its defensive corps "left the field" or when the Royals pitcher and all four Montreal infielders had left fair territory on their way to the dugout.

In the papers of Frederick E. Long, which reside at the Hall of Fame, historian/writer Richard Hershberger discovered an early day example where the fourth out rule could have been applied way back when if anyone on the field at the time had known the appeals process then in vogue. In a letter Boston player-manager Harry Wright wrote to Long on October 21, 1873, describing a game his club had played at Baltimore that afternoon, he concluded:

> Andy [Leonard] made an exceedingly brilliant catch in left field off a hit by [Lip] Pike he running with the ball and taking it at arm's length with a high jump. The bases were full and all started to run, the hit looking quite safe, but he returned it to second base, making a double play, closing the innings for a blank, one hand being already out. Had Andy not made that catch, it would have been very bad for us, as it would have given them the lead, at the close of the fifth inning. They claimed that the man's run, who was on third base when the ball was hit, counted, he getting home before the third man was put out. The umpire decided against them, and then there was a row. They objected to his continuing to act.

Hershberger noted: The 1873 rule read, "A player running the bases shall, after touching the home base, be entitled to score one run, but if a fair ball be struck when two hands are already out, no player running home at the time the ball is struck can make a run to count in the score of the game if the striker or player running the bases, is put out before touching the first base."

This reader observed that since the rule did not apply when only one hand was out, the runner on third tallied a run that ought to have counted because the appeal was made at second base rather than third base. Seemingly no one on the Baltimore club was cognizant of the situation, a fairly complex one, but it is surprising that Wright, a walking rule book, did not seem to realize his club's errant decision. What's more, the run would have also counted according to the current rule unless the team in the field, in this case Boston, had awakened to its mistake before abandoning the field.

5.10 Substitutions and Pitching Changes (Including Visits to the Mound)

(a) A player, or players, may be substituted during a game at any time the ball is dead. A substitute player shall bat in the replaced player's position in the team's batting order.

For many years, a manager was allowed to substitute for a player in his lineup only when a disabling injury occurred. Even then, the opposing manager could refuse to allow the substitution if he felt the injury was not severe enough. Oftentimes an argument ensued, with the umpire forced by the rules to side against the team with the injured player. Unable to substitute, the loser of the argument then either had to struggle onward with the injured player or play a man short. Sometimes a team was forced to play short a man solely because it came to the park with only eight men and could not find a suitable player in attendance who would agree to fill in that day. This happened to the Cleveland Forest Citys on July 6, 1872, when they appeared at the park used by the Brooklyn Eckfords for a National Association contest after Al Pratt and Rynie Wolters—both of them pitchers—abandoned the club. Pressed into service in the box for Cleveland was left-hander Charlie Pabor, normally an outfielder but with enough pitching background to be arguably the game's first southpaw of consequence. When Pabor beat the Eckfords, 24–5, with only two outfielders behind him, the headline in the *New York Times* the following day was: "The Eckfords Beaten by Eight Men."

There can be no doubt that players in the nineteenth century were a hardy breed. In 1878, the Boston Red Caps went through the entire National League season with only ten players, winning the pennant in the process. At that, the team's lone sub, Harry Schafer, got into just two official league games.

But most clubs were not as free of mishap as the 1878 Red Caps. One of the most famous instances when a team was compelled to finish a contest with only eight men came on July 22, 1884, in a match between the Providence Grays and Philadelphia Phillies at Providence. In the box for the Grays was Charlie Sweeney, who only the week before had been made the club's ace after Charley Radbourn was suspended for drunkenness and insubordination. Holding a 6–2 lead over winless Philadelphia rookie Jim McElroy after seven innings, Providence manager Frank Bancroft decided to save Sweeney's arm and ordered him to right field, bringing right fielder Cyclone Miller in to pitch.

As though offended by the idea, Sweeney stalked off the diamond and headed for the dressing room. Finding him there changing into his street clothes, Bancroft demanded he return to the field, but Sweeney refused to comply. The suspicion was that Sweeney wangled the showdown with Bancroft so that he could gain his release from Providence and sign with the St. Louis Maroons of the rebel Union Association. At any rate, the Grays had to play the rest of the game a man short, the rules at the time giving Bancroft no other recourse when a player who was not injured refused to remain in action. Providence somehow survived the eighth inning unscathed, but then the roof fell in. According to one account: "In the ninth Miller was hit freely, the ball going just where the [two remaining] outfielders could have handled it had they been in their regular places. Errors crept in fast, and the Philadelphias scored eight unearned runs."

After the disheartening 10–6 loss (which provided McElroy with his first and only major-league win), Providence released Sweeney, reinstated Radbourn, and went on to bag the National League flag. But teams continued to play shorthanded on occasion until 1889, when a limited substitution rule was drafted, allowing one player for each team (whose name was printed on the scorecard as an extra player) to be put into the game for any player on the field at the end of any complete inning, with the replaced player not permitted to return to the game.

The following year the rule was revised to let a second substitute for each team also enter a game at the end of a complete inning. In 1891, the rule was further liberalized so that it now resembled the current rule.

Beginning with the 1891 campaign, any player on the field could be sub-stituted for at any time during a game. Among other things, the revamped rule ushered in a new type of specialist: the pinch hitter. Previously, a player had sometimes been sent up to bat for a teammate but only when an injury compelled the opposition agree to the substitution. Like so many innovations, however, the concept of a pinch hitter was slow to take hold. In the early 1890s, pinch-hitters were used so infrequently that until 1896 the record for the most pinch hits in a season stood at a mere two, first done in 1893 by Jack Sharrott, a reserve with the Philadelphia Phillies.

According to baseball legend, the one player who more than any other forced the game's lawmakers to tighten the 1891 substitution rule was Mike "King" Kelly. There is an oft-told tale that one afternoon in the early 1890s, shortly after the rule was loosened to allow substitutes to enter a game at any time, Kelly, then with the Boston Beaneaters, was on the bench when a pop foul headed his way. Seeing that Beaneaters catcher Charlie Ganzel had no chance to reach it, Kelly sprang to his feet, announced himself in the game for Ganzel, and snared the pop. The problem here is that if Kelly really pulled off this stunt, one would imagine that so obvious a loophole in the rules would have been immedi-ately sealed. However, there was no further important legislation regard-ing substitutions until 1910, when it was mandated that the captain of a team making a substitute must immediately notify the umpire, who in turn must announce the change to the spectators. By 1910, Kelly was not only out of the game but had been dead for some sixteen years. Hence the probability is strong that the Kelly tale, if not altogether apocryphal, has been embellished over the years. What's more, two contemporary players of Kelly's, Kid Gleason and Charlie Bennett, attested that his gambit was not bought by the umpire that day in any event.

5.10 (d)

A player once removed from a game shall not re-enter that game. If a player who has been substituted for attempts to reenter, or re-enters, the game in any capacity, the umpire-in-chief shall direct the player's manager to remove such player from the game immediately upon noticing the player's presence or upon being informed of the player's improper presence by another umpire or by either manager. If such direction to remove the substituted for player occurs before play commences with the player improperly in the game, then the substitute player may enter the game. If such direction to remove the substituted-for player occurs after play has commenced with the substituted-for player in the game, then the substitute player shall be deemed to have been removed from the game (in addition to the removal of the substituted-for player) and shall not enter the game. If a substitute enters the game in place of a player-manager, the manager may thereafter go to the coaching lines at his discretion. When two or more substitute players of the defensive team enter the game at the same time, the manager shall, immediately before they take their positions as fielders, designate to the umpire-in-chief such players' positions in the team's batting order and the umpire-in-chief shall so notify the official scorer. If this information is not immediately given to the umpire-in-chief, he shall have authority to designate the substitutes' places in the batting order.

Much ado was made when Chris Young of the Red Sox appeared twice in the same game on August 25, 2017, in a lopsided 16–3 loss to Baltimore in Fenway Park. Young began the game as the Sox' DH, batting in the seventh spot in the order. Given that the game was a complete blowout, Boston manager John Farrell selected a position player to pitch the top of the ninth inning, and chose one of his players already in the game, first baseman Mitch Moreland, for the task. Because Moreland—who had batted cleanup the entire game—replaced a pitcher, who does not bat, the Red Sox forfeited the designated hitter pursuant to Rule 5.11 (a), meaning that Moreland would continue hitting for himself in the four spot, and Moreland's first-base replacement, Hanley Ramirez, would also hit for himself and replace DH Young in the seventh slot in the batting order.

As luck would have it, the seventh-place hitter was due up second in the bottom of the ninth, and none other than Young stepped into the batter's box and hit a fluke single. Fortunately the inning ended without the Sox scoring, so Orioles reliever Mike Wright's ERA went unblemished. He was charged with a hit, however, when the game ended with the illegal substitution unnoticed by any of the umpires or Baltimore manager Buck

Showalter. Since it did so end, the portion of Rule 5.10 (d) applied, which states any play that occurs while a player appears in a game after having been substituted for shall count.

Rules pundits contended Young's "feat" was the first time in major-league history that a player returned to a game after having been removed from it and revealed how close Major League Baseball had come to a similar catastrophe earlier in the season. On July 25, 2017, at Dodger Stadium, plate umpire Lance Barrett misheard Minnesota manager Paul Molitor's double-switch request "Pressly for Polanco" as "Belisle for Rosario," causing Barrett to hurriedly wave shortstop Jorge Polanco, who had disappeared into in the Twins dugout thinking he was out of the game, back onto the field. By the time the entire muddle was sorted out with the replay command center in New York, a pitch had already been thrown to Dodgers right fielder Yasiel Puig, but after an 18-minute delay it was determined that Polanco—even though he had entered the dugout—was still in the game. Thus, the "no re-entry rule" was waived and MLB was able to breathe a sigh of relief that its perfect illegal substitution record was still unblemished—for exactly one more month.

But more thorough research by MLB gurus would have shown that Young's "feat" was far from being a first. As David Nemec and Eric Miklich recounted in their book, *The Complete Book of Forfeited and Successfully Protested Major League Games*, an early instance of a player appearing twice in the same game occurred on July 27, 1890, in an American Association contest between the Columbus Senators and Brooklyn Gladiators: "In the fifth inning of the very first game [umpire and former catcher Jim] Peoples worked involving his former team [Columbus], Columbus pitcher Hank Gastright was knocked out of the box and replaced by Elton Chamberlain, who was subsequently fined and banished to the bench in the seventh inning for refusing to pitch with a new ball. Contrary to the rules, Peoples then allowed Gastright to return to the game because Columbus claimed it had no other bona fide pitchers available. Rule 28, Section 2—new to the rule book in 1890—specifically addressed substitutions and should have been enforced here but was not.

> Two players, whose name shall be printed on the score card as extra players, may be substituted at any time, by either club, but no player so retired shall thereafter participate in the game. In

addition, thereto a substitute may be allowed at any time in place of a player disabled in the game then being played, by reason of illness or injury, of the nature and extent of which the umpire shall be the sole judge.

Instead, however, Peoples eventually forfeited the game to Columbus because—guess what—Brooklyn was unable to furnish Peoples with a new ball when he demanded one in the eighth inning with Brooklyn ahead, 13–8!"

> Rule 5.10 (d) Comment: A pitcher may change to another position only once during the same inning; e.g. the pitcher will not be allowed to assume a position other than a pitcher more than once in the same inning.

The proviso prohibiting pitchers from assuming a position other than pitcher more than once in the same inning was added to Rule 5.10 (d)—formerly Rule 3.03—largely to thwart managers like Paul Richards, who created undue delays with his perplexing maneuvers in the 1950s that would have made four-hour games the norm nowadays. On June 25, 1953, in the top of the ninth inning at Comiskey Park, with the the White Sox leading the Yankees, 4–2, and righty Hank Bauer leading off the frame, Richards, then at the helm of the White Sox, removed his southpaw ace, Billy Pierce, stationing him at first base and brought in right-hander Harry Dorish. After lefty Don Bollweg pinch-hit for Bauer and beat out a bunt single, Pierce returned to the mound to face lefty Gene Woodling and emerged from the inning a 4–2 victor who played a complete game but did not pitch one. Richards had first pulled this stunt two years earlier in a Tuesday afternoon game on May 15, 1951, at Fenway Park with Dorish, sending him to replace Minnie Minoso at third base while Pierce took the mound in relief to face Ted Williams in the top of the ninth inning of a 7–7 game. After Pierce retired Williams on a popup, Dorish again assumed the pitching chores and a new third baseman, Floyd Baker, came into the lineup. The Pale Hose eventually won, 9–7, in 11 innings, with Dorish getting the win. Richards's move in this case was particularly daring inasmuch as Minoso, then a rookie, was the Sox' best all-around player and Pierce had been scheduled to start the following day but was held back until May 18.

Richards also employed the maneuver twice more in 1954, once with right-hander Sandy Consuegra and finally with southpaw Jack Harshman. Without a rule to prevent it, a manager with Richards's kind of mind could orchestrate a lefty-righty switch again and again during an inning, or for that matter during every inning if he happened to have a right-handed pitcher with the same versatility as Harshman, who was originally a first baseman, and a bench loaded with players who could play first base. The machination obviously has the potential to make a game interminable, but was so seldom perpetrated anymore—even before the 2020 rule change requiring a new pitcher to either face three batters or end the inning—that mass confusion occurred when the Rays' manager Kevin Cash pulled this ancient rabbit out of his cap in a game with the Red Sox at Tampa's Tropicana Field on July 23, 2019.

With the score 3–2, Rays in the top of the eighth, Adam Kolarek took the hill for his second inning in relief of starter Charlie Morton. After Sam Travis, the first Boston batter was retired, Kolarek moved to first base, replacing Austin Meadows, and right-hander Chaz Roe took the mound to face righty Mookie Betts. After Betts flew out to left field, Cash brought Kolarek back to the mound to face Raffy Devers, with Nate Lowe taking over at first base. Before Kolarek could throw his first pitch to Devers, Red Sox manager Alex Cora stormed out of the dugout. Few, if any, in attendance had any notion what Cora's grievance was with the umpiring crew, headlined by home-plate ump Angel Hernandez, except that it seemed to concern something with Tampa's new batting order. When play eventually resumed, Devers grounded out on the first pitch thrown in more than 20 minutes to end the frame. Then the fun resumed. Cora returned to once again lay out his complaint to the umpires and word began to spread in the stands that Boston was playing the game under protest. The source of the problem was the designated hitter rule (5.11), which lists a lot of scenarios that terminate the use of the designated hitter but does not explicitly detail what the batting order should be when a pitcher goes to another position and a new pitcher comes in. Rule 5.11 (a) (8) just notes that the DH is gone when this occurs in an American League game. Rule 5.11 (a) (5) covers the DH going to the field and the new pitcher having to bat in the DH spot, unless more than one substitution is made, in which case the manager designates the spots. From all reports, Cash failed to do this when Lowe entered the game throwing everyone into a quandry, most conspicuously of all the umpiring crew. Hernandez, a frequent catalytic presence in controversial officiating decisions, later said that that in the absence of any instructions from Cash he had full authority to take it upon himself to decide who in the Tampa Bay lineup now hit where. Even if true, Boston had no grounds for a protest according to Rule 7.04, because nothing that happened after Kolarek re-entered the game as a pitcher had any bearing on the final outcome, which remained 3–2 Rays.

An example of a legal position switch by a pitcher under the current rule occurred in a game in San Francisco on September 1, 1979. With Pittsburgh leading 5–3, Pirates closer Kent Tekulve got the first two outs in the ninth inning. Jack Clark then singled and lefty-hitting Darrell Evans came to bat representing the tying run. Pirates skipper Chuck Tanner moved Tekulve to left field and brought in southpaw Grant Jackson to face Evans. Jackson got the save when Evans flied out to none other than Tekulve. Had Evans reached base, Tanner no doubt have brought back Tekulve to face the next batter, righty Mike Ivie, but whether he would have put Jackson in left field in the event Ivie kept the rally alive, bringing up lefty-swinging Terry Whitfield we will never know.

Houston fans witnessed a much more intriguing example in a game between Pittsburgh and the Astros on August 18, 1965, at the Astrodome. Pirates ace Bob Veale, with an 8–1 lead, began the bottom of the ninth on cruise control but was hastily replaced by right-hander Al McBean, Pittsburgh's customary closer, after the first four Houston batters reached base. McBean entered the game with the score 8–3 and two runners on base, not a save situation under today's rules since the potential tying run was neither at the plate nor on deck. But after McBean allowed three consecutive hits, the score was shaved to 8–6 and the potential winning run was at the plate in the person of Joe Morgan. Pirates skipper Harry Walker brought in lefty Frank Carpin to face the lefty-hitting Morgan, but with a trio of right-handed hitters to follow he kept McBean in the game in left field, replacing Willie Stargell. After Carpin fanned Morgan, Bob Bailey moved to left field with Jose Pagan replacing him at third base, and McBean, now in a retroactive save situation, returned to the hill. He promptly surrendered a double to Jim Wynn, scoring Walt Bond and bringing the score to 8–7 with still only one out.

Jim Gentile, pinch-hitting for first baseman Frank Thomas, was then walked intentionally, loading the bases for catcher Ron Brand, playing out of position at third base that day. Many managers would have yanked McBean at this point. Walker stuck with him, however, and was rewarded when Brand grounded into a game-ending double play.

5.10 (e)

A player whose name is on his team's batting order may not become a substitute runner for another member of his team.

Rule 5.10 (e) Comment: This rule is intended to eliminate the practice of using so-called courtesy runners. No player in the game shall be permitted to act as a courtesy runner for a teammate. No player who has been in the game and has been taken out for a substitute shall return as a courtesy runner. Any player not in the lineup, if used as a runner, shall be considered as a substitute player.

Until 1950, courtesy runners were permitted with the consent of the opposing team. This rule enabled catcher Pat Collins to set a record that will almost certainly never be equaled. In the second inning of a game on June 8, 1923, against the Philadelphia Athletics at Shibe Park, St. Louis Browns third sacker Homer Ezzell had to heed a call of nature after reaching base. A's pilot Connie Mack permitted the Browns to use Collins as a courtesy runner while Ezzell took care of business. Collins later pinch-hit for pitcher Ray Kolp in the top of the ninth and walked, making him the only documented player to date to pinch-run and pinch-hit in the same game. Observe that Collins's usage as a substitute twice in the same game technically was yet another early day violation of Rule 5.10 (d).

5.10 (f)

The pitcher named in the batting order handed the umpire-in-chief, as provided in Rules 4.02 (a) and 4.02 (b), shall pitch to the first batter or any substitute batter until such batter is put out or reaches first base, unless the pitcher sustains injury or illness which, in the judgment of the umpire-in-chief, incapacitates him from pitching.

5.10 (g)

If the pitcher is replaced, the substitute pitcher shall pitch to the batter then at bat, or any substitute batter, until such batter is put out or reaches first base, or until the offensive team is put out, unless the substitute pitcher sustains injury or illness which, in the umpire-in-chief's judgment, incapacitates him for further play as a pitcher.

Note that Rule 5.10 (g) inserted this addendum in the 2019 rule book, applicable for the moment to National Association play only, although the independent Atlantic League also employed it: As of 2020, the rule will also apply for the first time in MLB play.

> *The starting pitcher or any substitute pitcher is required to pitch to a minimum of three consecutive batters, including the batter then at bat (or any substitute batter), until such batters are put out or reach first base, or until the offensive team is put out, unless the starting pitcher or substitute pitcher sustains injury or illness which, in the umpire-in-chief's judgment, incapacitates him from further play as a pitcher.*

Only time will tell if this 5.10 (g) addendum permanently becomes a rule at all levels of the game.

5.10 (h)

If an improper substitution is made for the pitcher, the umpire shall direct the proper pitcher to return to the game until the provisions of this rule are fulfilled. If the improper pitcher is permitted to pitch, any play that results is legal. The improper pitcher becomes the proper pitcher as soon as he makes his first pitch to the batter, or as soon as any runner is put out.

Comment: If a manager attempts to remove a pitcher in violation of Rule 5.10 (h) the umpire shall notify the manager of the offending club that it cannot be done. If, by chance, the umpire-in-chief has, through oversight, announced the incoming improper pitcher, he should still correct the situation before the improper pitcher pitches. Once the improper pitcher delivers a pitch he becomes the proper pitcher.

5.10 (i)

If a pitcher who is already in the game crosses the foul line on his way to take his place on the pitcher's plate to start an inning, he shall pitch to the first batter until such batter is put out or reaches first base, unless the batter is substituted for, or the pitcher sustains an injury or illness which, in the judgment of the umpire-in-chief, incapacitates him from pitching. If the pitcher ends the previous inning on base or at bat and does not return to the dugout after the inning is completed, the pitcher is not required to pitch to the first batter of the inning until he makes contact with the pitcher's plate to begin his warm-up pitches.

All four of these contingencies to Rule 5.10 essentially are designed to achieve the same result: that each new pitcher entering a game must pitch to at least one batter before he can be removed. A nascent form of the essence of these contingencies first appeared in rule books prior to the 1910 season. Managers like John McGraw made it necessary to stipulate that any player who assumes the position of pitcher must pitch to at least one hitter before he can be replaced on the mound. Prior to 1910, whenever one of the New York Giants' starting pitchers ran into trouble and McGraw had no one ready, he would replace the besieged hurler with a substitute player, sometimes even himself, who would then stall on the mound until the relief pitcher they really wanted was warmed up. Since the first sub—whether it be McGraw or one of his utility men—would exit without having thrown a single pitch, his name would usually not even appear in the box score.

Despite the presence of Rule 5.10 (f), a pitcher can still receive credit for a mound appearance without throwing a single pitch in earnest. Many pitchers have entered in relief and promptly picked off a runner to end an inning or even a game before they delivered a pitch. In such an instance, a pitcher still is credited for having worked a third of an inning. Perhaps the most significant incident when this occurred was the 1954 All-Star Game at Cleveland. In the top of the eighth, with the National League leading, 9–8, the NL had runners on first and third with two out when Washington Senators lefty Dean Stone was brought in to relieve right-hander Bob Keegan of the White Sox in order to face Brooklyn's lefty slugger Duke Snider. Before Stone could even deliver a pitch, Red

Schoendienst, who was on third base, took a long lead and then suddenly broke for home. Stone hurriedly threw the ball to Yankees catcher Yogi Berra in time to catch Schoendienst stealing for the third out. The National League clamored that Stone had balked, but home-plate umpire Eddie Rommel stood behind his call, and after the American League tallied three runs in the bottom of the eighth to go ahead, 11–9, Stone was credited with the win when that score stood.

Once announced into the game, a hurler can gain a mound appearance even without toeing the rubber while the ball is in play. On June 21, 1957, Jim Brosnan, later the author of several fine baseball books, including *The Long Season*, came out of the Cubs bullpen to face the New York Giants in the top of the 10th inning. While taking his warmup tosses, Brosnan slipped off the rubber and pulled the Achilles tendon in his left ankle. The umpire-in-chief properly waived the rule requiring Brosnan to face at least one batter and allowed Cubs manager Bob Scheffing to bring Dave Hillman into the game. Danny O'Connell and Bobby Thomson swiftly tagged Hillman for solo home runs to give the Giants a 12–10 victory.

The following year Brosnan played a role in a very different situation that featured a pitcher entering and leaving a game without throwing a pitch. On June 29, 1958, with the Cardinals leading, 4–3, they brought reliever Billy Muffett into a game against the Phillies in the bottom of the eighth frame at Connie Mack Stadium. The game was summarily suspended due to the Philadelphia Sunday curfew, however, before Muffett completed his warmup tosses. On July 29, when the game was resumed with different umpires, Brosnan was allowed by the suspension rules then in effect to replace Muffett. He held the Phils scoreless in both the eighth and ninth innings to earn a retrospective save.

A pitcher can also be credited with a start even though he never throws a single pitch. On September 15, 1950, St. Louis Cardinals scheduled starter Cloyd Boyer hurt his arm while warming up prior to a game at Brooklyn. Red Munger replaced Boyer and received credit for a complete-game 6–2 win over Don Newcombe, even though Boyer was deemed the starting pitcher. A similar event occurred fifty-five years earlier, some fifteen years before there was a rule that a starter, unless injured, had to face a minimum of one batter. On September 27, 1895, in a National League game at Washington, Boston manager Frank Selee penciled in future Hall of Famer Kid Nichols as his starting pitcher. But when Boston posted 12 runs and a multitude of hits in the top of the first inning, including a single by Nichols, Selee decided not to waste his ace. Before facing a single Washington batter, Nichols was removed from the game in favor of rookie Bill Yerrick, who gained an easy 14–2 complete-game victory, as had Munger, despite not being the official starting pitcher. But unlike Boyer, Nichols was not credited with a start even though he had actually appeared in the game, if only as a hitter.

Brosnan and Boyer recovered from their injuries to enjoy lengthy careers, but Robin Yount's older brother Larry was not as fortunate. The elder Yount's entire taste of life in the majors consisted of a single warmup toss for the Houston Astros. After being called up from the Astros' Oklahoma City farm club in 1971, Yount was summoned in relief to face the Atlanta Braves in the ninth inning of a game on September 15. In his exuberance he aggravated an old elbow injury on the first preliminary pitch he delivered and had to be removed. But even though Larry Yount never faced a single batter, his name is in the record books as having appeared in a major-league game.

The compelling question now is can there be a situation in which an umpire will allow a pitcher who is not injured to exit from a game before he pitches to the required one batter? Yes, there can, and Western International League fans saw one of most singular examples of it on June 17, 1952.

While outfielder John Kovenz of the Tri-City Braves was at bat in the ninth inning, pitcher Bill Wisneski of Victoria was removed when his first serving to Kovenz was a ball. Eric Gard came on in relief. As Gard wound up to make his first pitch, Kovenz stepped out of the box. When Gard paused in his windup, plate umpire Herman Ziruolo shouted, "Balk!" and waved the tying run in from third base.

Storming in from the mound to protest that he thought time had been called when Kovenz stepped out, Gard brushed against Ziruolo and was promptly tossed out of the game. Another Victoria reliever, Ben Lorino, then took the hill, finished pitching to Kovenz, and went on to blank Tri-City and earn credit for a 10-inning 10–9 win. Gard is only one of several hurlers to be thumbed from a game before they could pitch to the required one batter, but Kovenz may be the lone hitter ever to face three pitchers in a single turn at bat.

Another compelling question is has there ever been a situation at the major-league level since 1910 when a pitcher was mistakenly removed before he faced the minimum of one batter? And again, there has. As but one example, on July 4, 1946, in the first game of a doubleheader at Detroit's Briggs Stadium, Cleveland player-manager Lou Boudreau sent Joe Krakauskas to the mound in the eighth inning in relief of Pete Center and then pulled him in favor of Joe Berry after he reached a 3-and-0 count on Detroit shortstop Eddie Lake. Lake eventually walked, but no damage was done as the score remained 8–4 Detroit, which was the final tally. As of yet, no researchers have reported whether any action was taken by the American League office against umpires Hal Weafer, Joe Rhue, and Art Passarella for allowing Boudreau to make an illegal pitching change.

A more egregious example came on May 9, 2013, at Houston's Minute Maid Park in the seventh inning of a game between the Angels and the Astros. With runners on first and second and two out, Astros manager Bo Porter summoned Wesley Wright from the pen to replace Paul Clemens. With his team trailing, 5–3, Angles skipper Mike Scioscia called on Luis Jimenez to pinch hit for J. B. Shuck. Porter immediately countered by bringing on Hector Ambriz to face Jimenez, but Scioscia instead sent Scott Cousins out to bat for Jimenez and then announced he was playing the game under protest because Wright had not faced a batter or been injured. Porter later claimed the rules allowed him to replace his pitcher when the second pinch-hitter was announced, but the rules of course clearly say otherwise. When the Angels won, 6–5, the protest was withdrawn, but umpire Fieldin Culbreth nevertheless was suspended for two games for permitting Porter's gaffe to occur. Culbreth took the fall because he was the crew chief; all four umpires should have known the rule but apparently took Porter's word for what it said.

5.10 (l) Visits to the Mound Requiring a Pitcher's Removal From the Game

A professional league shall adopt the following rule pertaining to the visit of the manager or coach to the pitcher:

(1) This rule limits the number of trips a manager or coach may make to any one pitcher in any one inning;

A form of the rule limiting a manager or pitching coach to one trip to the mound per inning first appeared in the 1967 manual. Its purpose is to prevent managers and pitching coaches from traipsing back and forth endlessly between the dugout and the mound to confer with their battery men. The one-visit limit helps so much to speed up games that it becomes all the more difficult to believe that in the early part of the century, when managers could hold as many mound pow-wows as they pleased, contests often took little more than an hour. If a manager or pitching coach pops out of the dugout a second time in an inning, it can only be to make a pitching change. However, a second mound visit is allowed if a pinch-hitter is inserted for the batter due up next, but even then a pitching change must be made. Visits to the mound by teammates in the game are also limited depending on the length of the game and whether or not it is a postseason game.

5.10 (m)

Limitation on the Number of Mound Visits Per Game

In 2019, this rule was revised to limit the number of mound visits without making a pitching change to five per game instead of six. These visits include catcher, infielder, and outfielder conferences with a pitcher.

5.11 Designated Hitter Rule

Any League may elect to use Rule 5.11 (a), which shall be called the Designated Hitter Rule.

(a) The Designated Hitter Rule provides as follows:

(1) A hitter may be designated to bat for the starting pitcher and all subsequent pitchers in any game without otherwise affecting the status of the pitcher(s) in the game. A Designated Hitter for the pitcher, if any, must be selected prior to the game and must be included in the lineup cards presented to the Umpire-in-Chief. If a manager lists 10 players in his team's lineup card, but fails to indicate one as the Designated Hitter, and an umpire or either manager (or designee of either manager who presents his team's

lineup card) notices the error before the umpire-in-chief calls "Play" to start the game, the umpire-in-chief shall direct the manager who had made the omission to designate which of the nine players, other than the pitcher, will be the Designated Hitter.

Rule 5.11 (a) (1) Comment: A correction of a failure to indicate a Designated Hitter when 10 players are listed in a batting order is an "obvious" error that may be corrected before a game starts.

Although the notion of a DH had first been proposed as early as the late 1880s and there was even a failed league vote on whether to adopt the DH in 1892 after it was prosed by Pittsburgh official William Temple (for whom the Temple Cup is named), the first major-league official to present persuasive case for the addition of a DH to the rules oddly enough was National League president John Heydler, back in 1928. Senior loop owners felt that action lagged when pitchers batted and were solidly behind Heydler's proposal, but it fell flat after American League moguls vetoed it, believing the game already had enough offensive punch. Forty-five years later, when the concept was next seriously entertained, the two leagues were still at opposite poles, only by then each had undergone a complete 180-degree reversal. In 1972, the last season that pitchers batted for themselves in both leagues, NL teams outhit AL clubs by nine points and tallied 824 more runs. The following year, with its pitchers no longer batting except as occasional pinch-hitters, the AL topped the NL in batting by five points and scored 252 more runs.

Designated hitters first appeared in World Series action in 1976, when the Cincinnati Reds swept the New York Yankees. Dan Driessen served as the Reds' DH in all four games, whereas the Yankees divided the assignment among Carlos May, Lou Piniella, and Elliott Maddox. For reasons that made little sense in 1976 and still seem quixotic at best, major-league officials voted to allow DHs every other year in Series play. Series participants continued to use DHs only in even years until 1986 when the present rule was adopted, limiting their use to games hosted by American League teams.

In 1985, the last time that pitchers were required to bat for themselves in every World Series game, pitchers for the Kansas City Royals and the St. Louis Cardinals went a combined 0-for-30.

Since the designated hitter rule now seems here to stay in the AL and to remain anathema forever to NL magnates, it is time to consider the offshoot of it that seems destined to generate the most controversy in future years. Although some reactionaries will never stop lamenting that the perfectly symmetrical game Alexander Cartwright and his colleagues devised was irrevocably impaired the moment all nine men in the field were no longer required to take their fair turn at bat. Cartwright's crew of rulesmakers never intended for there to be pinch-hitters or defensive substitutions either, and few now quibble with their usage. Almost every serious baseball analyst and historian is disturbed, however, by the way the DH rule has enabled so many players to compile career and single-season stats that seem bogus in comparison to the accomplishments of players who had to do full duty both in the field and at bat.

Included among the ersatz achievements are the hit, home run, and RBI career totals compiled by Dave Winfield, Paul Molitor, Harold Baines, Brian Downing, Frank Thomas, Orlando Cepeda, Rico Carty, Tony Oliva, George Brett, Al Kaline, Rusty Staub, Alex Rodriguez, Reggie Jackson, Eddie Murray, and Jim Rice, to name just a few of the many players whose careers were extended when they were relieved of any necessity to play in the field—and to say nothing as yet about the case of David Ortiz. Ortiz played in 2,048 major league games, compiled 541 home runs, a .931 career OPS, and a 56.7 offensive WAR. However, he played 50 or more games in the field just once in his 20-year career and finished with a -20.9 defensive WAR even though he seldom ventured outside the dugout when his team was in the field (89 percent of the games he started were as a DH). Ortiz is arguably the most glaring example of a one-dimensional player even though he likely will make the Hall of Fame in 2022, the first year he is eligible. But less obvious is the impact of the DH rule on pitchers' career totals. In 1990, Frank Tanana became the first pitcher to post 200 wins, even though he had yet to score a run in a major-league game. One must doubt, too, that Phil Niekro would still have been a starting pitcher at age forty-eight and amassed 318 wins if he had not been exempted from having to bat and run the bases during the last few years of his career.

5.11 (a) (2)

The Designated Hitter named in the starting lineup must come to bat at least one time, unless the opposing club changes pitchers.

When the DH was established in the American League in 1973, Earl Weaver was beginning his sixth season as manager of the Orioles. At the time, the new position came with just one stipulation: The designated hitter had to be selected prior to the game and included in the lineup cards presented to the home-plate umpire. In short order Weaver, cut from the same cloth as Paul Richards, found a loophole he could exploit at his pleasure. Rather than simply naming a decent hitter who was either a poor fielder or a player who needed rest from fielding duties, Weaver would often pencil in as his DH a pitcher he had no intention of using that day and then send up the hitter he actually wanted when that spot in the lineup was first due up. The move allowed Weaver to summon from his bench the ideal batter in his estimation depending on the game situation at the time.

In 1979 alone, Weaver pulled his "Phantom DH" trick 21 times. Surprisingly, however, the American League did not add contingency (2) to the rule book until after the 1980 season.

It should surprise no one that Weaver, in a sense, borrowed a page from the master of similar trickery—Paul Richards. Fifteen years before the DH rule was implemented, Richards presented a starting lineup that had *three* pitchers in the batting order. On September 11, 1958, in a meaningless late-season game at Kansas City, Richards, the king of unorthodox stratagems, started Billy O'Dell on the mound, batting ninth, but in addition listed pitcher Jack Harshman in center field, batting fifth, and rookie right-hander Milt Pappas in the seventh spot, playing second base. Harshman and Pappas had started two of the Orioles' previous three games on the mound and hence were not slated to pitch under any circumstances that day. Richards's one-off plan depended on the Orioles' first four hitters in the lineup enginering a scoring opportunity in the first inning against KC starter Ned Garver, in which case he would pinch-hit for Harshman and later in the frame, if necessary, for Pappas. At the close of the top of the first he would then, regardless of his experiment's outcome, send his regulars, Jim Busby and Billy Gardner, to center field and second base, respectively. To a degree, Richards met with success even though he was partially foiled by KC helmsman Harry Craft. With Dick Williams (later one of the many future managers who had learned at Richards's feet) on second base and two out, Craft ordered Garver to walk Baltimore's cleanup hitter Bob Nieman intentionally to force Richards's hand with Harshman. Richards's response was to bring in Gene Woodling to bat for Harshman. But Woodling flied out to right fielder Roger Maris to spoil Richards's latest brainstorm and bring Busby and Gardner into the game. As for the final outcome that day, Garver hurled a complete-game four-hitter and won, 7–1.

5.11 (a) (3)

It is not mandatory that a club designate a hitter for the pitcher, but failure to do so prior to the game precludes the use of a Designated Hitter for that club for that game.

Almost always an AL manager's failure to properly utilize a DH is entirely the result of carelessness rather than by plan. A prime example occurred on July 22, 1999, when the Cleveland Indians hosted the Toronto Blue Jays. The Indians at the time happened to have two outfielders named Ramirez: Manny and Alex. Tribe manager Mike Hargrove opted to play them both, listing Manny as the DH and cleanup hitter and Alex as the right fielder, batting seventh. But when Cleveland took the field in the top of the first, Manny was in right field rather than Alex. Whether Hargrove was responsible for the confusion or one of his coaches, the outcome was the same; once Manny took the field the Tribe lost its privilege to employ a DH and Alex Ramirez lost his spot in the batting order. Instead, Cleveland starter Charles Nagy, a .105 career hitter, albeit in just 19 at-bats, had to hit in the seventh spot. He went 0-for-2 and absorbed a 4–3 loss to the Jays' David Wells.

5.12 Calling "Time" and Dead Balls

(a) When an umpire suspends play, he shall call "Time." At the umpire-in-chief's call of "Play," the suspension is lifted and play resumes. Between the call of "Time" and the call of "Play" the ball is dead.

Bear in mind that any umpire can call time, even foul line umpires in postseason games. Many games would doubtless have had a different outcome were it not for the strict enforcement of this rule. In a contest on August 28, 1960, at Baltimore's Memorial Stadium between the Orioles and the Chicago White Sox, pinch-hitter Ted Kluszewski slammed a three-run homer in the eighth inning off the Orioles' Milt Pappas to vault the Sox from a 3–1 deficit to an apparent 4–3 lead. But the blow was erased because third-base umpire Ed Hurley had called time a split second before Pappas fed Kluszewski the gopher ball.

Ted Kluszewski participated in the 1959 World Series fourteen years after playing end on the 1945 Indiana Hoosiers, the only season Indiana won an outright Big Ten football championship.

Hurley had observed Earl Torgeson and Floyd Robinson playing catch outside the Sox bullpen in foul territory and stopped play while he told them to get inside the restraining barrier. Made to bat over, Kluszewski lined out to center field to end the inning, and Chicago went on to lose the game, 3–1.

In 1976, Don Money of the Milwaukee Brewers lost an apparent game-winning walk-off grand slam homer in a similar manner. As he came to bat on April 10 at County Stadium against Dave Pagan of the New York Yankees, the bases were jammed in the bottom of the ninth and his team trailed, 9–6. Concentrating only on the task at hand, Money failed to notice that Yankees manager Billy Martin was waving to his outfielders to reposition themselves. New York first baseman Chris Chambliss saw Martin gesturing, however, and asked first base umpire Jim McKean for time.

McKean granted the request just before Pagan released the ball. When Money drove the pitch into the left-field stands, Milwaukee fans erupted in the belief that the blow was a grand slam, giving the Brewers a last-ditch 10–9 victory.

Money started circling the bases while many of his teammates headed jubilantly for the clubhouse. But throughout the celebration McKean continued to wave his arms until finally he got everyone's attention, whereupon he announced that he had to disallow the four-run homer because he had called time.

Returning to the batter's box, Money hit a sacrifice fly to bring the score to 9–7, New York, which is how it stood when the game ended moments later.

Before we leave this rule, it must be pointed out that more than one pitch or play can be nullified after an umpire's unrecognized call of "Time" is belatedly acknowledged. During a May 6, 1959, game at Briggs Stadium (later Tiger Stadium), leading off in the fifth inning Boston Red Sox third baseman Frank Malzone fouled off a pitch from Detroit's Paul Foytack and then looked at a called strike. Down 0-and-2 in the count, Malzone suddenly breathed a new life upon hearing first-base umpire Ed Hurley cry that he had called time before the first strike.

Unnoticed by the other three arbiters, Hurley had gone down to the Boston bullpen as Malzone stepped into the box to warn a player who was riding the umpires. When Hurley returned to his position and found that two strikes had been registered in his absence, he told plate umpire Joe Paparella to erase them because he had not been prepared to call a play at first base. Paparella tried to compromise and leave at least one strike on the board, but Hurley insisted time had been out for both pitches.

Standing in against Foytack with a fresh 0-and-0 count, Malzone smacked the Tigers' right-hander's next pitch for a home run.

5.12 (b)

The ball becomes dead when an umpire calls "Time." The umpire-in-chief shall call "Time:

(1) When in his judgment weather, darkness or similar conditions make immediate further play impossible;

A game nowadays is suspended when darkness halts it because the stadium lights fail or a local ordinance prevents them from being turned on. At one time, however, a team was not allowed to turn on the lights in its home park during the course of a game unless it was a scheduled night or twi-night doubleheader event. When darkness intervened the game was stopped at that juncture. If it had gone the necessary five innings, it was considered an official game. When darkness forced a halt short of five innings, unless the home team led after 4 ½ frames had been completed all record of the game vanished.

An unfortunate example of the old tradition occurred on June 1, 1947. That afternoon, after a crowd of 47,132 in Cleveland Stadium sat through a 33-minute rain delay prior to the first game of a scheduled doubleheader between the Indians and the Yankees, the weather broke long enough to play two innings before another storm front forced a second stoppage that lasted an hour and 18 minutes. When the game resumed in the mud and fog, New York and Cleveland waged a slugfest that took four and a half hours to finish, including the two rain delays. Finally, with the clock approaching 6 p.m. and New York ahead, 11–9, Yankees relief ace Joe Page stifled a Tribe rally in the bottom of the ninth to preserve Al Lyons's lone win with the Bronx Bombers.

After the two teams repaired to their dressing rooms, the crowd had to endure another wait before the second game began. By the time the clubs took the field again it was nearly 6:30 p.m. and the fog made the hour seem even later. Cleveland owner Bill Veeck would happily have turned on the lights, but the rules in 1947 forbade it. Yankees leadoff hitter Snuffy Stirnweiss stepped reluctantly to the plate to face Indians right-hander Al Gettel. After each pitch Stirnweiss turned to home-plate umpire Red Jones and complained that he was having trouble seeing the ball. Finally Stirnweiss took a called third strike and even before he could turn to complain again, Jones threw up his hands and announced that he was calling the game on account of darkness. Although the crowd loudly voiced its dissatisfaction, the *New York Times* reporter at the game said: "But it seemed the sensible thing to do." No one thought to grumble then about Veeck not being allowed to use the stadium lights so that the twin-bill could be completed.

Although an umpire-in-chief is the sole judge whether to terminate or interrupt a game for one of the reasons cited in this rule, players will nevertheless try to give a stubborn arbiter a nudge. There have been instances of batters coming to the plate carrying flashlights to clue an umpire that playing conditions warranted stopping the game. Usually these dramatic asides are ignored, but sometimes a man in blue will listen since insufficient daylight or artificial light is not the only impediment to stop play. In a game on May 20, 1960, between the Chicago Cubs and the Milwaukee Braves the umpires allowed play to continue into the fifth inning at Milwaukee's County Stadium, even though outfielders on both teams griped incessantly that a heavy fog that had blown in from

Lake Michigan early in the proceeding was cutting their visibility to near zero and umpire Frank Dascoli, working the plate, admitted he could not always see the outfielders.

Finally, in the bottom of the fifth, with the game still scoreless, the three Cubs outfielders convinced all four umpires to stroll out to center field to inspect conditions. What they saw persuaded them to ask Frank Thomas, a Cubs player not in the game, to stand at the plate and fungo a fly ball to the outfield. When none of the umps could see the ball coming their way, the game was halted and all record of it was erased. There have been many other instances before and since when fog interfered with play, but the only other recorded time in National League history when it forced a stoppage before the game became official came in 1956 at Brooklyn and also involved the Cubs.

Weather conditions and light outages are not the only circumstances where an umpire might elect to call "Time" and not resume play until the intrusion causing the stoppage has abated. Among the most bizarre situations in recent years is the "Bug Game" at Cleveland's Jacobs Field on the night of October 2, 2007, in Game Two of the American League Division Series between the Indians and the Yankees. Hoping to even the series at one apiece, the Yankees held a 1–0 lead in the bottom of the eighth inning with rookie Joba Chamberlain working in relief of New York starter Andy Pettitte. Chamberlain had already begun to be troubled by swarms of midges the previous inning that strangely did not seem to bother Cleveland's starter Fausto Carmona (a.k.a. Roberto Hernandez). He began the eighth frame by walking Indians leadoff hitter Grady Sizemore and then letting him take second base on a wild pitch. At that point Chamberlain called for more bug spray since midges were crawling all over his neck and face and additional swarms of them circled his head. When the spray had little effect, Yankees manager Joe Torre began begging for time to be called. Home plate umpire Laz Diaz demurred. Cleveland second baseman Asdrubal Cabrera then sacrificed Sizemore to third base where he seemed doomed to languish when DH Travis Hafner lined out to first base. But with two out and Victor Martinez at the plate, Chamberlain threw a second wild pitch, bringing Sizemore home. He then followed by walking both Martinez and first baseman Ryan Garko with Torre continuing all the while to request that play be stopped to no avail.

Chamberlain eventually got out of the inning without further damage by striking out shortstop Jhonny Peralta and the midges had no further impact on the game. But Cleveland prevailed, 2–1, when Hafner singled home left fielder Kenny Lofton in the 11th inning.

What enticed the midges to zero in so ferociously on Chamberlain while scarcely bothering everyone else on the field remains a mystery, but a more significant one is why Torre did not replace Chamberlain after two were out with his bullpen ace Mariano Rivera. Rivera would have needed only to retire Martinez, who was 0-for-3 on the day, and then retire three more batters in the ninth inning to cement a Yankees 1–0 victory. As it developed, he shut down the Tribe cold in the ninth and then escaped a jam in the 10th inning generated by catcher Jorge Posada's muffed third strike before turning the game over to Luis Vizcaino, the losing pitcher. Meanwhile Torre's protestations that play should have been stopped while Chamberlain was under siege went nowhere, and Chamberlain, a star in the making prior to the "Bug Game"—he fashioned an 0.75 WHIP during the regular season—was never again more than a journeyman reliever in his 10-year career.

5.12 (b) (3)

When an accident incapacitates a player or an umpire;

(A) If an accident to a runner is such as to prevent him from proceeding to a base to which he is entitled, as on a home run hit out of the playing field, or an award of one or more bases, a substitute runner shall be permitted to complete the play.

Although allowed by this rule to do so, an umpire will seldom kill a play just because a player is injured. Runners have been retired after being knocked unconscious by errant throws or in basepath collisions, sometimes right in front of a base coach who was powerless to come to their assistance.

But while a base coach cannot physically help a stricken runner, a teammate who is also a baserunner can offer assistance. Purportedly, many years ago in a New Jersey sandlot game a player scored after collapsing at third base and dying of a heart attack when the runner coming along behind him picked him up and dragged him all the way home, making sure that his dead teammate's foot touched the plate before his own. No one has ever found conclusive evidence that this event actually occurred, but it is theoretically possible, even at the major-league level.

One of the most famous moments when a player's teammates failed to rally to his aid came on October 8 in Game Four of the 1939 World Series between the New York Yankees and the Cincinnati Reds at Cincinnati's Crosley Field. The two clubs were knotted at 4–4 in the top of the 10th when Joe DiMaggio singled to chase home Frank Crosetti.

Charlie Keller also tried to tally on DiMaggio's hit but seemingly was beaten on right fielder Ival Goodman's throw home to Reds catcher Ernie Lombardi even though the throw was slightly off line. Instead of giving himself up, Keller crashed into Lombardi so violently that the ball was jarred loose. As Lombardi lay in the dust beside the plate, dazed and semiconscious with the ball inches away from him, his teammates, as if expecting time to be called, stood by in a trance of their own and allowed DiMaggio to circle the bases and score the Yankees' third run on the play. But home plate umpire Babe Pinelli was not bound to call time until Reds pitcher Bucky Walters stood on the rubber with the ball in his hand. To add insult, both Goodman and Lombardi were charged with errors on the play and the Yankees won, 7–4, to sweep the Series.

5.12 (b) (8)

Except in the cases stated in paragraphs (2) and (3) (A) of [Rule 5.12], no umpire shall call "Time" while a play is in progress.

It is worth noting here that contingency (8) by inference corrects a common misconception. Many players, coaches, and managers have assumed that time was automatically out when they started to protest an umpire's decision only to discover the game was still very much in progress.

In the second inning of a game at Braves Field on September 7, 1923, between the Brooklyn Dodgers and the Boston Braves, Boston had Stuffy McInnis on third, Hod Ford on second, and rookie shortstop Bob Smith at bat. After Smith singled to tally both McInnis and Ford, Brooklyn catcher Zack Taylor began jawing with home-plate umpire Hank O'Day that Ford had run out of the baseline to elude Taylor's tag on the throw to the plate from right fielder Tommy Griffith. Smith took second base on the throw. Then, seeing that Taylor was still occupied with O'Day, Smith darted to third. When Taylor continued to pay the Braves' runner no attention while he argued, Smith snuck home. Taylor then started a new argument that time had been out, but that too went nowhere.

On April 30, 1990, New York Mets pitcher David Cone allowed the Atlanta Braves to gain two free runs when he got caught up in a debate with first-base umpire Charlie Williams.

With Dale Murphy on second and Ernie Whitt on first and two out, Cone raced to cover first on a grounder between first sacker Mike Marshall and second baseman Gregg Jefferies. Jefferies came up with the ball and tossed it to Cone, who crossed the bag

Hank O'Day served in his long baseball career as a major-league pitcher, umpire, and manager. He had moments when he excelled in all three roles, but his overall contributions led many pundits to scratch their heads when he was selected for the Hall of Fame by a special Veterans Committee in 2013.

with what he thought was the inning-ending out. But when Williams said Cone's foot had missed the bag, Cone blew a fuse.

Noticing Cone's back was to the infield as he argued with Williams, Murphy, who had taken third on the play, stole a few feet down the line and then broke for home when Cone didn't turn around. Other Mets, including Jefferies, tried unavailingly to call Cone's attention to Murphy. Seeing that Cone was oblivious, Ernie Whitt took third and then sprinted for home too after Murphy scored. Jefferies finally grabbed Cone and tried to spin him around so that he could see what Whitt was doing. But Cone continued to sputter until two runs had been tallied after what he was morally certain should have been the third out. The pair of freebies helped the Braves to a 7–4 win. Cone later admitted sheepishly. "I just snapped."

Rule 5.12 (b) (8) also helps correct another common misconception that time is automatically out when a bat flies out of a hitter's hands as he swings and sails into the playing field. Hall of Famer Pee Wee Reese had to learn the hard way that there was no such rule.

The Dodgers' all-time greatest shortstop was on first in a 1947 game on July 12 at Ebbets Field against the Chicago Cubs with Dixie Walker at the plate in the bottom of the third inning. A vicious swing and a miss by Walker on a pitch from Chicago lefty Johnny Schmitz sent the bat flying out of Walker's grip and toward first base. Reese stepped off the bag to

retrieve it for his teammate, and Cubs catcher Clyde McCullough immediately snapped the ball to first sacker Eddie Waitkus. Even as Waitkus
was slapping the tag on him, Reese began to proclaim that time must
surely be out. But first-base umpire Lee Ballanfant put him straight. Only
he was out.

6.00: Improper Play, Illegal Action, and Misconduct

Until 2009, right-hander Frank Chapman was believed to be one Frederick Joseph Chapman, born on November 14, 1872, and at age fourteen the youngest player in major-league history. But those vital statistics we know now belong to an upholsterer in Erie, Pennsylvania, who may never have played ball at all, let alone pitched a game in the majors. Thanks to researcher Richard Malatzky, we've learned Chapman was a minor-league pitcher whose real first name was Frank, and that he was born in 1861.

Chapman's lone major-league appearance came on July 22, 1887, in the uniform of the American Association's Philadelphia A's and ended on one of the strangest batter's inference calls ever made. Opposing Chapman that afternoon were the fledgling Cleveland Blues, who had joined the AA in 1887 as a replacement for the Pittsburgh Allegheny club (after Pittsburgh had jumped to the National League). By the bottom of the sixth inning, Philadelphia trailed, 6–2, but had a rally going with Harry Stovey on third and Lou Bierbauer on first with hard-hitting Ted Larkin at the plate. On a pitch to Larkin, Bierbauer jogged toward second base to draw a throw from Cleveland catcher Charlie Snyder and Stovey then raced for home when Cleveland second sacker Cub Stricker ran Bierbauer back to first. Seeing that Stovey would be out when Stricker suddenly wheeled and threw home instead, Larkin wrestled with Snyder, allowing Stovey to regain third base. Umpire Mitchell (first name unknown) at first called Stovey out, a call befitting today's Rule 6.01 (a) (3) on batter's interference, but then reversed himself and called Larkin out.

While Cleveland was rightfully arguing that Stovey should be the one ruled out, Mitchell, to the astonishment of everyone, abruptly forfeited the game to the A's. Just as astonishingly, AA president Wheeler Wikoff later upheld the forfeit. Because Cleveland was leading when the game was forfeited, no pitching decisions were awarded and Chapman was spared a likely loss. As for Mitchell, the forfeit came in the second of the only three games he umpired in the majors before departing without leaving behind a shred of biographical information.

6.01 (a) (5)

Any batter or runner who has just been put out, or any runner who has just scored, hinders or impedes any following play being made on a runner. Such runner shall be declared out for the interference of his teammate (see Rule 6.01 (j));

Rule 6.01 (a) (5) Comment: If the batter or a runner continues to advance or returns or attempts to return to his last legally touched base after he has been put out, he shall not by that act alone be considered as confusing, hindering or impeding the fielders.

The vast majority of the time, a player who continues to behave as if he were a base runner after he has been called out will be nailed for interference, but there have been notable instances when an umpire chose to rule otherwise. In the bottom of the sixth inning of Game Four of the 1978 World Series at Yankee Stadium on October 14, the Yankees trailed the Dodgers, 3–0, but had Thurman Munson on second base and Reggie Jackson on first with Lou Piniella batting. Piniella hit a line shot to Los Angeles shortstop Bill Russell, who dropped it. There was some question whether Russell dropped the liner on purpose, hoping to set up an easy double play, in which case Piniella would be out according to Rule 5.09 (a) (12) and Munson and Jackson would not be forced to vacate their respective bases. However, second-base umpire Joe Brinkman made no call, so the play continued. Russell retrieved the ball, tagged second to force Jackson, and then fired to first expecting to double up Piniella. But the ball hit Jackson, who was continuing to run, and bounced off down the right-field line into foul territory. Before the errant peg could be chased down, Munson scored and Piniella reached second.

It then fell on first-base umpire Frank Pulli to judge whether Jackson was guilty of interference. Instant replay angles gave the impression that Jackson not only had continued to run after being forced at second but also may have flicked his hip into the path of the throw. Pulli thought otherwise, contending that Jackson neither had intended to interfere with the play by continuing to run nor with the throw when he saw it coming toward him. The Dodgers vehemently dissented, but Pulli's call stood and the Yankees eventually scored two runs in the inning and wound up winning the game, 4–3, and eventually the Series.

6.01 (a) (10)

He fails to avoid a fielder who is attempting to field a batted ball . . .

6.01 (a) (10) Comment: When a catcher and batter-runner going to first base have contact when the catcher is fielding the ball, there is generally no violation and nothing should be called. "Obstruction" by a fielder attempting to field a ball should be called only in very flagrant and violent cases because the rules give him the right of way, but of course such "right of way" is not a license to, for example, intentionally trip a runner even though fielding the ball . . .

This rule allows an umpire considerable latitude, as the Boston Red Sox learned on October 14, 1975, in the bottom of the 10th inning in Game Three of the World Series at Cincinatti. With the score tied, 5–5, Cincinnati center fielder Cesar Geronimo led off with a single. Reds manager Sparky Anderson then sent up Ed Armbrister to pinch-hit for pitcher Rawly Eastwick. While attempting to lay down a sacrifice bunt, Armbrister became entangled with Red Sox catcher Carlton Fisk as Fisk sprang out from behind the plate to field the ball. The two seemed to lock together forever before Armbrister finally broke free to run to first, enabling Fisk to seize the ball and throw it to second baseman Denny Doyle, hoping to get Geronimo.

When Fisk's throw went into center field, the Reds ended up with runners on second and third, and plate umpire Larry Barnett wound up with Fisk and Red Sox manager Darrell Johnson in his face, howling that Armbrister should be out for interference and Geronimo made to return to first. Barnett insisted the collision did not constitute interference because it had not been intentional, and first-base umpire Dick Stello came to his support even though there was nothing in the rule at the time to stipulate that a batter's interference must be intentional for it to be deemed an illegal action. A few minutes later the Reds won the game, 6–5, on a single by Joe Morgan.

6.01 (a) (11)

A fair ball touches him on fair territory before touching a fielder. If a fair ball goes through, or by, an infielder, and touches a runner immediately back of him, or touches the runner after having been deflected by a fielder, the umpire shall not declare the runner out for being touched by a batted ball. In making such decision the umpire must be convinced that the ball passed through, or by, the fielder, and that no other infielder had the chance to make a play on the ball. If, in the judgment of the umpire, the runner deliberately and intentionally kicks such a batted ball on which the infielder has missed a play, then the runner shall be called out for interference.

In the early game there was considerable disagreement over whether a runner should be declared out when he was hit by a batted ball, since it so often was an unavoidable accident. The first effort to address this issue was in 1872, when a rule was created that any player who willfully let a batted or thrown ball hit him was automatically out.

In 1877, the rule was altered so that any baserunner, whether his act was willful or not, was out if he was struck by a batted ball before it had passed a fielder. The revision was necessary when it grew apparent that umpires could not be expected to judge whether a runner had intentionally let a ball hit him. Since an official scorer could not be expected to judge either whether the batted ball would have resulted in a hit or an out if a runner had not interfered with it, the vote was to count any batted ball that struck a runner as a single.

The lone exception to this rule occurs when a runner occupying his base is called out for being hit by a ball that has already been ruled an infield fly and could not possibly dodge it without stepping off his base and risking being doubled off. No official scorer in major-league history has ever been challenged, however, by the following fictious situation:

On the closing day of the season, Mike Stroke of the Hawks trails Bill Clout of the Eagles by one percentage point in the race for the league batting title. As luck would have it, the Hawks and the Eagles face each other in the final game. Clout elects to sit out the contest to protect his slim lead. To further aid his teammate's bid for the batting crown, the Eagles' pitcher, John Flame, intentionally walks Stroke each time he comes to bat.

Stroke's last plate appearance comes with two out in the ninth inning and his team trailing, 6–0. So effective has Flame been to this point against the other eight members of the Hawks' order that he is working on a no-hitter. The gem in the making of course only provides Flame with all the more incentive to purposely pass the dangerous Stroke for the fourth time in the game.

On his way to first base, Stroke roundly curses Flame, who merely sneers at him. Stroke seemingly is powerless to do anything to gain revenge against Flame and the Eagles for denying him a fair chance to claim the batting crown. But then, suddenly, an opportunity presents itself. Tim Speed, the Hawks' next batter, slices a sharp groundball toward the second baseman, and Stroke, running to second, makes what appears to be only a token attempt to avoid being hit by it.

Must the official scorer give Speed a hit and deprive Flame of a no-hitter? Rule 6.01 (a) (11) says he does, but happily no major-league official scorer to date has been made to face the unpleasant prospect of ending a no-hit bid on such a rude technicality when no one really can be certain of Stroke's intent.

However, when a Pacific Coast League game on July 6, 1963, between the Spokane Indians and the Hawaii Islanders (won by Spokane, 18–0) terminated with Islanders pinch-runner Stan Palys being hit by a batted ball with two out in the ninth inning to seemingly end a no-hit bid by Indians hurler Bob Radovich, PCL president Dewey Soriano happened to be in attendance. Soriano immediately contacted the press box and notified them that no base hit was to be awarded and to credit a putout to the first baseman unassisted because Palys was out for "unsportsmanlike play" rather than runner interference. Palys, in Soriano's judgment, had "danced up and down" in front of Spokane's first baseman, obviously staging himself to be hit by a grounder toward first rather than allowing the first baseman to make a play.

With base hits becoming more precious with each passing year in today's climate, would a major-league official ever dare do the same if Palys had been less blatant? Especially if, unlike Soriano, he had not witnessed it for himself? In all honesty, would Soriano have made the same decision if he had not seen the play with his own eyes but only received a report of it?

6.01 (b) Fielder Right of Way

The players, coaches or any member of a team at bat shall vacate any space (including both dugouts or bullpens) needed by a fielder who is attempting to field a batted or thrown ball. If a member of the team at bat (other than a runner) hinders a fielder's attempt to catch or field a batted ball, the ball is dead, the batter is declared out and all runners return to the bases occupied at the time of the pitch. If a member of the team at bat (other than a runner) hinders a fielder's attempt to field a thrown ball, the ball is dead, the runner on whom the play is being made shall be declared out and all runners return to the last legally occupied base at the time of the interference.

Note that hindering a fielder does not necessarily have to be a physical action or inaction. It can also be verbal and can come from either the dugout or the playing field. Until the early part of the twentieth century, players in all parks sat on benches only some 15 or 20 yards from the playing field and would often holler "Watch out!" to the opposing player chasing down a foul pop near their bench or "I've got it!" when two or more opponents were racing for a short fly ball. Generally umpires, most of the time working alone, would ignore complaints of interference or obstruction if a ball fell safely because of verbal chicanery simply by saying they didn't hear anything.

But it was a rougher game back then. Today, with every game having at least four umpires, one is almost certain to overhear any effort to convey verbal misinformation (albeit by some accounts Yankees base runner Alex Rodriguez got away with a bit of vocal mischief in a 2007 game against Toronto). Too, players on both teams will anger justifiably at such illegal tactics. What with the salary money at stake, no one wants to instigate an injury on a falsely induced collision involving a fellow player.

Observe that Rule 6.01, for all the contingencies it covers, has no comment on whether it constitutes interference if a runner deliberately kicks the ball out of the fielder's hand or glove as he is being tagged out on a slide into a base. The key word here is "deliberately." In 1871, the rule became that when a fielder holding the ball tagged a runner who was off a base, the runner was out even if he somehow knocked the ball out of the fielder's hand. This rule was rescinded in 1877, but an umpire could still call a runner out for interference if, in his judgment, an intentional effort was made to dislodge the ball from a fielder's grasp. Without the interference proviso it was felt, rightly, that some runners would stop at nothing to make a fielder drop the ball when a tag play was imminent.

Ty Cobb was notorious for kicking balls out of basemen's gloves without being called on it, but it was easier in Cobb's day when infielders wore skimpier gloves with only rudimentary webbing. A more recent miscreant was Eddie Stanky. On October 6, 1951, at the Polo Grounds, in Game Three of the World Series, Stanky fired up millions watching on TV—as well as his New York Giants teammates—with a foot maneuver that, momentarily at least, rattled the seemingly invincible New York Yankees to the core.

In the bottom of the fifth, after Giants pitcher Jim Hearn fanned, Stanky coaxed a walk out of Yankees starter Vic Raschi and then tried to steal second base. Catcher Yogi Berra's throw beat Stanky to the bag, but Stanky kicked the ball out of shortstop Phil Rizzuto's glove with a quick flick of his big toe (but again, this was nearly seventy years ago and gloves were still considerably smaller than they are today). When the ball rolled away into the outfield, Stanky took off for third base. Rizzuto was charged with an error on the play rather than registering what should have been the Giants' second out. Umpire Bill Summers turned a deaf ear to Rizzuto's shriek that Stanky's kick constituted interference, nor did he pay any attention to a Yankees protest that Stanky had never touched second base before picking himself up from the ground and darting to third.

Later in the inning, Berra dropped a throw home on what ought to have been the third out, and the Giants then broke the game open by scoring five runs in the frame—all of them unearned. The following morning, a Sunday headline on the *New York Times* sports page referred to the episode as Stanky's "Field Goal Kick." Much was made of how the play had not only shot the Giants to a 2–1 lead in the Series, but had given them all the momentum and left the heavily favored Yankees in disarray.

Unhappily for the Giants, the Yankees got lucky. It rained that Sunday, postponing Game Four at the Polo Grounds and allowing Yankees manager Casey Stengel to send Allie Reynolds to the mound the following afternoon with an extra day's rest. Reynolds hurled a 6–2 win to even the Series and revive the confidence of his teammates. The Yankees went on to win the world championship, four games to two, making Stanky's field goal kick no more than a footnote in Series lore.

6.01 (i) Collisions at Home Plate

(1) A runner attempting to score may not deviate from his direct pathway to the plate in order to initiate contact with the catcher (or other player covering home plate), or otherwise initiate an avoidable collision. If, in the judgment of the umpire, a runner attempting to score initiates contact with the catcher (or other player covering home plate) in such a manner, the umpire shall declare the runner out (regardless of whether the player covering home plate maintains possession of the ball). In such circumstances, the umpire shall call the ball dead, and all other base runners shall return to the last base touched at the time of the collision. If the runner slides into the plate in an appropriate manner, he shall not be adjudged to have violated Rule 6.01 (i).

Rule 6.01 (i) (1) Comment: The failure by the runner to make an effort to touch the plate, the runner's lowering of the shoulder, or the runner's pushing through with his hands, elbows or arms, would support a determination that the runner deviated from the pathway in order to initiate contact with the catcher in violation of Rule 6.01 (i), or otherwise initiated a collision that could have been avoided. A slide shall be deemed appropriate, in the case of a feet first slide, if the runner's buttocks and legs should hit the ground before contact with the catcher. In the case of a head first slide, a runner shall be deemed to have slid appropriately if his body should hit the ground before contact with the catcher. If a catcher blocks the pathway of the runner, the umpire shall not find that the runner initiated an avoidable collision in violation of this Rule 6.01 (i) (1).

In a game on May, 25, 2011, at San Francisco's AT&T Park, Giants catcher Buster Posey sustained a broken left ankle and torn ligaments in a violent home-plate collision when the Florida Marlins' Scott Cousins crashed into him while trying to score the go-ahead run in the 12th inning on a sacrifice fly. The force of the collision prevented Posey from handling the throw from right fielder Nate Schierholtz, which was on target. The injury truncated Posey's season to just 45 games. Cousins defended his part in the collision, telling the *San Francisco Chronicle* it was the only way he could have scored what proved to be the winning run in Florida's 7–6 triumph. "If I saw a clean lane to slide, that's the play I'm making," Cousins added. "I have speed and like to believe I'm going to beat the ball. But there was no chance on that play. It was a game-changing play in extra innings, and I had to play as hard as I could."

The play was nonetheless reminiscent of Pete Rose's horrendous crash into Cleveland catcher Ray Fosse during the 1970 All-Star Game that severely curtailed Fosse's career. Cousins's critics claimed that he could have avoided the collision by sliding to the third-base line side of the plate and brushing it with his hand. Posey also had his critics who contended he was blocking Cousins's path to the plate before having the ball in his possession.

In the wake of the Posey-Cousins collision and others like it both before and after 2011, MLB, at long last, laggardly adopted new rules regarding plate collisions—but not until nearly three years later, scarcely in time for them to go into effect for the 2014 season. The rules implemented then, under Rule 7.13, are essentially the same as those in Rule 6.01 (i).

6.01 (i) (2)

Unless the catcher is in possession of the ball, the catcher cannot block the pathway of the runner as he is attempting to score. If, in the judgment of the umpire, the catcher without possession of the ball blocks the pathway of the runner, the umpire shall call or signal the runner safe. Notwithstanding the above, it shall not be considered a violation of this Rule 6.01 (i) (2) if the catcher blocks the pathway of the runner in a legitimate attempt to field the throw (e.g., in reaction to the direction, trajectory or the hop of the incoming throw, or in reaction to a throw that originates from a pitcher or drawn-in infielder). In addition, a catcher without possession of the ball shall not be adjudged to violate this Rule 6.01 (i) (2) if the runner could have avoided the collision with the catcher (or other player covering home plate) by sliding.

Rule 6.01 (i) (2) Comment: A catcher shall not be deemed to have violated Rule 6.01 (i) (2) unless he has both blocked the plate without possession the ball (or when not in a legitimate attempt to field the throw), and also hindered or impeded the progress of the runner attempting to score. A catcher shall not be deemed to have hindered or impeded the progress of the runner if, in the judgment of the umpire, the runner would have been called out notwithstanding the catcher having blocked the plate. In addition, a catcher should use best efforts to avoid unnecessary and forcible contact while tagging a runner attempting to slide. Catchers who routinely make unnecessary and forcible contact with a runner attempting to slide (e.g., by initiating contact using a knee, shin guard, elbow or forearm) may be subject to discipline by the League President.

This Rule 6.01 (i) (2) shall not apply to force plays at home plate.

Rule 6.01 (i) has been enormously expanded from the previous rules addressing collisions at home plate. While the Posey-Cousins confrontation was catalytic in tardily bringing about a new set of rules governing plays at the plate, there were numerous collisions in the 40 some years since the Rose-Fosse episode between catchers and baserunners that were just as violent and some even worse. In 1987, Royals outfielder Bo Jackson, better known for his football exploits, broke Cleveland catcher Rick Dempsey's thumb as he plowed into him. Five years later, Astros third baseman Ken

Caminiti KO'd Atlanta catcher Greg Olson in a plate collision, sending him to the hospital.

Given the many examples of vicious collisions from recent times, imagine what the catcher-runner battles must have been like in the rough-and-tumble years prior to the arrival of Babe Ruth and the Liveball Era. Rather amazingly, they were few and far between. Early day catchers, for one, were in general a bigger and hardier breed than other position players, let alone pitchers, and used to not only use their bodies but even the ball itself as a weapon to deter overly ambitious runners. Too, they wore masks and chest protectors and eventually shin guards, whereas runners came armed with only their spikes. Players like Ty Cobb changed all that to a degree, but even Cobb spent considerable time on the disabled list owing to base running mishaps and unnecessarily hard tags.

Lest the reader think that Rule 6.01 (i) (1) or (2) has eliminated or even thoroughly clarified illegal contact between catchers and baserunners, incidents that could be judged to constitute rule violations but do not still occur, while incidents deemed rule violations are perfectly legal. One of the former that received special attention came at Wrigley Field on June 19, 2017, in the bottom of the sixth inning of a game between the Padres and Cubs. Anthony Rizzo led off the frame by tripling. After second baseman Ian Happ fanned, third baseman Kris Bryant flied out to center fielder Matt Szczur. Rizzo tagged at third base and raced for home as soon as the catch was made. His trip began on the foul side of the third-base line, but when he saw Szczur's throw would reach San Diego catcher Austin Hedges ahead of him, he swerved into fair territory and came at Hedges's knees and elbows first without making any effort to touch the plate. Hedges held on to the ball but was forced to leave the game afterward. Rizzo was merely chided in the press for actively seeking out the collision and wrongly defended by his manager Joe Maddon, who said, "The catcher is in the way. You don't try to avoid him in an effort to score and hurt yourself. You hit him, just like Riz did."

6.01 (j) Sliding to Bases on Double Play Attempts

If a runner does not engage in a bona fide slide, and initiates (or attempts to make) contact with the fielder for the purpose of breaking up a double play, he should be called for interference under this Rule 6.01. A "bona fide slide" for purposes of Rule 6.01 occurs when the runner:

(1) begins his slide (i.e., makes contact with the ground) before reaching the base;

(2) is able and attempts to reach the base with his hand or foot;

(3) is able and attempts to remain on the base (except home plate) after completion of the slide; and

(4) slides within reach of the base without changing his pathway for the purpose of initiating contact with a fielder. A runner who engages in a "bona fide slide" shall not be called for interference under this Rule 6.01, even in cases where the runner makes contact with the fielder as a consequence of a permissible slide. In addition, interference shall not be called where a runner's contact with the fielder was caused by the fielder being positioned in (or moving into) the runner's legal pathway to the base.

Notwithstanding the above, a slide shall not be a "bona fide slide" if a runner engages in a "roll block," or intentionally initiates (or attempts to initiate) contact with the fielder by elevating and kicking his leg above the fielder's knee or throwing his arm or his upper body.

If the umpire determines that the runner violated this Rule 6.01 (j), the umpire shall declare both the runner and batter-runner out. Note, however, that if the runner has already been put out then the runner on whom the defense was attempting to make a play shall be declared out.

This rule and many of its ramifications followed one of the most iniquitous base-running incidents in history and, in the absence of it, its perpetrator almost inconceivably went unpunished. In Game Two of the National League Division Series on October 10, 2015, at Dodger Stadium between the Dodgers and the New York Mets, the home team trailed, 2–1. In their half of the seventh inning with one out, the Dodgers had Enrique Hernandez on third and Chase Utley on first when Howie Kendrick came to bat. Kendrick rapped a sharp grounder to Mets second baseman Daniel

Murphy, who tossed the ball to shortstop Ruben Tejada to start a potential double play. Utley slid far to the right side of second base, missing it altogether and colliding with Tejada's leg as he was turning to make a throw to first. Tejada was flipped by the contact and was carried off the field with a fractured right fibula—but not before Utley was called out at second and trotted off the field, having never touched the bag. Since it appeared to Dodgers manager Don Mattingly that Tejada dragged his foot near second base but hadn't actually touched it, he requested a video review. When the force out call at second was overturned, Utley trotted back out to the base. After Mets skipper Terry Collins pointed out that Utley had never touched second before leaving the field, he was in effect grudgingly told that since second-base umpire Chris Guccione blew the call, Utley had no need to tag the bag before his departure.

The Mets lost the game, 5–2, but still won the series, three games to two. Utley was initially suspended for two games but fought it and ultimately had it erased. However, in February 2016 MLB and the Players Association agreed that "slides on potential double plays will require runners will make a bona fide attempt to reach and remain on the base. Runners may still initiate contact with a fielder as a consequence of an otherwise permissible slide. A runner will be specifically prohibited from changing his pathway to the base or utilizing a 'roll block' for the purpose of initiating contact with the fielder." Utley finished his 16th consecutive season in the majors in 2018 before retiring. Tejada was never again more than a part-time major leaguer and has spent most of his time since 2015 in the minors.

Following the rule change as a direct result the Utley incident, coincidentally a ticky-tack game-ending example of the current version of runner interference occurred on June 17, 2016, at the Mets' Citi Field in Queens, New York. Trailing the Atlanta Braves in the bottom of the ninth, 5–1, Mets first baseman James Loney walked with one out. The next batter, catcher Kevin Plawecki, hit a ground ball to Braves shortstop Erick Aybar who tried for two by firing the ball to second baseman Jace Peterson to retire Loney. But Peterson's throw to first baseman Freddie Freeman was not in time to catch Plawecki. However, second-base umpire Mark Wegner immediately flashed the sign that Loney's slide into second had interfered with Peterson's effort to turn two, bringing the game to abrupt halt.

Loney's slide was nowhere near being in the Utley category—he brushed Peterson with an elbow as he slid into second—but the contact, slight as it was, clearly impinged on Peterson's throw to first in Wegner's judgment, which is the key criterion on a current interference call of this nature.

6.02 Pitcher Illegal Action

(a) Balks

    (2) The pitcher, while touching his plate, feints a throw to first or third base and fails to complete the throw;

Prior to the 2013 season, a pitcher was permitted to feint toward third (or second) base, and then turn and throw or feint a throw to first base if his pivot foot disengaged the rubber after his initial feint. This was called the "fake to third, throw to first"

> See **BALKS** in the **DEFINITIONS OF TERMS** chapter for more on balks.

play and over the years caught many an unwary runner. Abolishing this bit of trickery made runners look less foolish, but also deprived spectators of witnessing an age-old gambit that many are still unaware is now illegal.

6.02 (b) Illegal Pitches With Bases Unoccupied

If the pitcher makes an illegal pitch with the bases unoccupied, it shall be called a ball unless the batter reaches first base on a hit, an error, a base on balls, a hit batter or otherwise.

    Rule 6.02 (b) Comment: A ball which slips out of a pitcher's hand and crosses the foul line shall be called a ball; otherwise it will be called no pitch. This would be a balk with men on base.

    (c) Pitching Prohibitions

    The pitcher shall not:

        (1) While in the 18-foot circle surrounding the pitcher's plate, touch the ball after touching his mouth or lips, or touch his

> mouth or lips while he is in contact with the pitcher's plate. The pitcher must clearly wipe the fingers of his pitching hand dry before touching the ball or the pitcher's plate.
> (2) expectorate on the ball, either hand or his glove;
> (3) rub the ball on his glove, person or clothing;
> (4) apply a foreign substance of any kind to the ball;
> (5) deface the ball in any manner; or
> (6) deliver a ball altered in a manner prescribed by Rule 6.02 (c) (2) through (5) or what is called the "shine" ball, "spit" ball, "mud" ball or "emery" ball. The pitcher is allowed to rub the ball between his bare hands.

Before the spitball was outlawed in 1920, a pitcher was free to bring his pitching hand in contact with his mouth anywhere on the diamond. He could even bring the *ball* in contact with his mouth for a while the Pittsburgh Pirates had a pitcher, Marty O'Toole, who loaded up for a spitter by licking the ball with his tongue. O'Toole's only season of note was 1912, when he won 15 games. There is a tale that the reason he went into a tailspin after 1912 came in one of his outings that season in an early July game against the Phillies when Phils first sacker Fred Luderus found an insidious way to emasculate his spitter. Luderus purportedly harbored a tube of liniment in his pants pocket and applied a dab of it each time the ball came into his hands. Balls in 1912 often lasted several innings and sometimes even an entire game. By the third inning O'Toole's tongue was so raw he had to be removed from the mound. Pittsburgh manager Fred Clarke, aware of what Luderus was doing, protested. But it went nowhere when Phils skipper Red Dooin pointed out that there was nothing in the rules to prevent it and, furthermore, Luderus was only trying to protect the health of his teammates who would otherwise be exposed to millions of germs. The problem with the tale is that the game in question, on July 9, was won by O'Toole, 2–0. Historian Dick Thompson postulated that the true reason for O'Toole's abrupt decline was overwork and never really learning to control his spitter, allowing batters to lay off it once they realized this.

Regardless, the proviso making it illegal for a pitcher to bring his pitching hand in contact with his mouth or lips was not added to the anti-spitball rule until 1968. There was a massive effort at the time to rid the game of the spitter after the majors were given little choice but to acknowledge that many pitchers were using it. The estimates ran as high as 50 or 60, an average of about three pitchers on a team. One hurler, Cal Koonce of the New York Mets, in an inconceivable moment of candor, admitted in a piece that appeared in the September 2, 1967, issue of *The Sporting News* that the spitter was an important weapon in his arsenal. Subsequently asked if he had really made such an admission, Koonce said, "I don't know what all the fuss is about. A lot of pitchers in the [National] league throw the spitter and everyone knows who they are."

It seems unbelievable, in any case, that for forty-eight years after the spitball was outlawed the Official Playing Rules Committee failed to stipulate that a pitcher could not spit on his pitching hand. Since 1968, the rule has been amended to allow a pitcher to go to his mouth if he is not on the mound.

When the spitball was banned, the majors introduced a corollary rule that any player who intentionally discolored or defaced a ball would be kicked out of the game and the ball removed from play. If the umpires were unable to detect a transgressor, then the pitcher would be ejected as soon as the ball was in his possession and socked in addition with a 10-day suspension.

For obvious reasons, this rule didn't fly and was subsequently redrafted so that it was not all bark and no bite. Realizing they were verging on overreacting to the spitball specter and the concomitant bad press that followed Ray Chapman's beaning death, major-league tsars privately tempered their stance, even as they continued to rail publicly against pitchers who loaded up the ball. After a livelier type of horsehide was slipped into play during the early 1920s, no one wanted to punish hurlers any more than they were already having to suffer as they watched their ERAs mount alarmingly. In 1922, George Uhle of Cleveland became the first moundsman since the 1890s to win 20 games with an ERA over 4.00. Eight years later Pittsburgh's Ray Kremer became the first pitcher ever to collect 20 wins with an ERA over 5.00 (5.02). In 1938, Bobo Newsom topped Kremer's negative mark with he won 20 for the St. Louis Browns with a 5.08 ERA.

The last time a pitcher threw a spitball in a major-league game without facing the possibility of being penalized for it was in 1934, when Burleigh Grimes was in his final season in the majors. Grimes was the last to remain active of the 17 hurlers who had been given special dispensation in 1920 to continue throwing spitters in the majors until their careers were over. When Grimes notched his 270th and final win on May 30, 1934, by beating the Washington Senators, 5–4 in a relief role for the New York Yankees, it was the last victory by a hurler legally permitted to throw a spitter.

Burleigh Grimes legally threw a spitball pitch in the major leagues for a record nineteen seasons.

For some twenty-four years after the anti-spitball edict was enacted, no pitcher was ejected from a game specifically for violating the rule. Finally, on July 20, 1944, in a Thursday night game at St. Louis against the New York Yankees, Nels Potter of the Browns was tossed out by home-plate umpire Cal Hubbard in the fifth inning with New York's Don Savage at the plate. Nearly a quarter century after the anti-spitball rule went into effect, Potter became its first victim when Hubbard tired of watching him blow on the ball in such a way that it looked like he was spitting on it. Potter insisted he was doing nothing wrong and got huffy with Hubbard. His defiance helped convict him, for it was never proven that he was spraying saliva on the ball when he blew on it. The game, which St. Louis won, 7–3, was nearly forfeited to New York when Brownie fans rained the field with bottles for some 15 minutes after Potter's ejection was announced.

A few years before the Potter incident, the Yankees were certain that Tommy Bridges of the Detroit Tigers was shutting them down with a spitter. When Yankees skipper Joe McCarthy finally induced umpire Bill McGowan to take a look at the ball, Tigers catcher Mickey Cochrane dropped it as he handed it to McGowan and then rolled it in the dirt down the third-base line when he went to pick it up. Variations of Cochrane's stratagem have been used time and again ever since 1920 by catchers and infielders when an arbiter has asked to examine a suspicious ball.

6.02 (c) (7)

Have on his person, or in his possession, any foreign substance.

Though Rule 6.02 (c) (7) does not so specify, it is also illegal for a pitcher to have on his person a jagged fingernail that he can use to nick the surface of a ball. But fingernails are not nearly as much of a worry to umpires as other devices that are at once more disruptive and harder to detect. On August 3, 1987, at a game in Anaheim, Joe Niekro—then with the Minnesota Twins—was caught red-handed with both an emery board and a strip of sandpaper in his hip pocket with one out in the bottom of the fourth inning with the score tied, 2–2, when plate umpire Tim Tschida confronted him on the mound. Niekro was suspended for 10 days, but few pitchers have made it so easy for officials to ferret out their methods for doctoring balls. When asked to empty his pockets, Niekro clumsy tried to throw the emery board away, but it landed nearly at his feet.

During a game at Baltimore's Camden Yards on June 21, 1992, Orioles manager Johnny Oates complained that New York Yankees pitcher Tim Leary was putting "sandpaper scratches" on the ball. The umpires checked Leary's glove and hand and found nothing, but TV cameras earlier showed Leary putting his mouth to his glove and later spitting something out of his mouth when he reached the Yankees dugout at the end of the inning. Asked later why he only inspected Leary's hand and glove, first-base umpire Dave Phillips said, "I don't want to put my hand into somebody's mouth."

When Steve Carlton was in his prime, sportswriters were quite willing to respect his desire not to give interviews. The loss to their readers was small, they felt. Carlton wasn't very interesting anyway. What was fascinating, though, was how he got away year after year with cutting the ball. No one ever figured out the instrument Carlton used, and he was scarcely about to break his code of silence to convict himself.

But if Leary's and Carlton's techniques for defacing a ball were too subtle to allow an umpire in indict them, Los Angeles Dodgers' hurler Don Sutton was not so fortunate. Pitching against the St. Louis Cardinals at Busch Stadium II on July 14, 1978, Sutton was given the heave in the bottom of the seventh inning by umpire Doug Harvey after he scrupulously collected three balls that had become mysteriously scuffed while in Sutton's hands. Even though Harvey could not determine how Sutton was doctoring the balls, he defended his ejection by saying, "I represent the integrity of the game and I'm going to continue to do it if necessary." Sutton responded by suing Harvey for jeopardizing his live-lihood. The threat worked. Sutton received only a warning for the inci-dent—never even a fine, let alone a suspension.

6.02 (c) (9) Intentionally Pitch at the Batter

If, in the umpire's judgment, such a violation occurs, the umpire may elect either to:
(A) Expel the pitcher, or the manager and the pitcher, from the game, or
(B) may warn the pitcher and the manager of both teams that another such pitch will result in the immediate expulsion of that pitcher (or a replacement) and the manager.

The starting points for an umpire who has to decide whether a pitcher is deliberately throwing at a batter are the pitcher's history, prior events in the game, and his own intuition. Whether or not the pitcher hits a batter is often irrelevant. In a game on May 1, 1974, at Three Rivers Stadium against the Cincinnati Reds, Dock Ellis of the Pirates hit the first three batters he faced in the game—Pete Rose, Joe Morgan, and Dan Driessen—and then threw four fastballs high and tight to cleanup hitter Tony Perez to force in a run. When Ellis nearly nailed Johnny Bench with his next two pitches, still no one thought there was malice aforethought in his wild steak. After all, Ellis had tossed a no-hitter four years earlier and claimed afterward that he did it while on LSD. Finally, though, Pirates manager Danny Murtaugh lifted Ellis before anyone was killed. Said Reds manager Sparky Anderson when asked later for his views on Ellis's performance: "No one would be crazy enough to deliberately hit the first three men. He was so wild he just didn't know where the ball was going." Later it emerged that several days before the game Ellis had purportedly boasted he would throw at everyone in sight once he took the mound.

In contrast, Texas Rangers reliever Bob Babcock was booted from a game against the California Angels on May 26, 1980, at Anaheim

Stadium after just one pitch—his first pitch of the season no less! Babcock entered the fray in the top of the seventh inning following a beanball war during the previous frame that had culminated in a benches-clearing brawl after Rangers third baseman Buddy Bell was tossed for charging the Angels' Bruce Kison on the mound. As a consequence, the umpires were especially vigilant. When Babcock's first delivery narrowly missed Dan Ford, leading off the inning for the Angels, all four men in blue were convinced he was headhunting on orders from Rangers manager Pat Corrales. Babcock tried to claim his foot had slipped off the rubber as he released the pitch, but no one was about to buy it. He was thumbed from the game by plate umpire Bill Haller almost as soon as the ball whizzed past Ford's head. The following inning Rangers pinch-hitter Johnny Grubb was hit by a pitch and he and Kison were both tossed when he too charged the mound. The game then fell into the hands of reliever Mark Clear and the Angels lost, 6–5, when their defense unraveled.

Babcock is not the only major-league hurler to be ejected after just one pitch. An even more notorious episode arose in a game at Atlanta's Sun Trust Park on August 15, 2018, when Miami starter Jose Urena drilled the Braves' rookie lead-off hitter Ronald Acuna Jr. in the left elbow area with his first pitch of the night in the bottom of the first inning. Acuna had entered the game having homered in a rookie-record five straight games, three of them against the Marlins. At first the umpires seemed inclined to treat Urena's pitch as simply an errant one. But when Acuna veered off toward the mound as he was starting to take his base and threw off the wrap he wore around his swollen elbow, Braves manager Brian Snitker led the charge out of the Atlanta dugout.

Braves outfielder Ronald Acuna Jr. set a frosh record in 2018 when he homered in five straight games. He conquered the sophomore jinx in 2019 by leading the National League in runs and stolen bases along with belting 41 homers, many of them as the Braves' leadoff hitter.

That quickly, the event disintegrated into a benches-clearing scuffle with both Urena and Snitker ejected from the game after the umpires huddled around crew chief Paul Nauert. The end result was that stiff warnings were issued to both teams, Atlanta won the game, 5–2, Urena escaped a suspension largely because he carried a reputation for wildness—the 2018 season marked his second in a row leading the National League in hit batsmen—and Acuna's home-run streak remained intact because he was hit by a pitch in his lone plate appearance. His streak ended the following night, however, in an 11–5 loss to Colorado.

6.03 Batter Illegal Action

(a) A batter is out for illegal action when:
  (2) He steps from one batter's box to the other while the pitcher is in position ready to pitch;

In sandlot games, an argument often arises if a batter switches from batting righ handed to hitting lefty or vice versa when an opposing team has not changed pitchers while he is batting. As Rule 6.06 (b) reads, however, a batter is free to switch to the opposite side of the plate after every pitch. Before 1907, a batter could switch sides even while a pitcher was in the midst of his delivery. Since then the rule has been that if the batter is in the batter's box and the pitcher is in position to deliver the ball, the batter cannot switch unless time is called by the umpire, allowing him to step out of the box and make the change.

Rule 6.03 (a) 2 makes an attempt by a batter to switch sides while time is in cause for an umpire to declare him out for an illegal action. In the early game it was not uncommon for batters, particularly foxy switch-hitters like Tommy Tucker, to do just that without penalty. One of the first victims of this rule (formerly 6.06 [b]) was Philadelphia Phillies outfielder and leadoff hitter Johnny Bates. In a game against the Cincinnati Reds at the Reds' Palace of the Fans on August 27, 1910, Bates, a left-handed hitter, was called out by home-plate umpire Mal Eason when he changed to the right side of the plate while Reds pitcher Fred Beebe was in motion. Bates nonetheless went 1-for-3 that day and scored a run in the Phils' 5–2 win.

Prior to the rule generated by Pat Venditte's recent arrival in the game, the problem became more complex for an umpire, however, when a switch-hitter faced a switch-pitcher. In a Western Association game in 1928, Paul Richards of Muskogee (the same Paul Richards who would later exasperate umpires with his ingenious tests of the rules as a major-league manager) baffled Topeka hitters by throwing left handed to lefty hitters and right-handed to righty hitters until switch-hitter Charlie "Swamp Baby" Wilson came up in the ninth inning as a pinch-hitter. Each time Richards changed his glove from one hand to the other Wilson matched him by moving to the opposite side of the plate. Said Richards in recalling the incident: "Finally I threw my glove down on the ground, faced him square with both feet on the rubber, put my hands behind my back and let him choose his own poison." In recounting the story, Richards would always end by slyly confessing he walked Wilson on a 3-and-2 count when he missed the plate with a slow left-handed curve.

> Rule 6.03 (a) (5) He uses or attempts to use a bat that, in the umpire's judgment, has been altered or tampered with in such a way to improve the distance factor or cause an unusual reaction on the baseball. This includes bats that are filled, flat-surfaced, nailed, hollowed, grooved or covered with a substance such as paraffin, wax, etc.
>
> No advancement on the bases will be allowed (except advancements that are not caused by the use of an illegal bat, e,g., stolen base, balk, wild pitch, passed ball), and any out or outs made during a play shall stand. In addition to being called out, the player shall be ejected from the game and may be subject to additional penalties as determined by his League President.
>
> 6.03 (a) (5) Comment: A batter shall be deemed to have used or attempted to use an illegal bat if he brings such a bat into the batter's box.

This rule was first inserted in 1975. Before then, if a batter was discovered to have struck a ball with a "loaded" or doctored bat, the hit counted and the offending bat was simply removed from the game (although the batter could be subject to further sanctions if it was a repeat violation or a particularly flagrant one). The procedure, if a bat was protested, was for the umpires to inspect it and then either allow it to continue in play or confiscate it for a more thorough examination if it looked suspicious.

Loaded bats have been part of the game almost from its inception. Players in the nineteenth century would often pound nails into the meat ends of their bats and then coat the nail heads with varnish or some other

Caught using a bat studded with nails in 1954, Cleveland third baseman Al Rosen sustained a badly broken finger shortly thereafter. The finger injury is thought to have stopped him from ever again being the great slugger he had formerly been, but it will never be certain whether he used the illegal bat in his MVP season in 1953.

substance that would conceal them from chary opponents. A much more recent incident occurred in 1954 when Cleveland third baseman Al Rosen was found to be using a bat studded with nails after slugging three home runs in a two-game set with the Boston Red Sox on May 18–19. At the time, Rosen was hitting .382 with nine homers and 38 RBIs in just 30 games, and coming off a season in which he had paced the American League in every important slugging department and almost won the Triple Crown. Soon after being deprived of his "magic" bat, Rosen suffered a broken finger. The dual setback caused a dramatic decline in his production. For the remaining 124 games of the 1954 campaign, Rosen hit well below .300 and notched just 15 home runs and 64 RBIs. The sharp drop, even though some of it was definitely attributable to Rosen's injury, fostered speculation that he may have been using a loaded bat for some time before he was caught.

Forty years later, another Cleveland slugger, outfielder Albert Belle, was suspended for 10 games after the corked bat he used in a game on July 15, 1994, was finally confiscated after a byzantine chase by umpires to recapture it following its theft from the umpires' dressing room. But no bat violation was more embarrassing to its culprit than the one seen by a national TV audience on June 3, 2003, in an interleague game at Wrigley Field between the Cubs and the Tampa Bay Devil Rays. In the bottom of the first inning, Cubs outfielder Sammy Sosa came to the plate with two on and one out against Tampa's Geremi Gonzalez. When Sosa grounded out to second base, his bat broke. He was immediately ejected from the game after plate umpire Tim McClelland examined it and found it was heavily corked. Sosa contended the bat had slipped into the game by accident and was used only in batting practice to entertain fans but was nonetheless suspended for seven games.

Probably the most bizarre loaded bat incident in the last half century came on September 7, 1974, at Shea Stadium while the Yankees were using it as a temporary home during a time when their own stadium was being renovated. In the second game of a doubleheader with Detroit, New York third baseman Graig Nettles broke his bat after lining a fastball from Woodie Fryman to left field in the bottom of the fifth . . . and six super-balls tumbled out of the barrel. Nettles was declared automatically out, with the out credited to Tigers catcher Bill Freehan, but was not ejected from the game by plate umpire Lou DiMuro even though three innings earlier he had homered for the game's only run, in all likelihood with the same bat. He was subsequently suspended for 10 games, however, by American League president Lee MacPhail who did not buy his excuse that the bat had been given to him by an admiring fan and he was unaware of its illicit contents. Rules authorities believe the Nettles incident more than any other prompted the creation of Rule 6.03 (a) (5).

6.03 (b) Batting Out of Turn

(1) A batter shall be called out, on appeal, when he fails to bat in his proper turn, and another batter completes a time at bat in his place.

Although the question is not specifically addressed in this rule, the absence of any proscription to the contrary licenses a vigilant fan to lean over the railing behind his favorite team's dugout and whisper to the manager that an opposition hitter is batting out of turn. Indeed, the only people in a ballpark who are forbidden by rule to call such a violation to a manager's attention are the official scorer and the umpiring crew. An umpire in particular is required to keep still, which is not to say that all arbiters know or abide by this rule. In her book, *You've Got to Have B*lls to Make It in This League*, Pam Postema recalled the following moment in a minor league game she was officiating:

> Once in a while I even showed up a manager or one of my own partners. For instance, one night I had the plate and noticed a batter step into the box who wasn't supposed to be there. He was batting out of order. Stupid rookie. Just as I was getting ready to call the batter out for hitting out of order, I heard the scorekeeper yell down to her husband, who happened to be one of the managers, "Woody, that's the wrong batter, honey," she said.

Too late, I called the guy out and quickly figured out who was supposed to be up next. Meanwhile, my partner, who didn't have a clue what the rule said, whispered, "Are you sure you're right?" Hey, it was no big deal to me. I knew the rule. I called it. End of discussion.

Postema's recollection makes it distressingly apparent that neither she nor her partner nor the official scorer nor the official scorer's manager-husband knew the present-day rule on a player batting out of order.

However, the rule in 1912 was a bit different. It was not left solely to the opposing team's manager to inform an umpire that a player had batted out of order.

Dick Cotter, a backup catcher in the NL for two seasons, is listed in all reference works today as having played his last major-league game on September 26, 1912. In actuality, he played his last game six days later on October 2 and emerged as its hero, but it didn't count. None of it counted because the custom during the 1910s dictated that all statistics from protested games that were thrown out were permanently eradicated. And who was responsible for the game being protested? Not Pittsburgh, the losing team, though technically its secretary officially lodged the protest but only after a writer at the game brought it to his attention long after both teams had left the field that he had grounds for a protest. That nameless writer, it need be said, along with several other scribes at the game, had made frantic efforts from the press box "to put the home team next to the mistake before it was too late."

The muddle began in the bottom of the ninth when Cotter, a right-handed hitter, pinch-hit for Wilbur Good, a left-handed hitter who had been sent up to bat for Cubs pitcher Jimmy Lavender and was called back when the Pirates replaced right-hander Howie Camnitz on the hill with southpaw Hank Robinson. Cotter ripped a single over first base that brought home Cubs outfielder Cy Williams with the run that tied the game, 5–5. Cotter then stayed in the contest, replacing catcher Jimmy Archer who had been pinch run for by Williams, while Charlie Smith replaced Lavender on the hill. After Smith held Pittsburgh scoreless in the visitors' half of the 10th frame, Chicago threatened in the home half, bringing Cotter to the plate with two out and a chance to drive in the winning run. Only Cotter this time was batting not in the ninth spot in the order, which Lavender had occupied, but the eighth spot, which had belonged to Archer. With two out and Vic Saier on second and Frank Schulte on third, Cotter lined a single over second base off Robinson to plate Schulte with the walk-off winning run—at least insofar as everyone connected with the Pittsburgh and Chicago clubs then believed.

Meanwhile, umpires Brick Owens and Bill Brennan had been aware that Cotter had batted out of turn when he hit in the eighth spot instead of the ninth, the spot he'd occupied when he entered the game, but looked the other way because they "thought it was up to the opposing team to claim the point, so did not declare Dick out." The *New York Sun* said both officials "waited for manager [Fred] Clarke to lodge a protest, but none was forth coming, and Owens, the-umpire-in-chief that day, declared that no further protests could be made, that the chance was lost when the Pirates rushed from the field." They learned otherwise before the evening was out when soon after they wired the protest on Pittsburgh's behalf to NL president Tom Lynch, Lynch read them the riot act.

Since the Giants had already clinched the NL pennant—ironically on the day that Dick Cotter played his final official ML game—the protested contest was not replayed because it meant nothing.

Except to Dick Cotter.

6.03 (b) (7)

When an improper batter becomes a proper batter because no appeal is made before the next pitch, the next batter shall be the batter whose name follows that of such legalized improper batter. The instant an improper batter's actions are legalized, the batting order picks up with the name following that of the legalized improper batter.

Rule 6.03 (b) (7) Comment: The umpire shall not direct the attention of any person to the presence in the batter's box of an improper batter. This rule is designed to require constant vigilance by the players and managers of both teams.

There are two fundamentals to keep in mind: When a player bats out of turn, the proper batter is the player called out. If an improper batter bats and reaches base or is out and no appeal is made before a pitch to the next batter, or before any play or attempted play, that improper batter is considered to have batted in proper turn and establishes the order that is to follow [for the remainder of the game].

Observe that this rule is a comparatively recent revision of the old rule that allowed a team manager to wait after noticing a batter has batted out of turn until the batting snafu produces a positive result for the offending team. Here is the old rule in action.

On August 2, 1923, in the first game of a doubleheader at Washington, St. Louis Browns skipper Lee Fohl, a compulsive batting order juggler, had not just two but four players batting out of order—outfielders Ken Williams and Baby Doll Jacobson, plus shortstop Wally Gerber and catcher Hank Severeid. The Williams-Jacobson mistake was rectified in the top of the first inning when Williams, who was listed in the fourth spot, batted third and walked, a positive result. Washington skipper Donie Bush protested immediately and Jacobson, who should have been hitting ahead of Williams, was declared out and Williams made to bat again. Even though Bush also noticed early in the game that Gerber and Severeid had switched positions in the batting order, he held his powder for their first three trips through the order because neither of them did anything positive. But in the ninth inning, when Gerber singled a runner to third with two out, Bush spoke up that Gerber was batting in Severeid's sixth spot in the order. His timing was impeccable. Plate umpire Red Ormsby ruled Severeid out to end the game and effectively erase Gerber's lone hit on the day.

Personally, this author prefers the old rule. Anything that requires a manager to strategize on the fly as the game progresses I'm for.

6.04 Unsportsmanlike Conduct
(c) No fielder shall take a position in the batter's line of vision, and with deliberate unsportsmanlike intent, act in a manner to distract the batter.

During one of his at-bats against the New York Giants at Braves Field on August 9, 1950, Boston third baseman Bob Elliott requested that umpire Augie Donetelli shift his positioning slightly—Donatelli, the roving umpire on a three-man crew, was in Elliott's line of vision, making it difficult for him to pick up the baseball. When Donatelli complied, Giants second baseman Eddie Stanky saw his chance to further rattle Elliott.

Before the next pitch, he sidled over to where Donatelli had been standing and began doing jumping jacks.

Elliott pretended not to see Stanky's antics, and the game proceeded without incident. On August 11, against the Phillies at Shibe Park, Stanky decided to see if his new "calisthenics" routine could rile Philadelphia's hotheaded catcher Andy Seminick. This time Stanky evoked the reaction he was aiming for—Seminick stepped out of the batter's box and demanded that home plate umpire Al Barlick make Stanky cease his antics. Barlick conferred with his three fellow umpires, one of them Donatelli, and Donatelli informed his crew that they had a problem. He had seen Stanky perform this same stunt just two days earlier and consulted the rule book after the game. Therein he discovered that Major League Baseball had lasted for nearly seventy years without ever having cause to outlaw jumping up and down in a batter's line of vision. Hence Barlick had no choice but to allow Stanky to continue for the rest of the game and then contact National League President Ford Frick afterward in an effort to get some clarification.

Failing to locate Frick prior to the next afternoon's game, the umpiring crew went to Stanky's manager, Leo Durocher, and requested that he tell Stanky to drop his jumping jacks act until an official ruling could be made. But Durocher, who had once said there was nothing Stanky could do well on the ball field except beat you, instructed Stanky to continue doing as he pleased. When Stanky did so and added waving his arms exaggeratedly that afternoon, tempers flared. In the second inning, Seminick broke Giants third baseman Hank Thompson's jaw with his elbow on a hard slide into third. By the fourth inning, second-base umpire Lon Warneke felt he was left with no choice but to eject Stanky when he again waved his arms with Seminick at bat, but it was too little too late. In sliding into second base later in the inning, Seminick took out Stanky's replacement, Bill Rigney, and detonated a benches-clearing brawl that took the NYPD's help to subdue it and Warneke having to eject both Rigney and Seminick. After the game, Frick was finally heard from. He instructed all his umpires in the future to eject fielders for "antics on the field designed or intended to annoy or disturb the opposing batsman." Though the language has changed and expanded, the rule has remained on the books ever since. A form of it actually first appeared in 1931 and may have been what Frick finally stumbled on when he was pushed for help by his umpires.

6.04 (e) (4.08)

When the occupants of a player's bench show violent disapproval of an umpire's decision, the umpire shall first give warning that such disapproval shall cease.

PENALTY: [If such action continues] The umpire shall order the offenders from the bench to the club house. If he is unable to detect the offender, or offenders, he may clear the bench of all substitute players. The manager of the offending team shall have the privilege of recalling to the playing field only those players needed for substitution in the game.

On numerous occasions, an umpire has invoked the ultimate power bestowed on him in Rule 6.04 (e) (4.08) and expelled every player on a team's bench from a game. One of the most volatile incidents occurred on September 27, 1951, in a game between the Brooklyn Dodgers and Boston Braves at Braves Field which resulted in the only ejection of a player who never participated in a major league game. Trying to hold a slim first-place lead over the onrushing New York Giants, the Dodgers were tied, 3–3, with Boston in the bottom of the eighth when Jackie Robinson speared a groundball and fired it home to catcher Roy Campanella seemingly in time to nail Bob Addis trying to score from third . . . but plate umpire Frank Dascoli called Addis safe. Campanella was swiftly dispatched for arguing, coach Cookie Lavagetto soon followed when the debate continued to rage, and finally Dascoli cleared the entire Dodgers bench.

Among the record 15 players who were banished was outfielder Bill Sharman, just up from the Dodgers' Forth Worth farm club in the Texas League after the club had finished its season. Sharman failed to get into a game with Brooklyn in 1951, however, and then quit baseball after one more season in the minors to pursue an NBA career. After joining Bob Cousy, Bill Russell, and Sam Jones to play on several championship Boston Celtics teams, Sharman eventually made the Naismith Memorial Basketball Hall of Fame, but he never had the thrill of seeing his name in a major-league box score, even though it once appeared in an umpire's report on players who were booted from the game.

7.00: Ending the Game

7.01 Regulation Games

A regulation game consists of nine innings, unless extended because of a tie score, or shortened (1) because the home team needs none of its half of the ninth inning or only a fraction of it, or (2) because the umpire-in-chief calls the game.

For the many historians who consider the National Association a major league, the first official major-league game took place on May 4, 1871, at Fort Wayne, between the Kekiongas of Fort Wayne and the Cleveland Forest Citys. The Kekiongas, behind pitcher Bobby Mathews, in an extraordinarily well-played game for the time, took a 2–0 lead into the top of the ninth. The visitors failed to score, but because the rules throughout the National Association era and as late as 1879 required that a full game be played even if the bottom of the ninth inning was meaningless—as was the case on this day—the Kekiongas had to take their raps.

Apart from giving fans a full nine innings for their money, the rule served no useful purpose and if anything invited abuses. Professional baseball in its infancy was rife with gamblers eager for an edge and also a fair number of players willing to provide them with one for a price. Games that went the full nine innings with the winner already determined in the top half of the ninth were prime meat—especially games between weak teams and strong ones. A popular scenario, once it was determined the heavy favorite would bat last, involved wagering the favorite would not score any runs in its last raps if enough players on the favored team were in on the bet and willing to cooperate. It generally proved to be a sucker's bet, and there were others if, say, the pitcher on a heavy underdog had been reached beforehand and coaxed to surrender an agreed upon minimum number of runs or hits in the bottom of the ninth. Fortunately, the majority of players continued to play their best after the final verdict was decided, but others just went through the motions, reluctant to expend extra energy or risk injury during a half inning whose only import was that all the statistics in it counted.

The last date all major-league games went a full nine innings regardless of which team led after the top of the ninth was on September 30, 1879, the final day of the only MLB season ever to feature the two top contenders—Providence and Boston—ending the campaign by meeting six games in a row to decide the NL pennant. Another memorable first occurred on Opening Day the following season: the first walk-off or sudden death hit in major-league history. On May 1, 1880, at Cincinnati, visiting Chicago batted last and trailed the Reds, 3–2, in the bottom of the ninth. After Chicago's vaunted rookie pitcher Larry Corcoran opened the frame with single, an error by Cincinnati shortstop Sam Wright put Chicago shortstop Tom Burns on board and both came home soon thereafter when Cincinnati right fielder Jack Manning threw Joe Quest's routine single over Reds catcher John Clapp's head, allowing the game to end, 4–3, the moment Burns, the trailing runner, touched home. Had there been a third runner on base and he too had scored, his tally would not have counted because the game officially ended the moment Burns, the winning run, crossed the plate.

7.01 (b)

If the score is tied after nine completed innings play shall continue until (1) the visiting team has scored more total runs than the home team at the end of a completed inning, or (2) the home team scores the winning run in an uncompleted inning.

Although this rule that normal play shall continue still applies in the major leagues, it may soon become obsolete. Already some minor leagues are experimenting with having each team start every extra frame with a runner on second and none out. What's more, the 2019 All-Star Game was chosen to showcase the experiment at the major-league level if the game was tied after 12 innings. (Happily, the American League won, 4–3, in regulation, obviating the need for experimentation.) The rule is an unpopular one thus far, even though its purpose is to promote more scoring and curb the number of protracted games that reduce their audiences with each passing inning and also, importantly, deplete the bullpens of both teams to a point where they end with a position player having to take the mound when the game is still in doubt, usually with farcical consequences.

If this rule were to become part of the major-league fabric, it is first going to require some deep thought on how to score it. Does a pitcher still retain his perfect game if he starts the 10th inning with a runner on second base? If so, does he lose both it and his no-hit bid if that runner is hit by a batted ball, making the third out in an otherwise unblemished inning? And who will start each extra frame occupying second base? The same runner each inning? A different runner each inning? The last out of the previous inning? A player chosen by the opposition? Or—perish the thought—if the game goes long enough and both benches are emptied, a player who's already been in the game?

7.01 (d)

If a regulation game is called with the score tied, it shall become a suspended game. See Rule 7.02.

Ties were frequent in the days when games could not be finished due to darkness or were forbidden from turning on their lights turned if the game began in daylight. A game nowadays that is halted with the score tied is treated as a suspended game and finished at a later time. However, ties do still exist. A recent one occurred on September 29, 2016, in a game at Pittsburgh's PNC Park when the Pirates and Cubs were deadlocked at 1–1 in the sixth inning when heavy rain stopped play for over an hour and the game was eventually called by plate umpire Brian Gorman. The tie was the first since 2005, and was declared such rather than a suspended game because the two teams were not scheduled to play again in 2016 and the Cubs had already clinched home-field advantage throughout the

National League playoffs while the Pirates were out of contention, eliminating any substantive reason to make up the game.

7.01 (e)

If a game is postponed or otherwise called before it has become a regulation game, the umpire-in-chief shall declare it "No Game," unless the game is called pursuant to Rules 7.02 (a) (3) or 7.02 (a) (4), which shall be a suspended game at any time after it starts.

Rule 7.01 Comment: The Major Leagues have determined that Rules 7.01 (c) and 7.01 (e) do not apply to any Wild Card, Division Series, League Championship Series or World Series games or for any additional Major League championship season game played to break a tie.

Prior to 2008, postseason games did not have different rules from regular season ones regarding suspended games. As a result, over the years there were several tie games in World Series play. For those who accept that the annual postseason World's Series contests between the American Association and the National League, which ran from 1884 through 1890, were the first World Series games between two rival major leagues, ironically the last such best-of-seven postseason—the 1890 World's Series between the Brooklyn Bridegrooms and the Louisville Cyclones—ended tied at three games apiece because Game Three on October 20 at Louisville had resulted in a 7–7 draw called by darkness after eight innings. And, due to miserable weather, it precluded any desire by either side to play a decisive Game Eight, as eventually did occur for the first time in the 1912 World Series.

The first application of the Rule 7.01 special comment came in Game Five of the 2008 World Series between the Tampa Bay Rays and Philadelphia Phillies at Philadelphia's Citizens Bank Park on October 27. The first suspended game in World Series history was halted by heavy rain and winds with the score tied, 2–2, in the bottom of the sixth after the Rays had tied the game in the top of the frame. Owing to lingering bad weather, the game was not resumed until October 29, and even then the temperature at game time was a blustery 44 degrees. The Phillies promptly scored a run in the bottom of the sixth and the game ended with Philadelphia winning, 4–3, on Eric Bruntlett's run in the bottom of the seventh and taking the World Series in five games.

Commissioner Bud Selig later decreed that the game would have been suspended even if the Rays had not tied it, regardless of what the rule book stated. The next month, Major League Baseball instituted a rule stating that no postseason games nor any games with potential postseason significance—such as All-Star Games and tiebreaker games for division titles or wild cards—could be shortened due to weather. All games in those instances are suspended and completed at a later date from the point of termination, even if they are not yet regulation games.

Yes, the rule at first included All-Star Games, but that part was dropped prior to the 2017 season. Their results no longer have any bearing on which league hosts the World Series opener and even desultory fans know their inclusion stems from the 2002 All-Star fiasco at Milwaukee that Selig ruled a 7–7 tie when both teams ran out of pitchers.

7.01 (g) (3)

If the home team scores the winning run in its half of the ninth inning (or its half of an extra inning after a tie), the game ends immediately when the winning run is scored.

EXCEPTION: If the last batter in a game hits a home run out of the playing field, the batter-runner and all runners on base are permitted to score, in accordance with the base-running rules, and the game ends when the batter-runner touches home plate.

The exception to the present rule enabling a team to win by more than one run when a game is ended by a sudden death home run was first added in 1920. Before then, the rule was firm that a team batting last could not win by more than one run when it won the game in walk-off fashion in the ninth or an extra inning. If with the score tied and the bases loaded a player hit a sudden death outside-the-park home run, rather than a grand slam he was given credit only for one RBI (the number of runs needed to win the game) and a single (the number of bases the runner scoring the winning tally needed to make). Among the 38 players who lost home runs to the old rule was Babe Ruth. When Ruth homered off Stan Coveleski for Boston on July 8, 1918, with Red Sox teammate Amos Strunk on first base to end a ten-inning 0–0 game with Cleveland, he was credited at the time with only a triple.

In 1968, the Special Baseball Records Committee—which was formed to resolve historical disparities or errors—voted to credit all the players who had hit sudden death home runs before 1920 with an additional career four-bagger. Ruth's home run total was hiked from 714 to 715, where it remained for all of about a year before the committee reversed its decision on May 5, 1969, and again assigned Ruth only a triple for his 1918 blow. It has remained a triple ever since, but other home runs that should have been reduced to the number of bases needed to score the winning run have slipped through the cracks and are still in the record books as home runs. A premier example occurred in Cleveland on July 10, 1880, when Jim McCormick of the Cleveland Blues was locked in a 0–0 struggle with Fred Goldsmith of the Chicago White Stockings heading into the bottom of the ninth. After shortstop Jack Glasscock reached first on a single, second baseman Fred Dunlap hit a long blast over center fielder Larry Corcoran's head and circled the bases, giving Cleveland a 2–0 victory and ending Chicago's then NL record 21-game winning streak. Technically, Dunlap's hit should have been a triple as per a new rule installed just that year, which dictated that the game ended as soon as Glasscock touched the plate, but the official scorer either forgot the rule change or didn't agree with it and credited Dunlap with an inside-the-park home run. So it has remained ever since

7.02 Suspended, Postponed, and Tie Games

A game shall become a suspended game that must be completed at a future date if the game is terminated for any of the following reasons:
(4) Darkness, when a law prevents the lights from being turned on;

The marathon 26-inning 1–1 tie game between the Brooklyn Dodgers and Boston Braves on May 1, 1920, at Braves Field came forty-nine years too soon. Rather than Brooklyn's Leon Cadore and Boston's Joe Oeschger probably throwing well over 200 pitches each to no avail, now the game would have been suspended when darkness made it impossible to continue (and the field was without lights, as they all were in 1920) and then resumed at the top of the 27th inning the next time the teams met. Before 1969, however, a game called at the end of a completed inning with the score tied after nine or more innings was declared a draw and then replayed from scratch later in the season.

The 1969 rule change enabled the Chicago White Sox and Milwaukee Brewers to break the record in 1984 for the longest game inning-wise in American League history. On May 8, 1984, the two clubs battled for 17 innings to a 3–3 stalemate at Chicago's Comiskey Park, resuming the struggle the following day. Harold Baines eventually slammed a walk-off homer off the Brewers' Chuck Porter with one down in the bottom of the 25th to give the White Sox a 7–6 triumph. Tom Seaver, who worked the final inning of the suspended game in relief and then started the regularly scheduled game and went 8⅓ innings, won both contests for Chicago. Note that Rule 7.02 (8) specifies that if a game is suspended before it becomes a regulation-length game and then resumed prior to another regulation game, the regulation game that day is trimmed to seven innings unless it should happen to be a postseason game.

Previously, the record for the longest game in American League history had been 24 innings, last done on July 21, 1945, at Philadelphia when the A's and Detroit Tigers were forced to settle for a 1–1 tie. Had the current rule been in effect then, the game would have been completed at a later date, as would have the Dodgers and Braves 26-inning classic. As it stands, the longest game in National League history played to a decision came on September 11, 1974, when the Cardinals beat the Mets, 4–3, at Shea Stadium on an errant pickoff throw in the 25th inning.

Meanwhile, that 26-inning tie continues to be the longest game inning-wise in MLB history. The contest lasted three hours and fifty minutes, and featured Boston second baseman Charlie Pick going a single-game record 0-for-11 and Braves shortstop Rabbit Maranville the only starter to bat .300 on the day, going 3-for-10. The following day, a Sunday, the Dodgers played at home against Philadelphia and lost, 4–3, in 13 innings. They then journeyed back to Boston that evening, and on Monday afternoon lost, 2–1, to the Braves' Dana Fillingim in 19 innings, giving them a total of 58 innings played in a three-day period and nothing to show for it (except the 26-inning tie). Nonetheless, they won the 1920 NL pennant by a comfortable seven-game margin over the New York Giants.

7.02 (b)

A suspended game shall be resumed and completed as follows:

(5) Any postponed game, suspended game (that has not progressed far enough to become a regulation game), or tie game that has not been rescheduled and completed prior to the last scheduled game between the two teams during the championship season must be played (or continued, in the case of a suspended or tie game) to a completed regulation game, if the League President determines that not playing such game might affect eligibility for the post-season and/or home-field advantage for any Wild Card or Division Series game.

Major-league teams nowadays not only devote maximum effort to complete suspended games and make up postponed games, but are in fact required to do so—especially when the game(s) in question could have a bearing on a pennant or division race. Such has not always been the case. This issue was first addressed after the 1908 season, when Detroit copped the American League pennant by a half-game over Cleveland. The margin of victory was a postponed game at Washington the Tigers had not been required to play, leaving Detroit at 90–63, whereas Cleveland, playing a full 154-game slate, finished at 90–64.

Cleveland fans were understandably upset, but White Sox followers also had a legitimate grievance. The White Sox finished a game and a half behind Detroit at 88–64 after failing to replay two games that ended in a tie. Had the Tigers played their postponed game and lost them, and the White Sox won both of their replayed games, the 1908 American League race would have ended in a three-way tie, with Detroit, Cleveland, and Chicago all at 90–64.

Few historians have noted that the 1908 season was the fifth in a row in which postponed games were a significant factor in the American League pennant race. In 1904, the first year that both major leagues adopted a 154-game schedule, Boston and New York tied in victories with 92, but Boston had three fewer losses. Philadelphia and Chicago both garnered 92 wins in 1905, but postponements reduced the A's slate to 148 games, whereas the White Sox played 152. The following year the Sox benefited by postponements, finishing three games ahead of New York as both teams were held to 151 contests; had the clubs been required to play out the schedule, New York could have tied the Sox at 93–61.

The 1907 season was the only time in major-league history that a pennant winner lost more games than an also-ran. A rainy summer in the East shaved nine games off the Philadelphia A's schedule, while Detroit lost only four contests to the weather. Philadelphia finished at 88–57, a game and a half behind Detroit's 92–58 mark. Had the full slate been played, the A's record conceivably could have been 97–57, leaving the Tigers five games back at 92–62.

Despite a pledge following the 1908 campaign to make up postponed games that had a potential bearing on a pennant race, there have been several occasions in the years since when this was not done. The most glaring was in 1915, when three teams were bunched within half a game of each other at the close of the Federal League season. Owing to postponements, the flag-winning Chicago Whales played just 152 games and finished at 86–66; the Pittsburgh Rebels with the same number of wins but one more loss ended in third place, a half-game back, at 86–67. Finishing second were the St. Louis Terriers at 87–67. The Terriers were just one percentage point off the pace and are the only team prior to the inception of division play in 1969 to lead its circuit in victories yet fail to win the pennant.

Some critics tend to excuse the Federal League, contending it was not a true major league, but no satisfactory explanation has ever been presented for the American League's failure to order meaningful postponed games to be made up in 1935 or an even more serious gaffe by the National League three years later. Detroit copped the 1935 American League flag by a three-game margin over the New York Yankees that could have turned into a one-game deficit if both clubs had fulfilled their 154-game commitments. In 1938, the Chicago Cubs triumphed by two games over the Pittsburgh Pirates, but could likewise have wound up one game in arrears had the Pirates played and won four postponed games while the Bruins were losing their two unplayed contests.

The 1918 and 1972 seasons also saw teams benefit from the full schedule not being completed, but for reasons that were unavoidable. Owing to America's involvement in World War I, the 1918 campaign was terminated on Labor Day with the huge disparities between the number of home and road games the Boston Red Sox and Cleveland Indians played contributing to a Red Sox triumph by 2½ games. In 1972, after a spring-training lockout delayed the start of the major-league season, it was ruled that all games that were canceled as a result of the lockout would not be made up. Detroit then proceeded to win the American League East crown over Boston by a scant half-game. This memory prompted both major leagues to make up all canceled games during the course of the season when another labor lockout delayed the start of the 1990 campaign.

7.03 Forfeited Games

(a) A game may be forfeited to the opposing team when a team:
  (1) Fails to appear upon the field, or being upon the field, refuses to start play within five minutes after the umpire-in-chief has called "Play" at the appointed hour for beginning the game, unless such delayed appearance is, in the umpire-in-chief's judgment, unavoidable.

Technically, the last time a major-league game was forfeited because a team failed to show up was in 1902, when the Baltimore Orioles were unable to field a full team for an American League game on July 17 with the St. Louis Browns at Baltimore. The Orioles were in total disarray at the time after ex-National Leaguer John McGraw jumped the club to join the New York Giants, and he and owner Andrew Freedman induced several key players to also jump to his club. Others were sent to Cincinnati, leaving the Orioles with only three players. To fill out their roster so that they could finish the season without further forfeits, player contributions came from other American League clubs and also the high minors. In consequence, only Baltimore's three core players participated in as many as 100 games and the Orioles became the first team to complete its full schedule without a pitcher who worked as many as 200 innings.

Before the Baltimore decimation, the last time a team was saddled with a no-show loss was on October 12, 1892, when the Cleveland Spiders failed to appear for a scheduled makeup game at Pittsburgh. The game the day before had ended in a 4–4 tie, stopped by darkness. Pittsburgh wanted to replay the game and according to the rules notified both the Spiders and the league office. Cleveland insisted it already had scheduled a benefit game back in Cleveland on the 12th and left Pittsburgh on the midnight train. At game time on the 12th, umpire John Gaffney declared the game a forfeit win for Pittsburgh.

By the 1890s, forfeits for nonappearance were a rarity, but less than ten years earlier, owing to the vagaries of train travel, they had been fairly common. In September 1884, the Washington Unions bagged two victories in the space of 12 days when railway delays prevented, first, the Pittsburgh Stogies and then the Cincinnati Outlaw Reds from reaching the Washington ballyard by game time; the Cincinnati forfeit was later overturned, however, by Union Association officials.

7.03 (a) (2)
Employs tactics palpably designed to delay or shorten the game;

It has been more than sixty years since a major league team last received the ultimate penalty for stalling or deliberately trying to delay a game. On July 18, 1954, facing the Philadelphia Phillies at home in Sportsman's Park, the St. Louis Cardinals trailed, 8–1, in the second game of a rain-delayed doubleheader with one out in the top of the fifth and darkness fast approaching. Since the game was not yet official and the rules then did not permit turning on the stadium lights to continue play, Cardinals manager Eddie Stanky thought he saw a way to escape defeat.

Eddie Stanky, known as "The Brat," exasperated umpires as both a player and a manager but was on three different National League teams that won pennants in a four-year span. He was ejected from more than 50 games in his checkered career.

After changing pitchers three times in the fifth inning, though the Phils had made just one hit, Stanky decided to go to his bullpen a fourth time; the umpires had already warned Stanky that his tactics bordered on stalling. Meanwhile, the inning was suddenly interrupted for eight minutes by a free-for-all brawl, principally between the Phils' Earl Torgeson and Cards catcher Say Yvars after Torgeson ranted that Cards pitcher Cot Deal was trying to hit him. When crew chief Babe Pinelli saw Stanky wave in Tom Poholsky from the bullpen, he picked up the field phone and announced that the game was forfeited to the Phils. Because the game went fewer than five innings, the official scorer did not send in a box score. Many of the Phils lost hits and RBIs, and Phils rookie Bob Greenwood was denied an almost certain victory in his first major-league start. The following day, Stanky was suspended for five games—partly for his role in the pre-forfeit donnybrook which culminated with him wrestling Phils pilot Terry Moore to the ground at home plate. But he could be permitted to chortle when Moore designated Greenwood to start again against the Cardinals, seemingly on a misguided hunch that the rookie would still have it after a short workday. Instead, Greenwood was removed in the first inning after the Cards' first four hitters all singled and later was saddled with a 5–1 loss.

7.01 (a) (3)

Refuses to continue play during a game unless the game has been suspended or terminated by the umpire-in-chief;

In *The Complete Book of Forfeited and Successfully Protested Major League Games*, Nemec and Miklich offer a perfect example of this rule in action on July 3, 1887, in an American Association game in Louisville between the Colonels and the pennant-bound St. Louis Browns. "A swirling misty rain began falling in the second frame with Louisville ahead, 5–1. Umpire [Ben] Young stopped play for 10 minutes, but when it continued to rain 'so lightly that the uncovered seats were not vacated by the people,' he ordered the game to resume. St. Louis player-manager Charlie Comiskey did so grudgingly, but after the Colonels posted two more runs in their half of the second, he wanted the game postponed because it 'began to sprinkle again.' Young denied his request, contending that the skies were doing no more than gently dampening the field. Comiskey 'refused to play, whereupon Young gave the game to Louisville.'" An excellent and innovative umpire according to most accounts, Young was drummed out of the AA almost immediately thereafter (the July 3 contest was his AA coda in fact), with Comiskey leading the movement to get rid of a man who would not buckle to his will, and never returned to the majors. He died in a railroad accident on September 1, 1890, while on his way to umpire a minor-league game. During transport from the accident site to the nearest morgue, Young's body was robbed of all money and personal effects.

7.01 (b)

A game shall be forfeited to the opposing team when a team is unable or refuses to place nine players on the field.

A major-league game has never been forfeited solely because a team was unable to put nine players on the field. Ever since the rules forbade a team playing shorthanded for any reason, clubs have always managed to scrape together a full crew, sometimes by dragging a player of local repute out of the stands. On June 15, 1889, in an American Association game at Baltimore, Louisville dredged up its entire outfield corps at the last minute in its 20th consecutive loss in what evolved into an all-time record 27 straight defeats. There have been many instances, however, when a team sustained a forfeit because it *refused* to put nine players on the field, or even any players, as happened to the Baltimore AL team in 1902 when it could not round up enough volunteers to fill out a lineup.

One of the odder cases involved a season-closing series in 1886 between the Washington Senators and Kansas City Cowboys. The two teams were locked in a struggle to avoid the National League cellar. Arguably the greatest nineteenth-century umpire, John Gaffney, who had misguidedly taken time off from umpiring to manage the last-place Washington club, sent a telegram to Kansas player-manager Dave Rowe on September 26, asking, "Will you play three postponed games in the morning?" Rowe's response, received on the 28th, stated, "Yes: go ahead. All O.K." But Rowe later claimed he thought he was responding to Gaffney regarding the playing of a postponed game on the morning of September 27 and refused to play any morning games with Washington thereafter. The seventh-place Cowboys consequently failed to put in an appearance for the morning game of a scheduled double-header on October 7, which was the first of three scheduled doubleheaders on three consecutive days. Umpire Joe Quest, a former Chicago second baseman, forfeited the contest to last-place Washington when he and the team appeared at Washington's Swampoodle Park for the appointed time of the morning game on October 7 and then stuck around to officiate the afternoon game, which the Nationals won on the field, 12–3. The same pattern persisted on October 8 and October 9, with Washington winning all three afternoon contests, giving them a season-high six-game winning streak. However, the streak was broken on October 11, the final day of the season, when Kansas City prevailed, 7–5, in its final game as a member of the National League and clinched seventh place, 1½ games ahead of Washington. The games were otherwise noteworthy in that Kansas City brought so few men to its season-ending series in Washington that novice pitcher Silver King occupied right field for the Cowboys on days when he wasn't pitching.

7.01 (c)

A game shall be forfeited to the visiting team if, after it has been suspended, the order of the umpire to groundskeepers respecting preparation of the field for resumption of play intentionally or willfully is not complied with.

Official control of groundskeeping crews was first given to the umpire-in-chief in 1906 for the purpose of making a playing field fit to resume action after a rain delay, but though tarps had been introduced as early as the 1880s, groundskeeping crews at that time were small and often swiftly overwhelmed if a sudden rainstorm hit. The umpire consequently was unlikely to make an issue out of it if the crew was slow in protecting the field. By the middle of the twentieth century, however, most teams had a sizable staff of groundskeepers, and expectations had risen accordingly. On August 15, 1941, with the Washington Senators leading the Boston Red Sox, 6–3, in the eighth inning at Washington's Griffith Stadium, a thunderstorm caused a 40-minute delay. By the time the squall abated, the field was too wet to resume play, so the umpires called the game and declared Washington the victor, 6–3. Boston manager Joe Cronin immediately lodged a protest, contending that the game could have continued if the Washington crew had not been laggard in covering the field. American League president Will Harridge agreed with Cronin and awarded the game to the Red Sox by forfeit. Harridge's verdict cost the Senators' Venezuelan righty, Alex Carrasquel, a likely win.

Midway through the 1993 season, the New York Mets nearly became only the second team in history to collect a forfeited win because of a rain-delay snafu. On June 29, the day after Mets pitcher Anthony Young sustained his record-breaking 24th consecutive loss, the 40-member Florida Marlins' grounds crew fumbled with a tarp for fifteen minutes at Joe Robbie Stadium before getting the infield covered after a storm had stopped play. The crew's ineptness eventually had players on both teams laughing hysterically in their dugouts while the public-address system played the theme to *Mission Impossible*. The Mets ultimately won the game in 12 innings, 10–9, on Tim Bogar's sacrifice fly (but nonetheless finished in the NL East cellar).

Some twenty-two years later, three seasons after the Miami (formerly Florida) Marlins had opened Marlins Park, which had a retractable roof, on April 6, Opening Day, the Marlins had an even more embarrassing weather-related experience. Although the weather forecast predicted a 20 percent chance of rain, Marlins president David Samson elected to gamble and keep the roof open. The season opener against the Atlanta Braves had reached only the second inning when spectators began to stampede for cover as a massive, dark storm cloud suddenly unleashed a steady rain onto the open park. Samson immediately commanded the roof to be closed and the field be covered by its tarp in the interim. Unfortunately, no one quite knew where the tarp was since it had never been used in this sort of situation. That was, until Samson remembered he had ordered it to be tucked to an out-of-way storage space far from the infield.

By the time it was found the cloudburst had ended and the retractable roof covered the entire park. Even though the field was soon playable again, the Braves nonetheless might have lodged a protest had they not led, 1–0, at the time. As it was, they won, 2–1, and most in the near-capacity crowd left the park in dry clothes after Martin Prado lined out to second for the last out of the game. To keep his job from his seat in the protected press box Samson apologized profusely over the phone during the storm to team owner Jeffrey Loria, who was seated in the driving rain near the Marlins dugout .

7.04 Protesting Games

Each league shall adopt rules governing procedure for protesting a game, when a manager claims that an umpire's decision is in violation of these rules. No protest shall ever be permitted on judgment decisions by the umpire. In all protested games, the decision of the League President shall be final. Even if it is held that the protested decision violated the rules, no replay of the game will be ordered unless in the opinion of the League President the violation adversely affected the protesting team's chances of winning the game.

Until fairly late in the twentieth century successfully protested games were not infrequent. But now, because of the money and logistics involved in either replaying or resuming a protested game, Rule 7.04 has been written so that it is all but impossible for a protest to succeed. Remarkably, there has been only one upheld protest since the 1986 season. It occurred on August 19, 2014, at Chicago's Wrigley Field in a game between the Cubs and the San Francisco Giants, when the skies opened after four and a half completed innings with the Cubs leading, 2–0. The Wrigley grounds crew was directed by the umpires to cover the field. However, the force of the rain was so powerful the tarp unveiling did not occur as rehearsed. The workers were unable to correctly lay the shroud over the entire infield and, as a result, much of the home plate area and left side of the infield were left to suffer the elements at their worst.

Once the fifteen-minute deluge ceased the tarp was removed, but most of the infield by then was underwater. After a four hour and thirty-four-minute effort by the grounds crew to restore the field to playable condition, plate umpire Hunter Wendelstedt, in front of an almost entirely empty house, accepted that the field was beyond repair and awarded the game to Chicago at 1:16 a.m. on August 20.

Later, on August 20, Giants manager Bruce Bochy protested the umpires' ruling and deemed the cylinder that the tarp was wrapped around a mechanical device that fit the definition of a reason for his club to protest that the game should have been suspended rather than terminated as per then Rule 4.12.

7.04 (3)

Light failure or malfunction of a mechanical field device under control of the home club. (Mechanical field device shall include automatic tarpaulin or water removal equipment);

The Giants further contended that the game should have been forfeited to them as the visiting team based on the rule cited above from the 2014 rule book that if, after it has been suspended, the order of the umpire to groundskeepers respecting preparation of the field for resumption of play are not complied with.

Later that day, Major League Baseball announced, for the first time since June 16, 1986, in a game at Pittsburgh, that a protest was upheld. The game was ordered to be resumed as a suspended game, nullifying the Giants' forfeit request. The league office issued the following explanation of the incident:

> An examination of the circumstances of last night's game has led to the determination that there was sufficient cause to believe that there was a "malfunction of a mechanical field device under control of the home club" within the meaning of Official Baseball Rule 4.12 (a) (3). Available video of the incident, and conversations with representatives of the Cubs, demonstrate that the Cubs' inability to deploy the tarp appropriately was caused by the failure to properly wrap and spool the tarp after its last use. As a result, the groundskeeping crew was unable to properly deploy the tarp after the rain worsened. In accordance with Rule 4.12 (a) (3), the game should be considered a suspended game that must be completed at a future date.
>
> In addition, Major League Baseball has spoken with last night's crew chief, Hunter Wendelstedt, and has concluded that the grounds crew worked diligently in its attempt to comply with his direction and cover the field. Thus, there is no basis for the game to be forfeited by the Cubs pursuant to Rule 4.16.
>
> The game was resumed on August 21 at 4:05 p.m. CDT, and ended with the Cubs victorious by the score of 2–1, despite being outhit 11–3. The regular scheduled game was played

three hours after the suspended game ended and the Giants won, 8–3.

Pay special attention to the last sentence of current Rule 7.04. *Even if it is held that the protested decision violated the rules, no replay of the game will be ordered unless in the opinion of the League President the violation adversely affected the protesting team's chances of winning the game.*

Here is an earlier day example of a protested game that went completely awry and would almost certainly never have been successfully protested under today's guidelines.

Often in bygone days a disputed play would develop so early in the contest that it seemed more feasible to start from scratch, especially when an inability to duplicate the circumstances surrounding the protested game would put one team at a disadvantage. A good example took place in the August 1, 1932, contest at Detroit between the Tigers and New York Yankees. The hilarity was first introduced when second baseman Tony Lazzeri came to bat in the second inning under the assumption that he was the fifth hitter in the Yankees batting order. Plate umpire Dick Nallin informed Lazzeri that he was listed in the sixth spot on the lineup card behind right fielder Ben Chapman. When Yankees manager Joe McCarthy pleaded that he'd made a mistake in filling out the card and Lazzeri always hit fifth ahead of Chapman, Nallin relented and allowed Lazzeri to bat.

Detroit manager Bucky Harris remained mum on the issue until Lazzeri singled. Then he immediately appealed to Nallin, saying that Lazzeri had batted out of order. When Nallin pointed out that Lazzeri had batted in the fifth slot with his permission, Harris changed his appeal to a protest that Nallin had no right to change the batting order after the game had started.

Dick Nallin, the umpire responsible for a Yankees-Tigers game to be played in full on three separate occasions before it counted.

After the Yankees won the game, 6–3, American League president Will Harridge upheld the protest and ordered the contest replayed in its entirety, since Lazzeri's illegal hit had been made way back in the second inning and led to the Yankees' first run. The two clubs met again a month later during the club's next visit to Detroit, but ran into a further snag when the replay, the second game of a September 8 doubleheader, ended in a 7–7 tie that was called on account of darkness.

The game was played for a third time the following day, again as the second game of a doubleheader. Detroit triumphed, 4–1, finally putting an end to the mammoth amount of work that was required to unravel the tangle Nallin's effort to be accommodating had created. At the close of the 1932 season, Nallin's tenure as an American League umpire was terminated by Harridge after 18 seasons. Except for his 1932 snafu, Nallin was regarded as a solid umpire. His career highlights were working the plate in Charlie Robertson's perfect game in 1922 and officiating in the infamous 1919 Black Sox World Series.

8.00: The Umpire

8.01 Umpire Qualifications and Authority

(a) The League President shall appoint one or more umpires to officiate at each league championship game. The umpires shall be responsible for the conduct of the game in accordance with these official rules and for maintaining discipline and order on the playing field during the game.

Mention the name John Lensor Boake to everyone presently connected with Major League Baseball and do not be surprised if you draw not even a single look of recognition. Who was he? Why, he umpired the first game between Cleveland and Fort Wayne in the first all-professional league, the National Association, on May 4, 1871! It was also the only National Association game he ever umpired. Boake was born in Philadelphia on September 4, 1841. How did he come to be in Fort Wayne at age twenty-nine on May 4, 1871? We have no clue, as he died in Kentucky in 1912 and is buried in Cincinnati. But we do know that he played left field for the Buckeye Base Ball Club of Cincinnati in 1866 and his brother William played center field, hence the likelihood the family moved from Philadelphia to Cincinnati at some point and Boake settled there permanently (since he is buried there). Why was he chosen to officiate that most historic game? Again, no clue. Such a degree of facelessness is the norm with a slew of the umpires in the National Association and even some in the early days of the National League. Among the very few men who made even a pretense of earning a living as a major league umpire prior to the mid-1880s was Billy McLean, who umpired a total of

435 games between 1872 and 1890, although only in the 1884 National League season did he work anything approaching a full slate of games (118).

Currently, there are 76 umpires in the major leagues, spread over 19 umpiring squads. Bruce Weber has written, "Major league jobs . . . open up about as often as vacancies on the US Supreme Court." In recent years, the number of umpires has increased, but no new umpires were added in 2019. The previous increases were largely due to the process of video replay expansion. In addition, in 2018, the Office of the Commissioner of Baseball appointed former MLB umpire, Justin Klemm, as director of instant replay.

In 1883, when umpires first became salaried representatives of their respective major leagues, both the National League and the American Association carried just four arbiters. Since both leagues were eight-team circuits, there were a maximum of four playing sites in each loop on a given day. One umpire was assigned to each site, and he was responsible for making his own travel arrangements, booking his own hotel accommodations, paying for cleaning his uniform, and so on. The four AA arbiters at the beginning of the 1883 season were John Kelly, William H. Becannon, Charlie Daniels, and Ben Sommer. Sommer and Becannon both had brothers who played major-league baseball, but Kelly was the prize of the four, a fight referee in the winter months. *Sporting Life* described him as "prompt, decided, energetic . . . possessed of excellent judgment," and he was duly nicknamed "Honest John." Daniels was the most experienced, having previously served in portions of five seasons in the National League. Yet *Sporting Life's* terse assessment of him was: "He is not a professional."

The AA paid its umpires $140 a month in 1883, plus $3 per diem for travel expenses. Meager as this salary might seem, it was more than the NL paid, and the AA accordingly had a better quality of officiating. Of the four umpires the NL hired in 1883, one was a college student who was fired a few weeks into the season, and by 1885 only Stewart Decker, a bank bookkeeper by trade, was still a member of the senior loop's staff—though not for long. He left the NL a third of the way into the season and remained away from it except for a short stint in blue in 1888.

In the 1880s, if an umpire took sick or was unable to work for other reasons, one of three things could occur: If an experienced umpire acceptable to both teams happened to be at the park that day, he would be pressed into service. If the visiting team had a substitute player that the home club was amenable to have officiate, the job was his for the day but without extra pay. In the event the two teams could not agree on either of these options, usually a knowledgeable spectator umped the game and it was deemed an exhibition contest.

As an example, the scheduled American Association game on May 3, 1883, between the Philadelphia Athletics and Pittsburgh Alleghenys became an exhibition match when umpire Charlie Daniels took ill and no satisfactory substitute was on hand. The crowd of around 1,200 was unaware of the change in the game's status until they had bought tickets and were in their seats. They then saw something considerably less than they had paid for when a spectator named Blackmore was drafted to umpire as Frank McLaughlin, normally a shortstop, took the box for Pittsburgh and opposed Lon Knight, the A's regular right fielder, with Pittsburgh winning, 15–2.

One question that surely leaps to mind here: Why would a home team agree to accept an opposition player as an umpire? The answer: So that the game would be a championship contest. For all games that counted in the standings (except those that took place on Sundays or holidays), the visiting club received an appearance fee—as little as $65 per game in the American Association until 1888—and the home team then got to keep all the money that was collected at the gate. If the game was declared an exhibition, the two teams split the take down the middle. Hence the home team, especially if a decent crowd was on hand, happily agreed to have a member of the visiting club officiate; usually a pitcher not slated to work that day.

Sometimes fans would sit through an entire game without learning until days later whether it was an exhibition or a regular contest. When rookie umpire John Valentine missed his train and failed to arrive for an American Association game between the Louisville Eclipse and New York Metropolitans on June 21, 1884, both teams stewed over whether or not to play an exhibition contest while the Louisville crowd howled that they'd paid good money to see a championship affair. Finally, Mets manager Jim Mutrie suggested a compromise. He agreed to play a game that would count in the standings but only if he chose the umpire. He then designated Mets pitcher Tim Keefe, since Keefe had the day off anyway because Jack Lynch was slated to hurl.

Louisville acceded to Mutrie's offer, but after the Mets won the game, 4–2, in 11 innings, the Falls City club filed a protest, claiming Keefe was not a fit umpire for a championship contest. Mutrie eventually consented to have the game thrown out, even though it deprived his club of a victory, in return for half of the day's gate receipts. Later in the season, AA officials reversed their position again and decided to count the game in the standings.

It should come as no surprise to learn that there were a multitude of protests in the 1880s questioning the fitness of a particular umpire. There were also many arbiters whose honesty was questioned. In 1882, the National League's Dick Higham became the only umpire in MLB history ever to be officially banished for dishonesty, ostensibly for betting on games in which he officiated. The senior loop assigned Higham to work a string of games involving the Detroit Wolverines. When Wolves president W. G. Thompson, who also happened to be the mayor of Detroit, began complaining that too many of Higham's close decisions were going against his club, he was ignored at first. But when the pattern persisted the league met in an executive session to hear Thompson's grievance. His case was so persuasive that he was finally allowed to inspect Higham's mail, much of which was in code and not particularly hard to decipher—or so Thompson contended. He claimed it was simple to deduce that Higham was in collusion with gamblers who were betting against Detroit on the umpire's assurance that their money was safe. Nonetheless, the vagaries surrounding Higham's expulsion, coupled with his own refusal ever to discuss it publicly or make any ostensible attempt to defend himself against the bribery charges, lent weight to those who feel that the full story did not emerge in 1882, and Higham may simply have grown too disgusted with the job to expend any energy trying to keep it.

Higham's ouster and the suspicion that embraced the work of several other umpires in that era induced the National League to adopt Rule 67, which stated:

> Any League umpire who shall in the judgment of the President of the League be guilty of ungentlemanly conduct or of selling, or offering to sell, a game in which he is umpire, shall thereupon be removed from his official capacity and placed under the same disabilities inflicted upon expelled players by the Constitution of the League.

By the mid-1890s, umpires were better paid, helping to make their honesty no longer a constant issue, and Rule 67 was eliminated. There have been umpires given the boot for life since Higham in 1882, but none ostensibly for crooked work on the diamond.

Because major-league games until late in the nineteenth century, for the most part, had only one umpire, fielders could almost literally get away with murder. While an umpire's eyes were watching a ball hit down the line to see if it would land fair, the first baseman was free to obstruct the batter as he approached the bag while the shortstop tripped the lead runner as he rounded second. Others, like first sacker Tommy Tucker, were skilled at pretending to dive for a wild pickoff throw and instead falling on top of a baserunner who otherwise would have had an unimpeded journey to the next base while baserunners, like Mike "King" Kelly, were legendary for skipping bases when an umpire's back was to them.

Third baseman John McGraw of the Baltimore Orioles was only slightly more subtle in his modus operandi. On an outfield fly, while the umpire watched to make sure it was caught, McGraw would grab the belt of the runner on third waiting to tag up and try to score and then release it when the umpire's head whipped around to catch the play at the plate. That split-second holdup was often enough to prevent a run. One day Honus Wagner was on third base as a member of the Louisville Colonels and had not been in the majors long, but he knew about McGraw. The moment a fly ball was hit to the outfield, he returned to third base and prepared himself as he felt McGraw seize his belt. When the ball was caught, Wagner took off for the plate and made it with ease. Back on third base with his mouth open stood McGraw holding Wagner's belt, which Wagner had undone while waiting at third to tag up, as he'd known in advance about McGraw's tactics. Precise documentation of this incident remains to be found, but its portrayal has been in existence for more than a century and is in absolute keeping with the rugged and imaginative way both McGraw and Wagner played the game.

As might be expected, the one-umpire system also licensed baserunners to evade the rules when they thought an arbiter was not watching them. Among the many tricks reputedly invented by the 1890s Baltimore

Orioles was bypassing third base when an umpire's back was to the runner. But in point of fact this shortcut was taken by baserunners long before the Orioles became a National League power. One the earliest documented instances of it came in a critical American Association game at Sportsman's Park on September 23, 1883, between the St. Louis Browns and Philadelphia Athletics.

The two teams had been in a season-long struggle for the AA pennant, and the Browns badly needed the game to stay in contention. In the ninth inning, St. Louis trailed, 9–1, and had two outs. Joe Quest was on first base for the Browns and breaking toward second as a groundball was hit. Seeing that the play would be made at first base, umpire Charlie Daniels turned his back to the diamond, and Quest wheeled around second and sprinted straight for home. When Philadelphia first sacker Harry Stovey dropped the throw, Quest was able to score. The partisan St. Louis crowd jeered the A's as they protested the run to no avail. However, Quest's tally only narrowed Philadelphia's lead to 9–2, and George Strief, the next batter, made the argument over his teammate's creative bit of baserunning moot when he flied out to end the game.

8.01 (c)

Each umpire has authority to rule on any point not specifically covered in these rules.

Even though the game has existed in more or less its present form for well over a century, practically every umpire who has worked at his craft for any length of time has run into a situation the rulemakers have still not satisfactorily addressed.

Umpire Wesley Curry rose to an unanticipated challenge in an American Association skirmish at Eclipse Park in Louisville on July 9, 1887, between the Falls City club and Brooklyn Bridegrooms. With Brooklyn leading, 4–2, Louisville loaded the bases. Reddy Mack then scored from third on an infield boot and hovered near the plate to coach teammate Bill White as he raced to beat the throw home from Bridegrooms shortstop Germany Smith. Seeing that Brooklyn catcher Bob Clark would get the ball before White arrived, Mack intentionally jostled Clark, preventing him from tagging his sliding teammate. While Mack and Clark continued to tussle, Joe Werrick proceeded to tally what fans thought was the third run on the play, putting the local club ahead, 5–4.

But Curry declared White out at the plate and also disallowed Werrick's run, claiming that Mack had illegally obstructed Clark. Although Curry's ruling seems now to have been the only viable verdict under the circumstances, at the time it triggered a storm of protest when Brooklyn ended up winning the game, 4–3. In 1887, there was still nothing in the rule book that dealt with the problem that had been thrust upon Curry. His dilemma was that, in the 1887 manual, only a baserunner could be guilty of obstructing a fielder, and the moment Mack crossed the plate he was by definition no longer a baserunner.

Wesley Curry, a former professional pitcher seen here in 1880s umpire's garb, made a gutsy groundbreaking decision in 1887 as an American Association arbiter.

Curry's decision, though it was reviled in Louisville and condemned even by many impartial observers, ultimately was viewed as entirely reasonable and resulted in the creation of an ancestor to Rule 8.01 (c)—formerly Rule 6.01 (a) 4—that deems any member of an offensive team who stands around any base and hinders a fielder guilty of interference.

8.02 Appeal of Umpire Decisions

(a) Any umpire's decision which involves judgment, such as, but not limited to, whether a batted ball is fair or foul, whether a pitch is a strike or a ball, or whether a runner is safe or out, is final. No player, manager, coach or substitute shall object to any such judgment decisions.

Because an umpire in the early days worked alone and rule makers recognized that he could not see everything, before 1881 he could either reserve making a decision on a matter of judgment until he had taken a poll of spectators and players who might have had a better view of a play than him or else reverse a decision he had already rendered if the testimony of a witness to a play was convincing enough to change his mind. Although it was frowned upon, some umpires continued to seek help from spectators until 1887. However, also in 1887, when batsmen for the first time were universally given their base if they were hit by a pitch, the rule was amended, restoring an umpire's right to consult with a player before rendering a decision. Underlying the revision was a recognition that the newly adopted rule made it necessary on occasion for umpires— especially when they were calling the game from behind the pitcher—to confer with batters and catchers before deciding if a hitter was struck by a pitch and a free base should be awarded.

By 1897, an umpire was no longer permitted to ask a player for help in making a decision. In fact, umpires were instructed not to reverse any decisions in which the sole question involved was whether there had been an error of judgment. Yet players and managers continue to object to umpiring decisions, and they always will regardless of the rule against it. How long and how vociferously they can object depends largely on the umpire. New umpires can expect to have the length of their fuses immediately tested. Only the caveat regarding contesting ball and strike calls stands firm. Almost all other decisions rendered as per Rule 8.02 (a) at the very least can be protested under the replay rule.

Rule 8.02 (c) Comment: A manager is permitted to ask the umpires for an explanation of the play and how the umpires have exercised their discretion to eliminate the results and consequences of the earlier call that the umpires are reversing. Once the umpires explain the result of the play, however, no one is permitted to argue that the umpires should have exercised their discretion in a different manner. The manager or the catcher may request the plate umpire to ask his partner for help on a half swing when the plate umpire calls the pitch a ball, but not when the pitch is called a strike. The manager may not complain that the umpire made an improper call, but only that he did not ask his partner for help. Field umpires must be alerted to the request from the plate umpire and quickly respond. Managers may not protest the call of a ball or strike on the pretense they are asking for information about a half swing. Appeals on a half swing may be made only on the call of ball and when asked to appeal, the home plate umpire must refer to a base umpire for his judgment on the half swing. Should the base umpire call the pitch a strike, the strike call shall prevail. Appeals on a half swing must be made before the next pitch, or any play or attempted play. If the half swing occurs during a play which ends a half-inning, the appeal must be made before all infielders of the defensive team leave fair territory. *Baserunners must be alert to the possibility that the base umpire on appeal from the plate umpire may reverse the call of a ball to the call of a strike, in which event the runner is in jeopardy of being out by the catcher's throw. Also, a catcher must be alert in a base stealing situation if a ball call is reversed to a strike by the base umpire upon appeal from the plate umpire.* The ball is in play on appeal on a half swing. On a half swing, if the manager comes out to argue with first or third base umpire and if after being warned he persists in arguing, he can be ejected as he is now arguing over a called ball or strike.

Much of the material in this comment added to Rule 8.02 (c) is a comparatively recent innovation. For more than half a century after the major leagues began to use at least two umpires in a game on a regular basis in the early 1900s, the team on defense had no recourse if a home-plate umpire's vision was blocked or some other circumstance prevented him from accurately gauging whether a batter swung at a pitch and he refused to consult with a colleague who might have had a better view. Now a defensive team can force the issue simply by signaling that they want a second opinion.

The italicized section in the above comment makes it clear that a runner has no grounds to protest if he is thrown out when he sets off for second base after the plate umpire has called a fourth ball on the batter, only to have a base umpire, on appeal, rule it a checked-swing strike. Nor, for that matter, can the catcher protest if the runner makes second uncontested before the base umpire calls the pitch a strike. In a 1906 game between the Pittsburgh Pirates and Chicago Cubs, Pirates player-manager Fred Clarke occupied third base with the bags loaded and a 3-and-1 count on the batter. When the umpire said nothing and gave no sign on the next pitch, Clarke assumed it was ball four, forcing him home, and started trotting toward the plate. Both the catcher and batter also thought it was a free pass. As the catcher tossed the ball back to the pitcher and the batter headed for first, Clarke touched the plate. Suddenly the umpire erupted and cried, "Strike two!" When everyone looked at him in amazement, he sheepishly admitted that he'd been unable to speak right away because something had been caught in his throat.

Since time had not been called, the umpire had no choice but to rule that Clarke's run counted. The official scorer in turn had to credit Clarke with a steal of home, albeit unintentional. Given this undeserved assist, Clarke finished his career with 15 thiefts of home.

8.02 (d)
No umpire may be replaced during a game unless he is injured

In the event a replacement is not available for an umpire who is injured or becomes ill during a game, the umpiring crew will work the rest of the game a man short. This is a fairly common occurrence nowadays and not much of a hardship, with four-man crews the norm in regular season games, and six in postseason clashes. Some seventy years ago, however, sometimes only two umpires were assigned to a game and a player occasionally had to fill in when an arbiter was sidelined. Hall of Fame umpire Jocko Conlan got his start in this fashion.

Jocko Conlan was never more than an average major-league outfielder, but chance furnished him with the opportunity to become among the best umpires and definitely the most dapper man in blue in his time. He usually wore a bow tie when he officiated.

In 1935, Conlan was a backup outfielder with the Chicago White Sox. On July 28, the Sox were playing a twin bill with the St. Louis Browns at Sportsman's Park on a torrid Sunday afternoon. At the close of the first game, umpire Red Ormsby was overcome by the heat, leaving his partner, Harry Geisel, to handle the second game alone. Since he was out of action anyway with a sprained thumb, Conlan volunteered to help out

Geisel by working the bases. When Ormsby was still too weak to officiate the following day, Conlan subbed for him again and was paid $50 by the American League, as was Browns sub Ollie Bejma who handled first base while Conlan worked third base.

Bejma never umpired another major-league game, but Conlan discovered that he liked the job. At the close of the 1935 season, when it grew evident to him that his playing days in the majors were numbered, he accepted an offer to umpire the following year in the New York-Penn League for $300 a month. In 1941, after a five-year apprenticeship in the minors, Conlan was hired as a regular umpire by the National League. He stayed at the job for twenty-five years, distinguishing himself not only for his officiating skills, but for making all signals with his left hand and wearing a bow tie during games.

8.02 (e)

If there are two or more umpires, one shall be designated umpire-in-chief and the others field umpires.

Although it's not a formal rule that umpires must rotate their jobs, working the plate one day, first base the next, and so on, it has become a sacrosanct tradition, and the umpires' union would swiftly take issue if the major leagues decided an umpire was so good behind the plate that he should be permanently assigned to calling balls and strikes. Time was, though, when a league could do just that with an umpire's consent. Bill Klem was so esteemed that he was a National League arbiter for sixteen years before he deigned to begin rotating the crew-chief role with his fellow umpires by working the bases. In his thirty-seven years as an ML umpire Klem worked the plate a record 3,547 times in 5,272 games.

8.03 Umpire Position

(a) The umpire-in-chief shall stand behind the catcher. (He usually is called the plate umpire.) His duties shall be to:
    (1) Take full charge of, and be responsible for, the proper conduct of the game; (2) Call and count balls and strikes . . .

In the early years, when an umpire worked a game alone, he generally stood in back of the catcher, even though most catchers then played so far behind the plate when the bases were empty that positioning himself behind them put an umpire at a considerable distance from the batter. In the late 1880s, "Honest" John Gaffney introduced umping in the center of the diamond or behind the pitcher with men on base. Most arbiters quickly grew to prefer working there if only for safety reasons.

When catching equipment improved, enabling receivers to move closer to the plate, umpires accordingly began to officiate behind catchers again when the bases were clear, albeit with some trepidation. Even though a mask had become a standard part of an umpire's apparel by then, the face gear most arbiters wore provided scant protection. In a Union Association game at Wilmington on September 4, 1884, umpire Patrick Dutton nearly became the first on-the-field fatality in major-league history when a foul tip off the bat of Cincinnati's Jack Glasscock hit him in the throat. Dutton went down as if he had been poleaxed and lay so still that Glasscock and Wilmington catcher Tony Cusick thought he was dead. But luckily, there was a Doctor Frantz at the game. Frantz rushed out on the field and discovered that Dutton had ceased breathing because a dislocated bone in his lower jaw was pressing on his windpipe. The doctor was able to manipulate the bone back into place, and Dutton soon regained consciousness. Over Glasscock's vehement protestations (since Cincinnati was leading at the time), the game was stopped before it became official out of respect for the fallen umpire.

Injuries, like the one Dutton suffered, discouraged many umpires from working behind the plate whenever it could be avoided; but standing behind the pitcher was no refuge either. It put an umpire's back to four infielders and three outfielders, all of which could make his job miserable even when he was able to keep them under surveillance. Lacking eyes in the back of his head, an arbiter often failed to note that a first sacker had dislodged the first-base bag and inched it backward until the distance to it had grown mysteriously to 95 feet, or that a batter had fanned because the second baseman was standing in his line of vision and waving a white handkerchief.

8.03 (a) (6)
Decide when a game shall be forfeited;

The last home-plate umpire to date to forfeit a game was Jim Quick at Dodger Stadium on August 10, 1995, and the events of that evening narrowly missed deciding the NL West winner that season. As Nemec and Miklich describe it in *The Complete Book of Forfeited and Successfully Protested Major League Games*, "a crowd of 53,361 packed Dodger Stadium for a special Ball Night Promotion that featured as an added attraction the ballyhooed rookie Japanese pitcher Hideo Nomo facing the Cardinals . . . The game was briefly delayed in the seventh inning when several fans started indiscriminately throwing their souvenir balls on the field, but tension did not really begin to mount until the bottom of the following frame. With the Cards ahead 2–1, the Dodgers had two on and two out with slugging first sacker Eric Karros at the plate. Karros was rung up on strikes and argued the called third strike too vigorously . . . Quick lived up to his name and swiftly ejected him. Fans then began winging balls on the field in protest. Pleas over the public address to cease fire were successful on this occasion.

"After the Cardinals were retired in their half of the ninth inning, Dodgers right fielder Raul Mondesi led off the bottom of the frame against St. Louis closer Tom Henke. With a count of 3-and-0, Mondesi looked at a Henke fastball that he thought was ball four. As he took a step toward fire base, however, Quick . . . called it a strike."

After Mondesi also was ejected for arguing, Dodgers manager Tommy Lasorda rushed onto the field. Once he too was ejected, "fans let loose a fresh torrent of baseballs from the stands. The umpires hurriedly brought the Cardinals in from the field and waited in the security of the Dodgers' dugout until the grounds crew had cleared the field. But no sooner had play resumed than the still angry fans unleashed another hailstorm of baseballs. Quick stopped play and forfeited the game to St. Louis."

The forfeit win meant nothing to the Cardinals, who were mired well below .500 for most of the season, but it nearly cost the Dodgers dearly. The strike-abbreviated 144-game season concluded with Los Angeles a mere one game ahead of the Colorado Rockies in the NL West Division standings.

Note that since the forfeit occurred with the winner by forfeit ahead in the score, 2–1, all stats from the game counted. The rationale for sticking a pitcher with a loss in a forfeited game that goes at least five innings if his team is trailing when the infraction occurs owes to the fact that in many instances a forfeit grows out of events that convince the guilty team it is going to lose the game anyway. Likewise, the pitcher on the team benefiting by the forfeit in some cases gets a gift win.

In rare cases a pitcher is deprived of a win that should have been his when his team is saddled with a forfeit loss at a juncture when it was leading in the game. Perhaps the most unjust example came in the last American League game hosted by Washington on September 30, 1971, when a crowd riot ended the fray with two out in the top of the ninth and the Senators leading the New York Yankees, 7–5. One out away from recording his eighth victory of the season, instead Paul Lindblad received a no decision for his day's work, as did Yankees pitcher Jack Aker, who was about to be tagged with his fifth defeat.

The 1971 season stats credit Yankees pitchers with only 81 of their team's 82 wins because one victory came by forfeit. In the nineteenth century, official scorers and team statisticians were not always so careful, even though forfeits were much more common at that time. For many years, the stats for a number of teams during the 1880s and 1890s failed to balance in any of the baseball encyclopedias, partly because forfeit wins and losses were not taken into account. In addition, pitchers in forfeited games were often erroneously credited with wins or losses that have since been deducted.

8.03 (b)

A field umpire may take any position on the playing field he thinks best suited to make impending decisions on the bases. His duties shall be to:
(1) Make all decisions on the bases except those specifically reserved to the umpire-in-chief;

Base umpires' positioning was fairly straightforward once both leagues mandated in 1952 that, whenever possible, a minimum of four umpires were scheduled to work each game. With the bases empty, the first- and third-base umpires generally stationed themselves in foul territory near the base that was their responsibility, and the second-base umpire in an area where he was the least likely to interfere with a fielder or be hit by a batted ball. In recent years, owing to the extravagant shifts that many teams employ against pronounced pull hitters, base umpires will often shift accordingly. As a result, there are times when a third-base umpire may be a better judge on a play at second base than the second-base umpire. Although there are no known statistics to support this, there is a distinct impression that nowadays, perhaps due to packed conditions on one side or the other of second base created by the innumerable shifts, more field umpires are being hit by batted balls and unintentionally interfering with fielders trying to make a play.

Many games had four umpires as early as 1947, and those that had only three would have base umpires assigned to both first and third base along with the home-plate umpire. Plays at second base were up for grabs but generally taken by the field umpire closest to the bag. There were regular-season games in the late 1940s, however, that had as many as six umpires, and some had as few as two. A shining example of the unmitigated clout wielded by the New York Yankees in that era came in 1949. The previous year, the American League pennant race had boiled down to a one-game playoff at Boston between the Red Sox and Cleveland Indians. Only the customary four umpires were assigned to that contest. In 1949, when the AL pennant was destined to be decided on the final weekend of the season in a two-game series between the Red Sox and Yankees at Yankee Stadium, no less than six umpires were slated to work the pair of games, with the two extra men working the left- and right-field foul lines. To make this possible, two umpires that otherwise would have worked the final weekend games at Washington between the Philadelphia A's and the last-place Senators were sent to New York, burdening the A's-Senators' games with only a two-man crew, Joe Paparella and Bill Grieve, quite likely the last two-man crew assembled on purpose. Meanwhile, the National League race in 1949, which also came down to the final Sunday of the season, featured games with pennant implications at both Wrigley

Field and Shibe Park, where at each site only the standard four-man crew was assigned.

The National League and American League have not always had the same rules regarding the responsibilities a home plate umpire has as opposed to a base umpire. As but one example, the balk incident cited in the chapter on definitions of terms that may have cost the St. Louis Cardinals the National League pennant in 1949 could not have happened in the same way that year in the American League. Originally, it was reported in accounts of the game that plate umpire Bill Stewart called the balk. But actually second-base umpire Jocko Conlan cited Giants pitcher Adrian Zabala for the infraction that forced Nippy Jones to bat over again. In the National League, any umpire in 1949 could cite a pitcher for failing to pause in his stretch before delivering a pitch, whereas the only American League official permitted to pass that judgment was the home plate ump.

In truth, the National League and American League have not always played by the same set of rules, period. Well after the peace agreement between the two leagues was signed in 1903 and both agreed to play under the same basic rules, there were still significant differences. We have already cited several, and here is another that has flown under the radar.

For those who think having two sets of rules on the DH in the two different parks used in a World Series is an abomination, having different rules for different World Series parks is nothing new. In October 1911, sportswriter Damon Runyon wrote of the two sets of rules to be used in the upcoming Series between the Philadelphia A's and the New York Giants. American League rules would prevail in Shibe Park, while National League rules would be used at the Polo Grounds. Runyon explained, "In the National League on an infield fly baserunners may stand away from the base and in case the fly is dropped they can go down to the next base at their own peril, without first returning to the base they occupied and touching it. In the American League base runners must return to the base and not leave it until the ball is caught or strikes the ground or a player."

There was also a different rule on balks. In the National League, if a pitcher dropped a ball while in the act of pitching it was an automatic balk and all baserunners advanced one base. If there was a man on third he was permitted to score. In the American League, it was not a balk; runners took their chances on being put out if they opted to try to advance on the dropped ball. These differences between the two leagues extended deep into the 1910s and even in some instances well beyond, but posed no problem for umpires because they were employed solely by the league in which the World Series game was taking place rather that by MLB in general, as has been the case since 1999.

8.03 (c)

If different decisions should be made on one play by different umpires, the umpire-in-chief shall call all the umpires into consultation, with no manager or player present. After consultation, the umpire-in-chief (unless another umpire may have been designated by the League President) shall determine which decision shall prevail, based on which umpire was in best position and which decision was most likely correct. Play shall proceed as if only the final decision had been made.

Although the crew chief has the final word if two or more umpires disagree on a rule interpretation or a matter of judgment, if the majority of his staff outweighs him, he will usually concur with the consensus point of view. Since umpires are afforded the same protection as jurors, the baseball public never learns how the opinion fell on a controversial play except in the rare event when one of the arbiters chooses to talk for the record.

A case in point occurred in Game Two of the 2005 ALCS at U.S. Cellular Field between the Chicago White Sox and Los Angeles Angels when home-plate umpire Doug Eddings allowed A. J. Pierzynski to take first base on what he claimed was an uncaught third strike with two out to extend the White Sox' turn at bat in the bottom of the ninth. Eddings's ruling became critical when Pablo Ozuna, a pinch-runner for Pierzynski, scored on Joe Crede's double to give Chicago a hard-fought 2–1 victory. The Sox then swept the next three games from the visibly deflated Angels, and went on to bring Chicagoans their first world championship baseball team in eighty-eight years. The video replays indicated that Angels catcher Josh Paul caught reliever Kelvim Escobar's pitch, but were inconclusive. Eddings's disputable decision was not the crux of the Angels' argument, however. What rightfully angered the Halos was the way he waffled before making it. In an ironic prelude to arguably the pivotal play in the 2005 postseason, Aaron Rowand, the batter before Pierzynski, swung at a third strike that clearly bounced in front of the plate. Eddings properly threw out his right arm to indicate a strike, waited for Paul to tag Rowand, and then raised his right fist to indicate Rowand was out. When Pierzynski followed by striking out swinging on a low pitch, Eddings stuck out his right hand to indicate the strike. Paul then rolled the ball back to the mound as Eddings raised his fist to indicate the batter was out. Suddenly, Pierzynski, who had started toward the dugout, did a 90-degree turn and sprinted toward first base. It appeared that Eddings instantly questioned the correctness of his call, which is normal. But according to baseball historian Dennis Bingham, who is also a longtime umpire, Eddings then deviated from three of the basic rules that trainee umpires are taught. In a situation like the one confronting Eddings, unless he saw the ball bounce he should have shouted "Batter is out!" as Pierzynski ran to first base. If Eddings realized belatedly that the ball had bounced, then he should have given the safe sign emphatically when Pierzynski reached first. In the event Eddings hadn't seen the play clearly, he should have called time once Pierzynski reached base and immediately asked third-base umpire Ed Rapuano (since Pierzynski was a left-handed hitter, offering Rapuano the best view) for his opinion and then either gone with Rapuano's ruling if he saw the play or called Pierzynski out if he did not.

But Eddings failed to do any of these things. Instead, he began pacing around after Pierzynski reached first, obviously in a quandary, and never made a resolute call one way or the other. Yet Eddings's fellow umpires, including crew chief Jerry Crawford, at least tacitly supported his decision, albeit we will probably never learn with what degree of conviction. Later on, Eddings said that he was certain the ball had bounced, entitling Pierzynski to run to first, but his actions during and after the play belied his claim. The situation was made worse by a press conference after the game in which Eddings, members of his umpiring crew, and the umpires' rep hemmed and hawed, amplifying the feeling that none of them really felt confident the right call had been made.

8.04 Reporting

(a) The umpire shall report to the League President within twelve hours after the end of a game all violations of rules and other incidents worthy of comment, including the disqualification of any trainer, manager, coach or player, and the reasons therefor.

(b) When any trainer, manager, coach or player is disqualified for a flagrant offense such as the use of obscene or indecent language, or an assault upon an umpire, trainer, manager, coach or player, the umpire shall forward full particulars to the League President within four hours after the end of the game.

(c) After receiving the umpire's report that a trainer, manager, coach or player has been disqualified, the League President shall impose such penalty as he deems justified, and shall notify the person penalized and the manager of the club of which the penalized person is a member. If the penalty includes a fine, the penalized person shall pay the amount of the fine to the league within five days after receiving notice of the fine . . .

No major-league player has ever been barred for life for fighting with an umpire, although prior to Judge Kenesaw Mountain Landis's installation in 1920 as the game's first commissioner, there were numerous physical confrontations between players and umpires that could have been grounds for permanent expulsion. Ty Cobb's pugnacious temperament got him into a multitude of fistfights with fans and fellow players, and even on at least one occasion with an umpire. Billy Evans, the most fastidious and also among the most mild-mannered arbiters of his day, nevertheless locked horns with Cobb during a September 24, 1921, contest at Washington where he was officiating the bases.

To Cobb's great pleasure, Evans accepted the invitation to meet him under the Griffith Stadium stands after the game. Witnesses to the bout later characterized it as quick and brutal, with Cobb, as expected, administering a sound thrashing to Evans. Evans agreed in advance of the fight not to report the incident to the American League office, now a violation of Rule 9.05 (b) that would have earned his immediate suspension, if not dismissal. But AL president Ban Johnson heard about it anyway and at first responded to news of the incident by saying, "only that he was sorry that he missed it." On second thought, however, he suspended Cobb for one game and forced the battered Evans to officiate the next few games with his face swathed in bandages.

Evans was not the only umpire in the early 1900s to engage in fisticuffs with a player, but he was among the last. After Judge Landis took office, umpires were no longer fair game for irate players whenever they delivered an unpopular decision. Had Landis been called upon to review an incident like the one in a game in the Baker Bowl between Philadelphia and the St. Louis Cardinals on July 10, 1911, involving Phillies outfielder Sherry Magee and rookie National League umpire Bill Finneran, he might have banished Magee for life when the outfielder slugged Finneran after he was ejected from a game for disputing a third-strike call on a pitch by the Cards' Roy Golden. Earlier in the game, Magee had argued vigorously with base umpire Cy Rigler when he was thrown out attempting to steal second base. After Magee was rung up by Finneran, he threw his bat in the air and was promptly ejected. He then rushed the rookie umpire.

The two men clinched for a second before Magee stepped back and delivered a crushing left to Finneran's face. As Magee then walked toward the Phillies bench, Finneran chased after him with blood pouring from his mouth and had to be restrained. Magee's excuse was that Finneran had called him a vile name in ordering him off the field. For what was described as his "brutal and unprovoked assault," Magee was suspended for the rest of the 1911 season by National League president Tom Lynch, and fined $200.

However, Lynch, himself a former umpire, lifted the suspension after Magee had been out of uniform just 36 days, in part because there was testimony that Magee, who suffered from epilepsy, might have been in the throes of a seizure when he struck Finneran.

In 1901, its inaugural season as a major league, the American League suffered

Tom Lynch, one of the few successful early-day umpires, was president of the National League in 1911 when he was hard put to render a satisfactory decision after a rookie member of his umpiring crew was flattened by Sherry Magee, the defending NL batting champion.

its own version of the nefarious Magee incident. On August 21, in a game at Washington, Chicago shortstop Frank Shugart slugged umpire Jack Haskell after Haskell claimed Bill Coughlin was entitled to score from third base on a pitch that got away from White Sox catcher Joe Sugden. Shugart initially was declared ineligible "for all time" to play in the American League, but less than a month after being banned he was reinstated by league president Ban Johnson and finished the season with Chicago.

In the 1890s, Magee's and Shugart's actions would not even have warranted a suspension. During a game on July 22, 1897, when Cincinnati Reds pitcher Pink Hawley flattened umpire Jack Sheridan after the two came to blows over one of Sheridan's calls, Sheridan contented himself with merely ejecting Hawley. In another contest that season, Cincinnati catcher Heinie Peitz charged umpire Tim Hurst. When Hurst fended Peitz off with his mask, Peitz belted him in the mouth. This incident was one of the rare times that Hurst was on the receiving end. Asked once why he became a major-league umpire, a job that required him to work a game alone and endure virulent abuse from players, fans, owners, and even, on occasion, reporters, Hurst said, "It's a hard life, lads, but you can't beat the hours." A boxing referee in the off-season, Hurst seemed to thrive on conflict. If a player questioned one of his calls too fervidly, Hurst would put his mouth close to the protestor's ear and offer the key to his hotel room, where everything was "nice and quiet" and there would be no witnesses when the player had his jaw broken so that he couldn't bellyache about an umpire's decision for the rest of the season. No one ever reached for Hurst's key. He was eventually booted out of the major-league umpiring ranks in 1909 by Ban Johnson for spitting on A's second baseman Eddie Collins.

But not all umpires in Hurst's day were as combative as he. Many that lacked his

Eddie Collins posted a .333 career batting average and 3,312 hits, but never won a batting title in his lifetime. Today, some authorities credit him with the 1914 American League hitting crown.

bellicosity quickly found themselves unable to keep control of a game. Consequently, few men lasted even as long as a full season at the job. In the 1895 campaign alone, fifty-nine different men served as umpires in regular-season games, and National League president Nick Young grew so desperate to fill the constant vacancies in his ranks that he hired most of his arbiters sight unseen or else gave the post to ex-players with no officiating experience who were down on their luck. Among them was Hank O'Day, who had pitched with Washington in the late 1880s to a young catcher named Connie Mack. By the mid-1890s, when O'Day became an NL arbiter, Mack was managing the Pittsburgh Pirates. Revered for his ecclesiastical demeanor when he later piloted the Philadelphia A's for half a century, Mack was not always a gentlemen in the rollicking 1890s. He and O'Day clashed so fiercely one afternoon that the umpire was forced to eject his former batterymate and then summon a policeman when Mack refused to leave. The O'Day-Mack incident and others like it led Boston sportswriter Tim Murnane, himself an ex-player, to observe: "The time will soon come when no person above the rank of garrotter can be secured to umpire a game."

At the turn of the twentieth century, among the few weapons an umpire had—apart from his fists—was the authority to fine players. In 1895 a rule was created allowing umpires to assess fines of $25 to $100 for specified misconduct. The following year, the sanction was broadened so that umpires could also fine players $25 for vulgar or indecent language; but even this power could not help an umpire when an entire team got on his case.

In a doubleheader at Louisville on July 16, 1897, the aforementioned umpire Tom Lynch heaved two New York Giants players, shortstop George Davis and first baseman Bill Clark, out of the first game and then refused to work the second contest after the opener ended in a near brawl. Jimmy Wolf, a Louisville native and an ex-Falls City outfielder, volunteered to sub in the nightcap. With New York up, 7–2, in the ninth, Giants starter Mike Sullivan hit a wild streak—or so judged Wolf—and reliever Amos Rusie was no improvement. Ball after ball was called by Wolf until Tom McCreery walked to force in the tying run. The Giants then surrounded Wolf, and the crowd surged onto the field to protect one of Louisville's favorite sons. The police eventually had to haul several Giants players off the field so that the game could continue, with Louisville winning, 8–7.

During the nineteenth century, there were also numerous occasions when the police had to escort umpires to safety after a game. In an American Association contest between Cincinnati and Washington on May 31, 1884, umpire Terry Connell forfeited the game to Cincinnati when Washington manager Holly Hollingshead, wearied of watching every decision Connell made go against his men, pulled them off the field with the Ohio club ahead, 6–0. Connell no sooner announced the forfeit than the crowd in the nation's capital swarmed onto the diamond to vent their wrath.

Finding himself surrounded, Connell backpedaled toward the outfield. To help him escape with his life, the Cincinnati club concealed its carriage behind a gate in the ballpark fence. At a prearranged signal, the gate was flung open and several policemen pushed the terrified umpire through it and lifted him into the carriage. With the crowd in mad pursuit and the driver frantically whipping the horses, Connell fled down the street in a cloud of dust.

What finally gave an umpire enough protection to make his job tolerable was not so much a change in the rules as a change in a custom. Prior to the 1898 season, the National League conceded the possibility that the traditional one-umpire system might no longer be adequate by outlining the responsibilities each umpire would have in a game where two officials were assigned, but most games still had only one man in blue. Toward the end of the first decade of the twentieth century, largely upon the lead of the American League, both major leagues permanently began appointing two umpires to work almost every game, thereby providing more protection (as well as better coverage of the action). Three became the norm by the 1920s, and beginning in 1952 fans grew accustomed to seeing four umpires on the field for every game.

Why did major-league owners wait so long to begin using two umpires in each game? The obvious answer is to save money, but an equally important reason was that the owners of the stronger teams for a long time preferred the way games could be manipulated into victories with only one umpire officiating to improving the quality of their product. The players knew better. A players' rebellion when salary restrictions were imposed after the 1889 season ended in the players forming their own league, called fittingly the Players' League. Among the innovations the players introduced was to schedule two umpires to work every game, one behind the plate and the other on the bases. Unfortunately, the lesson was lost on the owners once the Players League rebellion was suppressed.

GENERAL INSTRUCTIONS TO UMPIRES

Among the 13 General Instructions given to umpires these two somewhat ironically follow one another.

> Do not allow criticism to keep you from studying out bad situations that may lead to protested games. Carry your rule book. It is better to consult the rules and hold up the game ten minutes to decide a knotty problem than to have a game thrown out on protest and replayed.
>
> Keep the game moving. A ball game is often helped by energetic and earnest work of the umpires.

Heavy as the pressure now is to keep games moving as rapidly as humanly possible, there is no limit to the amount of time an umpiring crew can take to "decide a knotty problem." Long before the rule book stated that the first requisite for an umpire is to get decisions right, arbiters regarded it as an unwritten principle of their profession. In a May 20, 1922, game between the St. Louis Browns and New York Yankees that in the long run would have considerable bearing on the American League pennant race, an umpires' conference resulted in a decision change that forced play to continue well after everyone present thought the contest was over. With St. Louis trailing, 2–1, with two out in the top of the ninth, two Browns pinch-hitters in succession, Chick Shorten and Pat Collins, singled to bring leadoff batter Jack Tobin to the plate. Tobin hit a dribbler to Yankees first sacker Wally Pipp, who tossed the ball to pitcher Sam Jones, racing to cover. When Jones crossed the bag ahead of Tobin, base umpire Ollie Chill gave the out signal and the Yankees left the field. Shorten rounded third base, however, and kept running until he crossed the plate as Browns manager Lee Fohl, coaching at first, began arguing with Chill that Jones was juggling the ball when he first tagged the bag. Because his view was obstructed by Jones's back, Chill missed seeing that the ball was not securely in Jones's possession, but when Fohl appealed to plate umpire Brick Owens, Owens agreed that Tobin should have been ruled safe.

Before the dispute ran its course, many of the 49,152 in attendance left the Polo Grounds—then the home the Yankees shared with the New York Giants—and most of the players had adjourned to their respective clubhouses. Finally, after a 20-minute delay, Chill reversed his call and both teams were ordered to return to the field and resume play. After Jones's game-ending putout was turned into an error, allowing Shorten to tally the tying run, the Browns proceeded to notch six more unearned runs in their time at bat and win, 8–2, but nevertheless ended the season in second place, one game behind the Yankees.

> Each umpire team should work out a simple set of signals, so the proper umpire can always right a manifestly wrong decision when convinced he has made an error. If sure you got the play correctly, do not be stampeded by players' appeals to "ask the other man." If not sure, ask one of your associates. Do not carry this to extremes, be alert and get your own plays. But remember! The first requisite is to get decisions correctly. If in doubt don't hesitate to consult your associate. Umpire dignity is important but never as important as "being right."

This general instruction explains why an umpire will often refuse to confer with the other members of his crew even when every player, fan, and TV camera at the stadium is morally certain that he blew a critical judgment call. Its general tone dissuades an umpire from consulting with his colleagues unless he is willing to admit he is not sure of his decision. An umpire who admits this too often is not long for his job.

On October 26, 1985, at Royals Stadium, in the bottom of the ninth

Whitey Herzog managed the Kansas City Royals in 1976 when they made their first postseason appearance, facing the New York Yankees in the ALCS. The Royals lost, but nine years later, under Dick Howser, won their first world championship when a famous disputed call enabled them to go on to prevail over the St. Louis Cardinals, then managed by Herzog.

As a rookie shortstop with the Kansas City Athletics in 1961, Dick Howser won The Sporting News Rookie of the Year Award. Seven years earlier, in 1954, Howser had batted .196 as a second baseman, lacking the arm strength to play shortstop in his senior year of high school at Palm Beach High in West Palm Beach, Florida. He received no college scholarship offers and went out for the Florida State team as a walk-on, wearing cutoff jeans and a sleeveless sweat shirt. But today, the annual college baseball MVP Award is named in his honor.

inning of Game Six of the 1985 World Series, Kansas City pinch-hitter Jorge Orta led off by hitting a bouncing ball to Cardinals first baseman Jack Clark. Probably no one in the country watching on TV or in person except first-base umpire Don Denkinger and rabid Kansas City fans believed that Orta beat Clark's toss to reliever Todd Worrell, covering the bag. St. Louis manager Whitey Herzog begged Denkinger to get help, but the ump adamantly refused, maintaining it was his play to call and he had gotten it right. Later, Denkinger insisted that Worrell had pulled his foot off the bag an instant before Clark's throw reached him. Worrell was not charged with an error, however, as the miscue eluded everyone else in Royals Stadium, as well as several dozen TV cameras. When the Royals posted two runs in the bottom of the ninth to win, 2–1, and then blew the Cards away, 11–0, the following night, many Mound City fans still feel they were robbed of the 1985 world championship by an umpire's bad call. But unbiased observers also remember the pop foul Clark missed later in the inning and Darrell Porter's passed ball, either of which could have taken much of the onus off Denkinger if it had not occurred.

In any event, Denkinger's handling of the situation was regarded by fellow umpires as exemplary, even if his decision may always cause him to be vilified in St. Louis.

Denkinger and almost all his colleagues worked in a time when an umpire's faulty decision had never been overturned days, let alone years, after the fact. But in 2016, that all seemed about to change . . . briefly. Six years earlier, on June 2, 2010, in a game at Detroit's Comerica Park between the Tigers and Cleveland Indians, Bengals pitcher Armando Galarraga had taken a perfect game into the ninth inning. He retired the first Tribe batter, Mark Grudzielanek, on a drive to deep center that Austin Jackson caught in spectacular fashion on the warning track. Catcher Mike Redmond grounded out to short, putting Gallaraga one out away from a perfect game—the first in Tigers history—as he faced rookie shortstop Jason Donald, batting in the ninth spot. The perfecto seemed a certainty when Donald hit a routine bouncer to first baseman Miguel Cabrera, who made a perfect throw to Galarraga, covering first. Donald was beaten by a step, but first-base umpire Jim Joyce inexplicably called him safe, ruining both the perfect game and a no-hitter. Galarraga managed to save his 3–0 shutout win by inducing center fielder Trevor Crowe to ground out, third to first, after Donald had wormed his way around to third base on defensive indifference. After the game, when Joyce saw the video replay, he immediately acknowledged he had been wrong in believing Donald beat the throw to first. Later he hugged Galarraga and apologized profusely. Meanwhile, Tyler Kepner of the *New York Times* wrote that no call had been "so important and so horribly botched" since Denkinger's in

Detroit pitcher Armando Galarraga, the day after his ruined perfecto, stoically bringing the Tigers' June 3, 2010, scorecard to the home plate umpire that day, a tearful Jim Joyce.

the 1985 World Series and there was a clamor in 2010 and again in 2016 for, first, Bud Selig and then his successor as commissioner, Rob Manfred, to overrule Joyce's blown call. For a time it appeared as if Manfred might actually do it as a parting gift since Galarraga was now out of the majors, but eventually the baseball tradition that a bell once rung can not be unrung prevailed.

Nonetheless, these two palpably mistaken calls—arguably more than any other controversial umpiring decisions in recent memory—led to the adoption of instant replay review in two separate stages. The first commenced on August 28, 2008, at the behest of commissioner Bud Selig. "I believe that the extraordinary technology that we now have merits the use of instant replay on a very limited basis," Selig said. "The system we have in place will ensure that the proper call is made on home run balls and will not cause a significant delay to the game."

Unfortunately for Galarraga, "very limited" replay review applied *only* to questionable home runs until the 2014 season when Major League Baseball, after much dithering, announced that it would expand its video review process to allow challenges on most plays that occurred on the field with certain exceptions. Judgment calls including, but not limited to, pitches called a ball or a strike, obstruction, interference, the infield fly rule, and checked swings were not reviewable. Originally, managers were granted one challenge over the first six innings of games (two if the first challenge was successful) and two from the seventh inning until the end of the game, however many innings that took. In addition, beginning in the seventh inning, the umpire-in-chief was authorized to initiate a review if he felt one was warranted. Calls that were challenged were to be reviewed by a crew in MLB headquarters in New York City, who were to make the final ruling in a timely fashion.

Unhappily, the new wrinkle, while generally a popular one, has worked against almost every other new wrinkle MLB has adopted in the past decade to shorten the length of games. This was evidenced as early as 2008, less than a month after video review came into play on questionable home runs. On September 26 at San Francisco's AT&T Park, in a game between the Giants and Dodgers, San Francisco catcher Bengie Molina smacked a long drive to right field off Dodgers reliever Scott Proctor that struck a few feet to the left of the park's famous "Splash Hits" sign. Molina, a slow runner, managed to leg out only a single on the blow and was immediately replaced at first base by Emmanuel Burriss, who had been told in advance by Giants manager Bruce Bochy that he would pinch-run for Molina if the catcher reached base, and popped out of the dugout before anyone could intervene.

No sooner had Burriss reached the bag than shortstop Omar Vizquel told Bochy he thought the ball had struck the green metal awning along the right-field wall, which by park rule is an automatic home run. Bochy found a ball with green paint on it and showed it to the umpires. Crew chief Tim Welke then decided to hold a conference with his colleagues. After a few minutes they disappeared inside the stadium since the park did not as yet have field replay, leaving the crowd clueless as to what was transpiring. When the umpires returned to the field and Welke signaled Molina's hit was a home run, Bochy immediately tried to put Molina back in the game since he had been replaced after the hit was initially ruled a single and timeout was called. However, the rule at the time stated that replay would not be allowed if play continued before it was requested, and the Giants' insertion of Burriss could be construed as a continuation of play, disallowing a replay review even though the evidence presented indicated one was necessary. Bochy cut through the red tape by announcing the Giants were continuing the game under protest, but Selig was spared having to rule on it when the Giants won, 6–5, in 10 innings. Molina was credited with a home run, but Burriss was given the run that scored on it and the stoppage in action consumed well over 10 minutes.

What's worse, video replay has made it glaring evident that there are some very weak umpires now working in the majors. In Game Three of the American League Division Series on October 7, 2018, at Yankee Stadium between the Yankees and Red Sox, four calls at first base alone were overturned by the TV replay crew.

Baseball remains the only major sport where too many of its officials bait and squabble with players and managers in keeping with their ambitions to be part of the show. There is ample technology to eliminate on-field umpires and replace them with video officials that would able to make correct decisions at a much higher percentage than what is currently yielded, but most authorities agree that the game would be irrevocably bastardized if umpires were no longer part and parcel of it.

Others argue that the technology is now in advanced enough to rule more accurately than umpires even on balls and strikes. PITCHf/x for some time now has been used to call balls and strikes in independent minor leagues. Since it has long since been acknowledged that every umpire has a slightly different strike zone and some have zones that vary from inning to inning and pitcher to pitcher, let alone from game to game, it soon may be that only the umpires' union may stand between its members and PITCHf/x, or a device even more refined being adopted for major league play.

The rules governing the video review process are still not found in the standard baseball rule book but are readily available online along with the process's complete history.

Anyone could be forgiven for believing this proper-looking, middle-aged woman was an educator. That was indeed Amanda Clement's profession when she posed for this photo. But in her younger days, Clement had been the greatest distaff umpire of her time.

Note that masculine pronouns still are used throughout Rule 8.00 in every reference to an umpire or his duties. Although that has been the case ever since the first rule book was written, there has never been a time when female umpires have been expressly prohibited from serving in the major leagues. In 1972, Bernice Gera became the first woman to break the unwritten gender barrier in Organized Baseball when she was hired to officiate in the Class-A New York-Penn League, but distaff umpires have been working for pay in all-male games for over a century. One of the earliest and best at her trade was Amanda Clement, who once held the woman's record of 275 feet for throwing a baseball.

A native of Hudson, Dakota Territory, Clement was born on March 28, 1888, a year before South Dakota became a state, and played first base for the Hudson town team in the early 1900s, gaining recognition not only for her playing prowess but also for her knowledge of the rules. As early as 1904, at age sixteen, she received her first assignment to officiate a local semi-pro game for pay when the scheduled umpire did not appear. After Clement received commendations for her work in the South Dakota semipro championship clash, invitations began appearing in her mailbox from neighboring North Dakota. Before she retired from the game to become a physical education director at Wyoming University, Clement called balls and strikes for some six seasons in the Dakotas, Nebraska, Iowa, and Minnesota. Because slacks were taboo for women a century ago, Clement umpired in a long, full skirt, white blouse, dark tie, and peaked cap. Clement, who never married according to women's baseball historian Leslie Heaphy, died on July 20, 1971, in Sioux Falls, South Dakota.

9.00: The Official Scorer

9.01 Official Scorer (General Rules)

(a) The Office of the Commissioner, with respect to Major League games, and the Minor League President, with respect to Minor League games, shall appoint an official scorer for each league championship, post-season or all-star game. The official scorer shall observe the game from a position in the press box. The official scorer shall have sole authority to make all decisions concerning application of Rule 9 that involve judgment, such as whether a batter's advance to first base is the result of a hit or an error. The official scorer shall communicate such decisions to the press box and broadcasting booths by hand signals or over the press box loudspeaker system and shall advise the public address announcer of such decisions, if requested. Club officials and players are prohibited from communicating with the official scorer regarding any such decisions . . .

League presidents were first required by rule to appoint official scorers in 1957. Now the job is in the hands of the commissioner's office since there are no more league presidents, even though the rule book continues to make frequent reference to them. Not until 1950 was it even stated in the rule book that an official scorer was an accredited representative of the league, although by then he had been long recognized as such. The pay for MLB official scorers in 1950 is unknown, but nowadays the position pays $180 per game. Even though the job on a daily basis can be so time consuming that it sometimes pays less than the minimum wage per hour spent, some official scorers love their work so much they would do it for free.

For many years, teams customarily awarded official scorers' jobs to favored sportswriters who could use the extra money the assignment paid. In the nineteenth century, a club was not required to divulge the identity of its official scorer. It was felt that shrouding the position in secrecy would protect the scorer from players and fans who might otherwise attack or subvert his decisions. From 1882 to 1891, the Chicago White Stockings kept the name of their official scorer a complete mystery. Later it emerged that Elisa Green Williams (the mother of the club's future treasurer C. G. Green), who signed her scoresheets as E. G. Williams, had been awarding hits and errors in all the team's home games. Williams would sit primly between two players' wives, seemingly no more than a spectator, although secretly she was keeping careful score of every play. After each game her son would mail her scoresheets to the National League office, unaware of what the envelope contained.

9.01 (b) (1)

In all cases, the official scorer shall not make a scoring decision that is in conflict with Rule 9 or any other Official Baseball Rule. The official scorer shall conform strictly to the rules of scoring set forth in this Rule 9. The official scorer shall not make any decision that conflicts with an umpire's decision. The official scorer shall have authority to rule on any point not specifically covered in these rules. The Office of the Commissioner, with respect to Major League scorers, and the League President, with respect to Minor League scorers shall order changed any decision of an official scorer that contradicts the rules of scoring set forth in this Rule 9 and shall take whatever remedial actions as may be necessary to correct any statistics that need correction as a result of such mistaken scoring decision.

Given the fact that their job was a sinecure and subject to the whims of the club that paid them, official scores—particularly in the nineteenth century—were frequently accused of favoring home team players in their rulings. Here is what one reporter had to say about Baltimore

Orioles outfielder Willie Keeler's march to the National League batting crown in 1897:

> John Heydler, who is one of the best known baseball scribes in the business, says exception should be taken to this over generous scoring and that Keeler's figure of .432 will not agree with any private accounts. [Second baseman] Frank Houseman of St. Louis also has objections to Baltimore scoring methods. He says: "Down in Baltimore, one day, Keeler sent two flies to Lally [left fielder Dan Lally of St. Louis], who muffed both of them. Then he hit to Hartman [St. Louis third baseman Fred Hartman] and the latter fumbled and then threw wild. Then Keeler made a good single. The next morning four hits appeared to Keeler's credit in the Baltimore papers. Talk about Cleveland stuffing Burkett's average, why, they are not in it with the oyster scribes of Baltimore."

Jimmy Ryan, considered by this author to be the true 1888 National League batting leader. Had he received his due award he would have been its first winner to bat right and throw left.

Keeler's batting average was later reduced to .424 when discrepancies were discovered in his hit and at bat totals. Yet to be revised are the suspect final averages of several other purported batting title winners of Keeler's time. A particularly murky season is 1888, when Chicago first baseman Cap Anson was crowned the National League's leading hitter with a .344 average, even though this

The most famous person born in Marshalltown, Iowa, Cap Anson, was still playing major league baseball at age 45. Actress Jean Seberg, arguably the second most famous person born in Marshalltown, was dead at age 40.

author's calculations indicate that he hit only .317 and the bat title properly belonged to Anson's teammate, outfielder Jimmy Ryan, with a .328 mark. Ryan appears never to have called for an investigation, but a good deal of enmity built up between him and his player-manager in the years following 1888, until Anson finally left Chicago after the 1897 season.

9.01 (3)

If the game is protested or suspended, the official scorer shall make a note of the exact situation at the time of the protest or suspension, including the score, the number of outs, the position of any runners, the ball-and-strike count on the batter, the lineups of both teams and the players who have been removed from the game for each team.

　　Rule 9.01 (b) (3) Comment: It is important that a suspended game resume with exactly the same situation as existed at the time of suspension. If a protested game is ordered replayed from the point of protest, the game must be resumed with exactly the situation that existed just before the protested play

Protested games have been part of major-league baseball since its inception, but the plethora of suspended games are a relatively recent development and require an official scorer to practice undue diligence since the rosters for many teams change almost daily. It is not uncommon for a player on one team in a suspended game to be in the uniform of the opposition when the game is resumed, and in some instances the official scorer may not be the same. This makes it extremely important that the notes of the original official scorer be thoroughly digested before a suspended game is resumed. Otherwise it is entirely possible that a player on Team A that left the game prior to its suspension might illegally participate in its resumption for Team B. But if that player on Team A is still in the game at the time it is suspended, he is available to play for Team B if he has joined it in the interim.

9.02 Official Scorer Report

The official score report prepared by the official scorer shall be in a form prescribed by the league and shall include:
The following records for each batter and runner:

There are 18 different batters' and runners' statistics that need to be in the report, ranging from (1) number of times batted, except for the four instances when no time at bat is charged—sacrifice hits, walks, hit by pitches, awarded first base via interference or obstruction—to (18) number of times caught stealing. In addition, at various junctures in history, the official scorer has also been saddled with the following duties:

During the 1980s, an official scorer was also required to furnish his league's office with the name of the player who collected the game-winning RBI in each contest. The experimental category lasted just nine seasons before it was given a quiet burial in 1989. At that, it endured much longer and was much better received by the baseball public than several other experimental categories over the years. The most interesting one may have been an official scorer's nightmare that was labeled "Total Bases Run." This invention survived all of one season: 1880. That year, National League official scorers were ordered to input the number of bases each player touched safely in their game reports. The totals were then computed to determine the Total Bases run champion for the season. Since the category had only a one-year life span, there was only one champion. The winner with 501 bases safely touched was Abner Dalrymple of the Chicago White Stockings, the owner of many other obscure records.

During the National League's inaugural season of 1876, a batter was socked with a turn at bat every time he walked. Punished most by the rule was free pass leader and batting champion Ross Barnes, who collected 20 walks and thus 20 extra times at bat. The rule was rescinded in 1877, but then resurrected ten years later. The upside in 1887, however, was that each walk was also scored as a hit. This bonus swelled batting averages to astronomical proportions. Tip O'Neill topped the American Association with a .492 mark and Cap Anson's .421 figure paced the National League.

In 1968, the Special Baseball Records Committee voted to treat a base on balls as neither a hit nor a time at bat, and made their judgment retroactive to 1876. This ruling meant statisticians had to recalculate batting averages for both the 1876 and 1887 seasons after bases on balls were deducted from the at-bat totals for each player. Averages jumped in the former year, though not a lot because there were very few walks issued in the 1870s; Barnes, who stood to gain the most, went from .404 to .429. But in the 1887 season, averages were shaved in some cases as much as 60 or 70 points. Tip O'Neill's .492 mark (actually .485 when correctly calculated), for one, dropped to .435.

Many baseball historians are still upset by the committee's 1968 ruling, believing that it affects the historical integrity of the game to act as if today's rules are better than those of the past. Dennis Bingham convincingly argues that what we want from the past, above all, is an accurate account of what happened, and that by allowing a "special committee" to change a scoring rule of the past, we have in a very real sense changed what occurred. A reasonable counter to Bingham's argument is that walks should not be accepted as hits (as per 1887) and as times at bat without being hits (as per 1876) because the rules in each case were in existence for only a single aberrant season and consequently were not a significant part of the evolutionary process of the game. A second counter is that the purist argument also can mislead as to what actually occurred because if statistical achievements were awarded in many cases where they would now not be, using pre-1898 stats vis-à-vis astronomical stolen base totals, for example, induces modern-day fans to believe something extraordinary happened that really did not. In 1887, for one, six players stole more than 100 bases—an extraordinary number. But if today's stolen base rule had governed that year, it is doubtful that most of them would have swiped even half as many.

A further point of interest: Had the 1887 walks rule been in effect in 2004, Barry Bonds would have batted a record .607.

9.02 (b)

The following records for each fielder:
There are five: putouts, assists, errors, double plays and triple plays participated in.
    (c) The following records for each pitcher:

There are 15 pitcher records, ranging from number of innings pitched to number of balks committed. In addition, the official scorer is responsible for entering the names of the winning and losing pitchers, the names of the pitchers on both teams starting and finishing the game, the name of the pitcher to be credited with a save (if any), the number of passed balls for all catchers in the game, and the names of players participating in each double and triple play. Time was—and not that long ago—when MLB came up with the splendid idea of rounding off innings pitched so that 200 innings became 200 and 200⅔ became 201. It soon went the way of GWH (game-winning hits), but at least GWH, though eventually regarded as a meaningless stat because the hit too often was something like a sacrifice fly in the first inning of a 12–0 game, did not demand retroactive record alterations since it was only in existence a short time. Rounding off innings pitched required changing the career stats for many pitchers in the game during the time it was in existence and, worse yet, created ersatz ERA leaders. A case in point is the 1981 strike season. To qualify for the ERA crown in 1981, a pitcher had to pitch one inning for each of his team's games played. Normally this would mean 162 innings, but the strike in 1981 had reduced each team's game totals to just over 100. The winner today would have been Sammy Stewart of Baltimore, with an ERA of 2.324 in 112⅓ innings pitched. Finishing second would have been Steve McCatty of the Oakland A's, whose ERA was 2.327 in 185⅔ innings pitched. But the rounding of innings pitched rule then in effect declared McCatty the official leader. Stewart's 112⅓ innings total was rounded down to 112, while McCatty's 185⅔ total rounded up to 186. McCatty got credit for an extra third of an inning without allowing a run, and Stewart lost a third of a scoreless inning he had actually pitched. That made McCatty's final ERA 2.32 and Stewart's 2.33. The findings were appealed, but the rules committee of the day upheld the result because it conformed to the established practice. The rule was changed the next year, probably principally due to this injustice, and fractions of innings were no longer rounded up or down. Hence why McCatty is still considered the AL ERA champ in 1981, but at least once source, Baseball-Reference.com, awards the crown to yet a *third* pitcher: Dave Righetti of the Yankees, because Righetti's 2.05 ERA was significantly lower than Stewart's or McCatty's, even though Righetti worked just 105⅓ innings, short of the number required by rule 9.22 (b) since the Yankees played 107 games. So go figure.

Even then, the official scorer's task is not complete. He or she still has to account for the names of batters who hit home runs with the bases full, along with six other stats. The final two are the length of the game, "with delays deducted for weather, light failure, or technological failure not related to game action" but not for the time spent attending to an injured player, umpire, manager, or coach. And lastly, "Official attendance, as provided by the home club." But his or her job is *still* not done, especially if there are extenuating circumstances like the game at hand being either forfeited or officially protested or suspended—or, in rare instances, he or she needs to exercise an official scorer's authority to rule on any point not specifically covered in the scorer's rules.

The time required to play a game has always been included in major-league box scores, but a century ago no one paid much attention to how long a game took to play, and official scorers were not compelled to be precise. Most rounded off the time of a game, usually to the nearest five minutes. A game that took an hour and eight minutes would thus be recorded as having lasted an hour and ten minutes. Games, in any event, that took longer than an hour and a half generally had frequent interruptions for arguments with umpires.

During the 1887 season, when bases on balls were counted as hits and many players went up to bat looking for walks, causing some games to drag on for over two hours, *Sporting Life* found the development so revolting that it predicted "the public will call a halt (to the new rule) by refusing to attend games." When club owners also began noticing that fans were leaving their parks in the seventh or eighth inning, they quickly took heed. The new rule was scrapped after only a one-season trial, and the average time of a game again fell to well under two hours.

9.03 Official Score Report (Additional Rules)

And there is yet more to the report for each game—a draconian amount in all. One can only pity an official scorer new to the job who has signed up for it on the assumption it demands little more input than what appears in each game's box score. About the only task of substance that is left for someone other than the official scorer to provide for a major league game is a play-by-play account of it. The reader is encouraged to compare the job description given for today's official scorers as contrasted with what it must have been as late as the early 1900s when RBIs did not yet exist, strikeouts and sacrifice hits were often not kept track of, the rules for ERA and assigning pitchers' wins and losses were still ill defined, and no particular effort was devoted to Rule 9.03 (c) How to Prove a Box Score, which states: "A box score shall balance (or is proven) when the total of the team's times at bat, bases on balls received, hit batters, sacrifice bunts, sacrifice flies and batters awarded first base because of interference or obstruction equals the total of that team's runs, players left on base and the opposing team's putouts."

9.03 (a)

In compiling the official score report, the official scorer shall list each player's name and fielding position, or positions, in the order in which the player batted, or would have batted if the game ended before the player came to bat

9.03 (a) Comment: When a player does not exchange positions with another fielder but is merely placed in a different spot for a particular batter (for example, if a second baseman goes to the outfield to form a four-man outfield, or if a third baseman moves to a position between the shortstop and second baseman), the official scorer should not list this as a new position.

These last examples to many modern fans may seem more like something that would occur in a softball game than a baseball game, but they were chosen for good reason. Against Ernie Lombardi, a catcher who was agonizingly slow and hit murderous top-spin shots that could fell an elephant, teams often played their middle infielders back on the outfield grass, technically creating four- and sometimes even five-man outfields. It was felt that even at that distance a ball Lombardi hit would get to a fielder so fast that there would still be time to retire the slow-footed slugger.

The shift, devised in 1946 by Cleveland player-manager Lou Boudreau to combat Ted Williams of the Boston Red Sox, packed three infielders on the right side of the diamond and left only third baseman Ken Keltner to the left of second base. However, Boudreau was not the inventor of the "Williams Shift." A similar alignment had been used by managers as far

Ernie Lombardi's .306 career batting average is the highest among National Leaguers who appeared in a minimum of 1,000 games as a catcher and played no other positions. Making his achievement all the more remarkable is how few of his 1,792 hits were "leg" hits.

back as 1922 against lefty pull hitters Cy Williams of the Philadelphia Phillies and Ken Williams of the St. Louis Browns, both of whom thrived on the short right-field porches in their home parks.

Official scorers at games where the Lombardi alignment or the various Williams shifts were deployed took no cognizance of the defensive alterations in compiling their score reports. The same attitude continues today and is even more pervasive what with the enormous increase in exaggerated shifts for pull hitters and wannabe pull hitters.

9.03 (b)

The official scorer shall identify in the official score report any player who enters the game as a substitute batter or substitute runner, whether or not such player continues in the game thereafter, in the batting order by a special symbol that shall refer to a separate record of substitute batters and runners. The record of substitute batters shall describe what the substitute batter did. The record of substitute batters and runners shall include the name of any such substitute whose name is announced, but who is removed for another substitute before he actually gets into the game. Any such second substitute shall be recorded as batting or running for the first announced substitute.

Before 1907, American League official scorers did not always credit players with a game played if they only appeared as pinch-runners or defensive replacements. The National League did not demand that these types of substitute appearances be recorded until 1912. As a result, many players who got into games only fleetingly never saw their names in major-league box scores, and some even failed to be included in the early editions of the Macmillan *Baseball Encyclopedia*, before researchers confirmed their existence.

Mistakes and omissions in early day box scores are still being unearthed. In the early 1990s, historian Dick Thompson established that Ivan "Pete" Bigler, for many years believed to be a "phantom" player whose name appeared in a 1917 St. Louis Browns box score through a typographical error, actually participated on May 6, 1917, in a game at St. Louis that resulted in an 8–4 win for the Browns' Alan Sothoron over Chicago. During the game in question, Bigler pinch-ran for pinch-hitter Bill Rumler, who had walked. Ironically, it was later discovered that Bigler and Sothoron were not only born in the same town—Bradford, Ohio—but had been teammates at Juniata College in Pennsylvania.

As for the nineteenth century, researchers are continually discovering new or misidentified players. Scarcely a month goes by without a name on the players' all-time register being changed or a statistic attributed for more than a century to a certain player found actually to belong to a different player.

Today, a player is officially credited with a game played once he legally enters it—even if not a single pitch is thrown after his entry. When none are thrown before the game is stopped for rain or for any other reason, he is considered to be in the game as a batter. If a pitch is thrown before a stoppage occurs, the record reflects that he is in the game on defense.

9.04 Runs Batted In

A run batted in is a statistic credited to a batter whose action at bat causes one or more runs to score, as set forth in this Rule 9.04.

(a) The official scorer shall credit the batter with a run batted in for every run that scores

(1) unaided by an error and as part of a play begun by the batter's safe hit (including the batter's home run), sacrifice bunt, sacrifice fly, infield out or fielder's choice, unless Rule 9.04 (b) applies;

(2) by reason of the batter becoming a runner with the bases full (because of a base on balls, an award of first base for being touched by a pitched ball or for interference or obstruction); or

(3) when, before two are out, an error is made on a play on which a runner from third base ordinarily would score.

Although RBIs did not become an official statistic until 1920, many sportswriters kept track of them on an informal basis prior to then. As far back as 1879, a Buffalo paper recorded RBIs in box scores of the Buffalo Bisons' National League games. In the mid-1880s, Henry Chadwick, the father of baseball writers, urged the inclusion of the RBI feature in all box scores. Finally, by the early 1890s, Chadwick carried his point and National League official scores grudgingly obeyed instructions to catalog RBIs. But most found it a burden, and the practice was soon abandoned. In 1907, the *New York Press* revived the RBI, but it did not become an official statistic again until the Baseball Writers' Association of America (BBWAA) championed its adoption in 1920.

RBI figures for most of the pre-1920 seasons have since been reconstructed from box scores and game accounts, but several American Association seasons are still incomplete, as is the entire 1884 Union Association campaign. In addition, many of the reconstructed figures are guesswork at best. A particularly significant one is the 0 RBI credited to Worcester first baseman Chub Sullivan in 1880 in 166 at-bats, which currently stands as the major league record for the most at bats in a season without an RBI. In October 2005, this author's research established conclusively that Sullivan had at least one RBI in 1880. On May 14, at Boston, he singled home Art Whitney from third base in the ninth inning after Whitney hit an apparent home run over the left-field fence but missed third base and was allowed to return there safely when umpire Billy McLean contended that Boston pitcher Tommy Bond failed to do "what should be done" to have Whitney ruled out.

Recent research has ascertained even more significant findings. In 1961, Baltimore first baseman Jim Gentile had an RBI that went unrecorded at the time, hiking his total for the season to 141. That additional RBI enabled Gentile to tie Roger Maris for the American League RBI crown that season. Lou Gehrig's AL season record RBI total of 184 in 1931 is also now open to question.

9.05 Base Hits

(4) the batter reaches first base safely on a fair ball that has not been touched by a fielder and that is in fair territory when the ball reaches the outfield, unless in the scorer's judgment the ball could have been handled with ordinary effort;

There are six scenarios under which an official scorer is required to award the batter with a base hit, the value of which is determined by seven contingencies. There are also provisions under Rule 9.05 (4) when an official scorer on occasion is obliged to award a hit even though the defensive team does not make an ordinary effort to retire a batter. The most common situation occurs in a tie game with the home team at bat in the bottom of the ninth or in extra innings with a runner on third and less than two out. Sometimes, when a batter hits a long fly ball that will inevitably permit the winning run to tag up and score, the defensive team will make no attempt to catch it. The official scorer customarily awards the batter a single in these cases of defensive indifference.

Probably the most infamous hit that an official scorer was forced to award owing to defensive indifference was on October 3, 1976, when two Kansas City Royals teammates, third baseman George Brett and designated hitter Hal McRae, went down to their final at-bats of the season in a game against the Minnesota Twins, neck and neck in their battle for the American League batting crown.

In the top of the ninth, the Royals trailed the Twins' Jim Hughes, 5–2, with one out when Brett hit a routine fly ball that dropped in front of Twins left fielder Steve Brye and then bounced over Brye's head and rolled to the wall. Before Brye could chase down the ball and relay it home, Brett tallied an inside-the-park home run, enabling him to finish the season with a .333 batting average.

McRae then stepped to the plate, also at .333, albeit a fraction of a point lower than Brett's mark subsequent to his ITP home run. When he hit a groundball to shortstop Luis Gomez that was obviously going to result in his being thrown out, McRae angrily shouted at Twins manager Gene Mauch as he ran toward first base. McRae's wrath swiftly brought Mauch out of the dugout. A fight nearly ensued when McRae (who was African American and Brett Caucasian) accused Mauch of ordering Brye to let Brett's fly ball drop safely and implied a racial motivation.

Mauch denied that he had coaxed his players to steer the batting crown Brett's way if the chance arose, but Brett joined in McRae's grievance when he went on record with a statement that his fly ball definitely should have been caught. Brye later waffled, saying at first that he had misjudged the ball, but eventually he acknowledged that most American League players preferred to see Brett rather than McRae win the batting crown because Brett was a full-time player whereas McRae served as no more than a designated hitter. Whether Jim Hughes was among them, since Brett's faux homer socked him with an earned run and later in the inning the Royals brought the tying run to the plate before being retired, is not a matter of record. In any event, it was Hughes's final big-league start.

> Rule 9.05 (a) Comment: In applying Rule 9.05 (a), the official scorer shall always give the batter the benefit of the doubt. A safe course for the official scorer to follow is to score a hit whenever normal fielding on a batted or thrown ball fails to result in a putout.

This special comment evokes the question if it applies with equal force when a no-hitter is in the making, especially in light of the commonly held belief that an official scorer is obliged to follow a rule that the first hit of a game should always be a clean one. Even though there has never been any such rule, there have been several occasions when an official scorer has gone out of his way to label a hit an error, sometimes even after the fact, in order to preserve a no-hitter.

One of the most renowned instances came in St. Louis's Sportsman's Park on May 5, 1917, when Browns southpaw Ernie Koob won a 1–0 no-hitter over the Chicago White Sox. The official scorer, John Sheridan, was late that day getting to the park and so missed seeing Buck Weaver's sharp grounder in the first inning that Browns second sacker Ernie Johnson, filling in for injured Del Pratt, fielded with his chest. Many newspapers the next day called the sizzler a hit as per the wire service report. But when Sheridan had time to digest what was at stake, after the game ended he took a poll of his fellow writers and players on both teams as well before electing to charge Johnson with an *ex post facto* error on the play. As proof that Sheridan's decision occurred after the game was in the books, the *Chicago Sunday Tribune* headline the following day was KOOB TAMES SOX IN ONE HIT GAME, 1–0, evidence that the play was still considered a hit at the time the *Tribune* went to bed. Even *St Louis Post-Dispatch* sportswriter W. J. O'Connor acknowledged the no-hitter was "hardly immaculate . . . it was slightly tainted, stained with doubt at its very incipiency."

Sheridan's handling of the situation resulted in a pledge by both Chicago and St. Louis baseball writers to safeguard the game against any more such controversial scorer's decisions in the future. The pledge was largely forgotten by the following afternoon when Bob Groom of the Browns, after a hitless two-inning relief appearance in the first game of a twin bill, shut out the pennant-bound White Sox 3–0 in the second game and duplicated Koob's no-hit feat in the process to mark the only time in history that two pitchers on the same team have registered no-nos on successive days.

> ### 9.07 Stolen Bases and Caught Stealing
> The official scorer shall credit a stolen base to a runner whenever the runner advances one base unaided by a hit, a putout, an error, a force-out, a fielder's choice, a passed ball, a wild pitch or a balk . . .

This introduction explains why when Rickey Henderson stole 130 bases in 1982 to break the modern record, the "modern" qualifier was added. In 1886, official scorers were instructed to credit a runner with a stolen base for every extra base he advanced of his own volition. Beginning that year, any time a runner went from first to third on a single or advanced a base on a fly ball he earned a theft that was worth as much as a steal he made on the pitcher. A runner was also credited then with a stolen base even if he ran beyond or overslid the bag he was trying for and was subsequently tagged out.

In 1887, two players in the National League and four in the American Association swiped more than 100 bases, led by Hugh Nicol of the Cincinnati Red Stockings with 138, still the all-time record. There is no way now of determining how many of Nicol's steals fit the current definition, but it is probably significant that he averaged more than one a game and had more thefts than hits. In 125 contests, Nicol collected just 102 hits and posted a .215 batting average, lending considerable weight to the theory that he garnered a lot of steals via the old standard since he had relatively few baserunning opportunities.

In 1892, a proviso was added to the stolen base rule, spelling out that a theft would only be credited to a runner if there was either a possible chance or a palpable effort made to retire him. Eliminated were instances where a runner moved up a base on a fly ball too deep for an outfielder even to make a throw, or where a runner went from first to third on a hit into the gap while the batter loafed to a single. But there was still a lack of uniformity among official scorers. Some continued to bestow a stolen base whenever a runner hustled, while others went by the letter of the rule. As a result, the 1892 proviso was dropped before the 1897 season.

Finally, in 1898, the modern stolen base rule was adopted, removing credit for any extra bases advanced on a batted ball. Where in 1887, a runner scoring from first base on a single would have been credited with two stolen bases—third and home—now he is credited with none.

9.07 (d)

When a double- or triple-steal is attempted and one runner is thrown out before reaching and holding the base such runner is attempting to steal, no other runner shall be credited with a stolen base.

Before 1909, a runner earned a theft even if a teammate at the front or the back end of an attempted double or triple steal was nabbed.

9.07 (e)

When a runner is tagged out after oversliding a base, while attempting either to return to that base or to advance to the next base, the official scorer shall not credit such runner with a stolen base.

Likewise, when a runner becomes entangled with a fielder after successfully stealing a base but fails to maintain contact with the base in disentangling himself and is tagged while off it, the stolen base is eradicated. If, however, the runner occupies the base and then steps off it of his own accord and is tagged by a fielder essaying to pull a hidden ball trick, he receives credit for the steal.

9.07 (g)

The official scorer shall not score a stolen base when a runner advances solely because of the defensive team's indifference to the runner's advance. The official scorer shall score such a play as a fielder's choice.

Until 1920, a runner could be awarded a stolen base when a defensive team was indifferent to his advance. An important point here: Making no palpable effort to nail a runner attempting to steal is not automatically characterized as indifference. Former Orioles catcher Gus Triandos, the only documented player with a perfect 1.000 steal percentage in over 1,000 games, profited from this rule. Triandos's only career steal attempt came in the ninth inning of the second game of 1958's season-ending doubleheader at New York on September 28 between Baltimore and the Yankees. Triandos, a right-handed hitter, batted for lefty swinger Joe Ginsberg, and singled off reliever Zach Monroe. His steal attempt was successful when the Yankees were so surprised that no throw was made. But the official scorer ruled correctly that a theft should be awarded because the situation warranted a throw. The Yankees were only ahead, 6–3, at the time and had yet to record an out in the inning.

9.08 Sacrifices

The official scorer shall:

(a) Score a sacrifice bunt when, before two are out, the batter advances one or more runners with a bunt and is put out at first base, or would have been put out except for a fielding error, unless, in the judgment of the official scorer, the batter was bunting exclusively for a base hit and not sacrificing his own chance of reaching first base for the purpose of advancing a runner or runners, in which case the official scorer shall charge the batter with a time at bat;

Rule 9.08 (a) Comment: In determining whether the batter had been sacrificing his own chance of reaching first base for the purpose of advancing a runner, the official scorer shall give the batter the benefit of the doubt. The official scorer shall consider the totality of the circumstances of the at-bat, including the inning, the number of outs and the score.

Having to judge whether a batter is trying to sacrifice or bunting for a base hit has been a problem for official scorers ever since 1894, when sacrifice bunts first became an official statistic and a rule was adopted not to charge a player with a time at bat on a successful sacrifice. Because the note to Rule 9.08 (a) says the batter must be given the benefit of the doubt, many times an official scorer has no option but to award a sacrifice, even though the game situation plainly indicates a batter ought to have been hitting away.

In Game 38 of Joe DiMaggio's 56-game hitting streak in 1941, on June 26 at New York, with the Yankees ahead of the visiting Browns by a narrow 3–1 margin, Tommy Henrich was reluctantly credited with a sacrifice when he bunted with one out in the bottom of the eighth and Red Rolfe occupying first to stay out of a potential double play so that DiMaggio, hitless on the day, would be assured of getting one more at bat. It paid off when DiMaggio laced a two-out double off Browns starter Elden Auker to keep his streak alive. Clearly, with New York ahead, 3–1, and one out already recorded, Henrich sensibly would not be sacrificing himself but trying to ignite a rally in a game still so close, and one might question whether the Brownies' scorer would have been so generous to Henrich had the game been played to St. Louis.

Tommy Henrich, the perpetrator of a dubious sacrifice hit that assured Yankees teammate Joe DiMaggio of a final opportunity in Game 38 to extend what eventually became his record 56-game hitting streak in 1941.

9.08 (d)

Score a sacrifice fly when, before two are out, the batter hits a ball in flight handled by an outfielder or an infielder running in the outfield in fair or foul territory that
(1) is caught, and a runner scores after the catch, or
(2) is dropped, and a runner scores, if in the scorer's judgment the runner could have scored after the catch had the fly been caught.

Rule 9.08 (d) has a mercurial history. The 1908 season was the first in which a player was not assessed with a time at bat if he advanced a teammate at least one base with a fly ball. No distinction was made, however, between sacrifice flies and sacrifice bunts until 1920, when the RBI was made an official statistic and it became important to determine how many RBIs were the result of fly ball outs. In 1931, a decision was made to eliminate the sacrifice fly rule and charge a player with a time at bat. Batting averages dropped accordingly, but stayed so high during the 1930s that the rule change was little noticed.

The sacrifice fly was revived on an experimental basis in 1939, but only in cases where a fly out scored a runner. For reasons that are impossible to fathom now, the experiment lasted only one season. In 1940, the sacrifice fly was again abolished and the rule remained dormant until 1954, when it was once more hauled out of mothballs and given another trial. Since then, the rule has endured with only one significant change. In 1974, an addendum made it clear that a sacrifice fly should be credited if a batter hit a fly ball that brought home a run after it was caught by an infielder running into the outfield to chase a pop fly. Many official scorers had already been giving sacrifice flies in such cases, as well as on foul flies caught by infielders that enabled a runner to score. Among the leading victims while sacrifice flies were nonexistent between 1931 and 1953 were Stan Musial, Joe DiMaggio, Luke Appling, and especially Ted Williams. All lost points off their batting averages during many of their prime years, and in Williams's case even a two-point increase in his career batting average would advance him from a tie for seventh to fourth place on the all-time list. But perhaps the greatest casualties were Johnny Mize and Hank Greenberg, two legendary sluggers who were qualifiers in only one season that included sacrifice flies (1939).

9.09 Putouts and 9.10 Assists

For the most part, the rules for crediting fielders with putouts and assists have always been very similar to what they are now, but there have been some notable

The first year the sacrifice fly was permanently resurrected as a stat, the Dodgers' Gil Hodges set a record that still stands for the most in a season, with 19 in 1954. Largely owing to the sac fly rebirth, Hodges batted .304 that year, a career high. Had the sac fly been recognized as a stat 13 years earlier, Ted Williams would have hit .413 in 1941 rather than a mere .406.

differences. The 1878 season was the first in which an official scorer was authorized to credit an assist to a fielder if a batted or thrown ball bounced off him to another fielder, who then made an assist or a putout. Until the late 1880s, pitchers were often erroneously given an assist every time they struck out a batter. Before 1931, a pitcher was also given an assist if a catcher snared a pitched ball in time to nail a runner trying to steal home. That same year the rule was first drafted to credit a putout to the fielder closest to the play when a runner is hit by a batted ball.

One of the new scoring rules for 1977 mandated giving an assist to any fielder who made a play in time to retire a batter, even if a subsequent error by another fielder prevented the out from being recorded. This rule was an ancestor of the current rule to the same purpose and allowed official scorers in the nineteenth century to credit assists to pitchers even on strike-outs that went awry. Interestingly, however, while the pitcher might get an assist on such a play, he would not always receive credit for a strikeout. The most remarkable example of this quixotic rule in action occurred on July 7, 1884, in a Union Association fray between Boston and Chicago. In the box for Chicago that day, with everything working for him, was Hugh "One Arm" Daily. Daily not only shut down the Boston Unions, 5–0, on just one hit, a three-bagger by Beantown catcher Ed Crane, but he fanned 19 batters to tie Charlie Sweeney's then-existing major-league record, set only a month to the day earlier. In actuality, Daily should have had 20 strike-outs. One was lost to a third-strike passed ball by Chicago receiver Bill Krieg. The Union Association, in its lone year as a major league, refused to credit a pitcher with a whiff unless the batter was retired. On another missed third strike in Daily's dream game, Krieg managed to toss out the batter at first in the nick of time. Krieg thus had 18 putouts on the day and one assist. Meanwhile, Daily notched 22 assists—all but two of them on strikeouts or, in one instance, a miscarried strikeout.

Since 1889, a third strike has been scored as a strikeout but not an assist in every league even if it results in a wild pitch or a passed ball that permits a batter to get to first base.

9.09 (2)
When a runner is called out for being touched by a fair ball (including an Infield Fly), the official scorer shall credit the putout to the fielder nearest the ball

Even though it has never happened in a major-league game, the reader can infer from this rule that it is possible for a fielder, particularly a middle infielder, to be credited with all three of his team's putouts in an inning without ever touching the ball. Here is but one way that can occur and hold a team scoreless despite it getting five hits in the inning: Batter A singles; Batter B singles Batter A to second; Batter C grounds a ball that hits Batter A, with the shortstop getting the putout, and Batter B moves to second while Batter C is credited with a single; Batters D and E follow with almost identical ground balls toward short that each hit the lead baserunner. The shortstop thereby notches three putouts while his pitcher logs a 5.00 WHIP for his work in the scoreless inning. By the way, the maximum number of hits a team can collect in an inning without scoring is six.

9.12 Errors

(a) The official scorer shall charge an error against any fielder:
(2) when such fielder muffs a foul fly to prolong the time at bat of a batter, whether the batter subsequently reaches first base or is put out;

Although it has yet to occur on the major-league level, a pitcher could conceivably toss a perfect game in which his team made an infinite number of errors. Rule 9.12 (a) (2) explains how it can be done; every muffed foul fly that extends a batter's turn at bat is an error regardless of whether or not the batter subsequently reaches base. Meanwhile, a number of major-league perfectos have been destroyed solely by errors. The ultimate in absurdity occurred to Jim Galvin, ironically the author of the first documented professional perfecto in history in an August 17, 1876, contest between his St. Louis Reds and the independent Cass club of Detroit at a tournament between pro and semipro teams in Ionia, Michigan.

In a National League game at Buffalo on August 20, 1880, Galvin topped Worcester's Fred Corey, 1–0, on a muddy field despite having six errors made behind him—the most ever by a team behind a pitcher who was otherwise perfect. Galvin had to overcome two boots each by second baseman Davy Force and third baseman Dan Stearns, plus a dropped throw by first baseman Dude Esterbrook and a fumbled grounder by shortstop Mike Moynahan. Esterbrook atoned for his miscue by tripling home outfielder Joe Hornung for the game's lone run. Because of the swarm of enemy baserunners, few at the game even noted that Galvin had hurled a no-hitter, the first ever by a pitcher on a visiting team.

9.12 (a) (8)

[An error shall be charged to any fielder] whose failure to stop, or try to stop, an accurately thrown ball permits a runner to advance, so long as there was occasion for the throw. If such throw was made to second base, the official scorer shall determine whether it was the duty of the second baseman or the shortstop to stop the ball and shall charge an error to the negligent fielder.

The 1904 season was the first in which an official scorer was licensed to charge a fielder with an error for failing to cover a base. Previously, the error had always been given to the fielder who threw the ball—i.e., the catcher on a steal attempt—even when the throw would have been on target if a teammate had been where he was supposed to be.

Many followers of the game believe there should also be a rule that charges a team with an error rather than an individual player—or in some cases no one at all—in situations where an error of omission or an error in judgment occurs, such as when two or more fielders allow a pop fly to drop untouched between them. For one year—and one year only—there was such a rule, instigated by representatives of the AA's St. Louis Browns. In 1888, all batted balls that allowed a player to reach base safely but were neither hits nor errors that could be justifiably assigned to a fielder, were deemed "unaccepted chances." In part because the new category could not be conveniently fit into box scores, it was dropped after the 1888 season at the same winter meeting where four balls and three strikes were permanently set (but there is no reason it could not be resuscitated). Every pitcher who has been charged with an earned run owing to a play that should have been made but could not be labeled an error will agree that the notion of an unaccepted chance is perfectly logical.

As for assists, Rule 9.10 (b) says:

> The official scorer shall not credit an assist to
> (1) the pitcher on a strikeout, unless the pitcher fields an uncaught third strike and makes a throw that results in a putout;

Early on, box scores often showed pitchers with an inordinate amount of assists. The natural assumption was that opposing hitters were bunting on them a lot, typically because they were poor fielders (a la Tom Ramsey, who posted a glamorous .761 fielding average in his six-year pitching career). But, as previously has been discussed, the high assist totals generally came from official scorers who improperly awarded pitchers with an assist any time they recorded a strikeout and some who only credited an assist if the batter who fanned had to be thrown out at first by the catcher. Contingency (1) under Rule 9.10 (b) has never been witnessed by this author except in a Little League game.

9.12 Errors

(a) The official scorer shall charge an error against any fielder:
    (1) whose misplay (fumble, muff or wild throw) prolongs the time at bat of a batter, prolongs the presence on the bases of a runner or permits a runner to advance one or more bases, unless, in the judgment of the official scorer, such fielder deliberately permits a foul fly to fall safe with a runner on third base before two are out in order that the runner on third shall not score after the catch;

Just twice has this author witnessed a fielder deliberately let a foul fly fall uncaught to prevent a runner on third with less than two out from tagging up and scoring; one occasion was in a high school game and the other in a men's senior league game. But it does happen now and again in major-league games, and then often because an alert teammate has shouted to the fielder within range of the ball, "Let it drop!" or something to that effect. One outfielder who had the presence on his own to let a foul fly drop was Cards left fielder Matt Holliday in the top of the 12th inning of a game against the Brewers on April 28, 2014, at Busch Stadium III. With the score tied, 3–3, and Milwaukee's Jonathan Lucroy on third base with one out, Holliday purposely let Greg Davis's deep fly to left drop untouched in foul territory. His heads-up play went for naught when Davis then tripled to right to score Lucroy and Milwaukee ultimately won, 5–3.

> Under Rule 9.12 (a) (1) Comment there is this paragraph:
> "The official scorer shall not score mental mistakes or mis-judgments as errors unless a specific rule prescribes otherwise. A fielder's mental mistake that leads to a physical misplay—such as throwing the ball into the stands or rolling the ball to the pitcher's mound, mistakenly believing there to be three outs, and thereby allowing a runner or runners to advance—shall not be considered a mental mistake for purposes of this rule and the official scorer shall charge a fielder committing such a mistake with an error. The official scorer shall not charge an error if the pitcher fails to cover first base on a play, thereby allowing a batter-runner to reach first base safely. The official scorer shall not charge an error to a fielder who incorrectly throws to the wrong base on a play."

Yes, players—even big leaguers—lose track of outs and throw balls into the stands, intending to give a lucky fan a souvenir. If the bases are empty when it happens, there is no problem. With runners on, however, the ball is immediately dead and they each advance two bases. On June 16, 2016, in a night game at Philadelphia's Citizens Bank Park between Toronto and the Phillies, Phillies center fielder Odubel Herrera, mistakenly thinking there were three outs after catching a fly ball off the bat of the Blue Jays' Michael Saunders, trotted out to the stands and threw the ball into them, helping to turn a one-run inning into a four-run inning. It mattered little since the Jays won, 13–2, but a similar humiliating gaffe by Montreal's Larry Walker on April 24, 1994, was instrumental in an Expos loss to the Dodgers in a Sunday night game at LA.

In the second inning with one out and Jose Offerman on first, Walker caught Mike Piazza's fly ball to deep right and casually flipped it into the stands. Offerman ended up on third base and the Dodgers posted two runs in the frame when Tim Wallach, the next batter, homered off rattled

Expos pitcher Pedro Martinez. The Dodgers went on to win the game, 7–1. There are numerous other examples of this type of brain lock that we could offer, but practically all of them, curiously (or perhaps not), are from seasons since the 1994 strike. We all would give plenty to know the first time such a howler occurred in a major-league game, but there is no doubt it rarely, if ever, happened in the days when fans were all but arrested if they did not return balls hit into the stands to the playing field. Today's players are actually encouraged to provide spectators with souvenir balls at every opportunity. Their efforts, in particular those by first and third basemen recording an inning-ending out, have been thwarted by the new major-league park rules requiring a solid stretch of netting to protect spectators along the first- and third-base lines from foul shots into the stands. Instead of simply tossing a ball to someone who catches their fancy, they now have to lob it over the netting and put it up for grabs.

9.12 (f)

The official scorer shall not charge an error when a runner or runners advance as the result of a passed ball, a wild pitch or a balk.
(1) When the fourth called ball is a wild pitch or a passed ball and as a result
　　(A) the batter-runner advances to a base beyond first base;
　　(B) any runner forced to advance by the base on balls advances more than one base; or
　　(C) any runner, not forced to advance, advances one or more bases,
　　the official scorer shall score the base on balls and also the wild pitch or passed ball, as the case may be.

In the game's early years, scorers would often charge pitchers and catchers with errors in addition to wild pitches and passed balls, respectively. Now, the official scorer needs only to account for each extra base a runner takes. A passed ball or a wild pitch is explanation enough.

9.16 Earned Runs and Runs Allowed

An earned run is a run for which a pitcher is held accountable. In determining earned runs, the official scorer shall reconstruct the inning without the errors (which exclude catcher's interference) and passed balls, giving the benefit of the doubt always to the pitcher in determining which bases would have been reached by runners had there been errorless play. For the purpose of determining earned runs, an intentional base on balls, regardless of the circumstances, shall be construed in exactly the same manner as any other base on balls.

(a) The official scorer shall charge an earned run against a pitcher every time a runner reaches home base by the aid of safe hits, sacrifice bunts, a sacrifice fly, stolen bases, putouts, fielder's choices, bases on balls, hit batters, balks or wild pitches (including a wild pitch on third strike that permits a batter to reach first base) before fielding chances have been offered to put out the offensive team. For the purpose of this rule, a defensive interference penalty shall be construed as a fielding chance. A wild pitch is solely the pitcher's fault and shall contribute to an earned run just as a base on balls or a balk.

Earned run averages for National League pitchers were calculated as early as 1876; that season, Louisville's Jim Devlin—yes, the same Jim Devlin who was banned after the 1877 season for taking bribes to throw games—allowed 309 runs but scarcely a third of them (109) were earned. After that season, there was a lapse of six years before the National League began calculating them again in 1883. Meanwhile, the upstart American Association kept track of pitcher ERAs for its entire 10-span as a major league (1882–91). But it was not until 1912 that the National League made calculating pitchers' ERAs a permanent fixture. The following season the American League began doing likewise annually. At that time, an earned run was assessed to a pitcher every time a player scored by the aid of base hits, sacrifice hits, walks, hit batters, wild pitches, and balks before enough fielding chances had been offered a defensive team to record three outs. In 1917, stolen bases were added to the list of permissible aids to the scoring of an earned run.

Before the 1931 season, runners who reached base on catcher's interference were added to passed balls and the other types of miscues that exempted a pitcher from being charged with an earned run. The 1931 rule reemphasized, however, that a run emanating from a batter who reached first on a wild pitch third strike was earned—even though the pitcher was charged with an error on the play—as the wild pitch was solely the pitcher's fault. All other errors that allowed a batter to reach base or prolonged his turn at bat excused the pitcher from being saddled with an earned run, including errors committed by him.

In most cases, pitchers' ERAs prior to the 1912 season have been reconstructed by dedicated researchers after laboriously poring over old box scores and game accounts. In some cases, a statistic that was computed well over a century ago was taken as fact for the lack of any method for verification. No one can really be sure now that Tim Keefe, by present scoring rules, really posted an all-time record-low 0.86 ERA by a qualifier in 1880 with Troy. It seems hard to imagine that Keefe could have allowed only 10 earned runs in 105 innings and yet lose six of his twelve decisions, whereas Troy's other Hall of Fame pitcher, Mickey Welch, won more than half his games despite a 2.54 ERA that was 0.17 runs above the National League average that season.

Even Dutch Leonard's twentieth-century record-low 0.96 ERA in 1914 has been scaled downward from 1.01 relatively recently as new information has come to light revealing that Leonard hurled 224 ⅔ innings that season rather than 222 ⅔, the total with which he was credited for well over half a century. Indeed, the career and single-season ERAs for almost every pitcher active prior to 1920 have undergone some adjustments since the first Macmillan baseball encyclopedia appeared in 1969.

Incidentally, the career and single-season ERAs for even some contemporary pitchers differ from one record book to another. Tommy John is an example. The final edition of the Macmillan encyclopedia in 1996 lists John with 4708 ⅓ career innings pitched and ERAs of 2.97 in 1979 and 2.64 in 1981. However, Baseball-Reference.com presently credits John with 4710⅓ career innings and ERAs of 2.96 in 1979 and 2.63 in 1981.

A mistake on either's part? Not at all. To simplify the math work, for the 1970 through 1981 seasons major-league statisticians were unwisely directed to round off the innings a pitcher worked to the nearest whole inning, only to revert in 1982 to the original rule that counted each third of an inning. Baseball-Reference.com incorporates all the thirds of an inning John had lost to the new ruling in his career and single-season stats, whereas the final Macmillan edition continued to deduct a third of an inning from John's stats in six different seasons. This sort of discrepancy has now been resolved for all pitchers from John's era. But as has been already discussed earlier, another quirk that developed as a result of the rule to round off innings pitched at the end of the season cost Baltimore's Sammy Stewart the AL ERA crown in the strike-shortened 1981 campaign. Stewart allowed 29 earned runs in 112 ⅓ innings for a 2.323 ERA, while Oakland's Steve McCatty was touched for 48 earned runs in 185 ⅔ innings for a 2.327 ERA. When the innings were rounded off to the nearest whole number, however, McCatty won 2.32 to 2.33.

9.16 (g)

When pitchers are changed during an inning, the official scorer shall not charge the relief pitcher with any run (earned or unearned) scored by a runner who was on base at the time such relief pitcher entered the game, nor for runs scored by any runner who reaches base on a fielder's choice that puts out a runner left on base by any preceding pitcher.

One oddity of the formula in Rule 9.12 (g) for determining when to charge a relief pitcher with an earned run is that it makes it possible for a reliever to be assessed an earned run for a tally that is unearned in his team's totals. If, say, a reliever enters in an inning when all the runs his predecessor allowed are unearned because of errors, and then promptly gives up a home run to the first batter he faces, the dinger is an earned run charged to his account, but an unearned run to the team's. Consequently, in many instances a team will have a season ERA that is lower than the aggregate season ERA totals of its pitchers.

9.17 Winning and Losing Pitcher

(a) The official scorer shall credit as the winning pitcher that pitcher whose team assumes a lead while such pitcher is in the game, or during the inning on offense in which such pitcher is removed from the game, and does not relinquish such lead, unless (1) such pitcher is a starting pitcher and Rule 9.17 (b) applies; or (2) Rule 9.17 (c) applies.

Rule 9.17 and its five contingencies have recently replaced Rule 10.19, which some authorities feel was more straightforward and simpler to grasp. In any case, the 1950 rule book was the first to formalize what previously had only been a custom not to award a starting pitcher a victory unless he worked at least five innings in all games that went six or more innings. Before then, exceptions had occasionally been made, especially when a pitcher had to be removed after being injured. One of the most flagrant exceptions occurred in the 1924 World Series, when Giants starter Hugh McQuillan was awarded the win in Game Three even though he worked only 3 ⅔ innings because his club led Washington, 3–2, when he departed in favor of the more deserving Rosy Ryan, who would have gathered the Giants' 6–4 win as per the 1950 rule change. McQuillan pitched again in relief twice later in the Series, negating the possibility that he suffered a disabling injury in his lone start.

In the nineteenth century, when teams often had only one standout hurler, pitching aces were frequently removed whenever they held a seemingly insurmountable lead. But removing a pitcher prior to 1889 meant having him swap positions with another player, who would then finish the game in the box. Sometimes a pitcher would be lifted as early as the second inning and sent to first base or right field on the premise that he could always be brought back into the box if the complexion of the game changed. No thought was given then to denying a hurler a win in such cases. In reviewing old records, however, some researchers have taken it upon themselves to deduct victories whenever a starting pitcher made only a token appearance.

One example where an effort has been made to rewrite history resulted in Providence's Charley Radbourn now being listed in record books with only 59 wins in 1884 rather than 60, an all-time mark that for over a century went pretty much unchallenged. But closer examination reveals that the win in question, in a game on July 28 at Philadelphia, was, via the rule as of 1950, properly assigned to the starting pitcher Cyclone Miller, who trailed, 4–3, when he left the box after the fifth inning but led, 7–4, when Providence scored four runs in the top of the sixth, after which Radbourn came in to pitch four scoreless frames to produce an 11–4 Providence win. The issue remains, though, that in many other similar games throughout pre-1950 baseball history, the wins were given to the winning team's most deserving pitcher, not necessarily the starter—even when he left the game with his club ahead. An even larger issue is that pitching wins and losses were only an informally kept statistic, as was a pitcher's ERA, in the game's embryonic years. When Cy Young finally took off his pitching toe plate for the last time in 1911, there were no headlines that proclaimed, "Young Departs with 511 Wins." His total, in fact, has been revised several times over the years.

9.17 (c)

The official scorer shall not credit as the winning pitcher a relief pitcher who is ineffective in a brief appearance, when at least one succeeding relief pitcher pitches effectively in helping his team maintain its lead.

In such a case, the official scorer shall credit as the winning pitcher the succeeding relief pitcher who was most effective, in the judgment of the official scorer.

Formerly Rule 10.17 (c), Rule 9.17 (c) can lead to some bizarre scoring decisions and in at least one instance, a decision that impacted on a Hall of Fame reliever's career record saves total.

In a night game at Camden Yards on September 12, 2013, between Baltimore and the Yankees, with his club ahead, 5–2, Yankees manager Joe Girardi called on setup man David Robertson to pitch the bottom of the eighth inning. Robertson retired the first two Orioles hitters he faced, but then yielded two successive singles followed by a three-run homer by Danny Valencia to tie the game at 5–5. Despite next serving up a double to J. J. Hardy, Robertson escaped the frame with the score still knotted. After the Yankees eeked out a run in the top of the ninth, Yankees relief kingpin Mariano Rivera came on in the bottom of the ninth to seal a 6–5 win for his club by setting the Orioles down 1-2-3 for what virtually everyone expected would be his 653rd career save, embellishing his already record total.

But instead of charging Robertson with a blown save and crediting him with the win, since he was still in the game when the Yankees went ahead, 6–5, in the ninth, the official scorer, Mark Jacobson, awarded the victory to Rivera, thus denying him what would have been his league-leading 44th save of the season. Jacobson's decision was correct on all counts but one that is nonetheless not often seen, as Rule 9.17 (c) is perhaps more inconsistently applied by official scorers than any other. It gave Rivera his 82nd and final career win, but froze his record save total at 652 since he retired after the 2013 season. When and if someone approaches Rivera's all-time saves record, it will be interesting to see how vividly this game, his last win instead of his last save, is remembered.

Here is an illustration of a more commonly seen application of Rule 9.17 (c). On August 16, 2004, at Arizona's Bank One Park (now known as Chase Field), Pirates reliever Jose Mesa came on in the bottom of the ninth to protect a 7–3 lead that would have meant a win for starter Sean Burnett (had Mesa been successful). Instead, Mesa gave up five hits and four runs to send the game into extra innings. Pittsburgh tallied a run in the top of the 10th and Mike Gonzalez held the Diamondbacks scoreless in the bottom half. If Mark Jacobson had been the official scorer for this game, Gonzalez probably would have gotten the win, but Diamondbacks scorer Rodney Johnson awarded it to Mesa instead, even though he was colossally ineffective in the single inning he worked and Gonzalez was given his only save of the season.

9.17 (d)

A losing pitcher is a pitcher who is responsible for the run that gives the winning team a lead that the winning team does not relinquish.

Rule 9.17 (d), at a glance, seems so clear that it requires no discussion. Yet until the twentieth century was well underway it was not unusual for an official scorer to saddle a starting pitcher with a defeat when his team lost, even if he left the game with his club *leading*. Likewise, a pitcher sometimes would collar a win in a game that he left while his team was trailing. In a 1912 meeting on April 20 at the Polo Grounds between the Giants and Dodgers, Giants rookie Jeff Tesreau got one such victory that seemed insignificant at the time but turned out to be of monumental importance. Tesreau was relieved by Rube Marquard in the top of the ninth inning of a game in which the Giants were trailing, 3–2, after he gave up three runs in the ninth. Marquard retired the only batter he faced to end the Brooklyn rally. When the Giants tallied two runs in the bottom

Had Rule 10.19 (a) been on the books in 1912, Rube Marquard would have begun the season with 20 straight wins. As it is, his 19–0 start is the best in history.

of the frame off Nap Rucker in relief of Eddie Stack, the official scorer put a "W" beside Tesreau's name. Nowadays, the win would go to Marquard, who was in the game when the winning run scored. Had Marquard garnered that extra victory, it would have enabled him to launch the 1912 season by winning his 20th straight decision. Instead, he had to settle for 19 straight wins, tying the then all-time record set by Tim Keefe in 1888 rather than establishing a new standard.

There is a strong temptation now among some baseball historians to correct these apparent injustices. As a result, the career won and lost totals of many pitchers, including not only Cy Young but several other Hall of Famers, have been revised in the past four decades. It becomes almost a matter of personal taste whether Tom Hughes had 16 wins for the Boston Braves in 1915 (as per the final 1996 Macmillan edition and Baseball-Reference.com) or 20 wins (as per the 1982 Macmillan edition). Hughes is by no means an extreme example. In any event, many decisions made by official scorers over a span of some fifty years have since been rescinded in an effort to bring a historical uniformity to all records.

9.18 Shutouts

A shutout is a statistic credited to a pitcher who allows no runs in a game. No pitcher shall be credited with pitching a shutout unless he pitches the complete game, or unless he enters the game with none out before the opposing team has scored in the first inning, puts out the side without a run scoring and pitches the rest of the game without allowing a run. When two or more pitchers combine to pitch a shutout, the league statistician shall make a notation to that effect in the league's official pitching records.

This rule might almost have been tailored to account for Ernie Shore, the perpetrator of the greatest one-game relief stint in history. On June 23, 1917, in the first game of a doubleheader at Fenway Park, Shore relieved Red Sox starter Babe Ruth after Ruth was booted by home-plate umpire Brick Owens for arguing a ball four call to Washington Senators leadoff hitter Ray Morgan. Enraged, Ruth charged Owens and threw a punch at him before he could be hauled off the field by a policeman. Had Ruth's attempted haymaker landed, the course of baseball history might have been permanently altered. Sox catcher Pinch Thomas was also tossed for objecting to the call. Thomas's replacement, Sam Agnew, gunned down Morgan trying to steal second, and Shore then retired the next 26 batters in a row and for over half a century received credit for both a shutout and a perfect game.

Shore's perfect-game honor is still the subject of controversy. Most historians now agree that no pitcher can earn a perfecto in a game where an opposing runner has reached base safely, or a complete game for that matter when he was not the starting pitcher. But Shore's combined no-hitter and shutout remain firm according to the rule book.

On May 31, 1988, Yankees reliever Neil Allen collected a whitewash in a similar manner when he blanked the A's, 5–0, at Oakland. Al Leiter started for the Yanks and on his first pitch was struck on the left wrist by Carney Lansford's smash, which resulted in a double. After Leiter was removed from the game, Allen was given all the time he needed to warm up as per the injury rule. He then preceded to toss nine innings of three-hit scoreless ball to receive credit for a shutout but not a complete game. Allen's 1988 stats reflect that he had no complete games but one shutout. It appears to be a misprint, until Allen's game log for the 1988 season is examined.

9.19 Saves for Relief Pitchers

A save is a statistic credited to a relief pitcher, as set forth in this Rule 9.19.

The official scorer shall credit a pitcher with a save when such pitcher meets all four of the following conditions:

    (a) He is the finishing pitcher in a game won by his team;

(b) He is not the winning pitcher;

(c) He is credited with at least 1/3 of an inning pitched; and

(d) He satisfies one of the following conditions:

(1) He enters the game with a lead of no more than three runs and pitches for at least one inning;

(2) He enters the game, regardless of the count, with the potential tying run either on base, or at bat or on deck (that is, the potential tying run is either already on base or is one of the first two batters he faces);or

(3) He pitches for at least three innings.

Until 1969, the term *save* was not even an official part of the game's lexicon. That season, major league rulemakers—at the urging of sportswriter Jerome Holtzman—first paid formal acknowledgement to a facet of relief pitching that many publications, *The Sporting News* among them, had already long since championed. But what *The Sporting News* deemed a save and what is now considered a save are not at all the same. In 1967, for example, *The Sporting News* named right-hander Minnie Rojas of the California Angels the American League "Fireman of the Year" for his 22 saves, whereas Ted Abernathy of the Chicago Cubs got the National League trophy for netting 26 saves.

Most record books now list Rojas with 27 saves in 1967 and Abernathy with 28. The reason for the disparity is because *The Sporting News* granted a save only when a reliever faced the tying or lead run during his mound stint or began the final inning with no more than a two-run lead and then pitched a perfect inning. In contrast, both major leagues awarded a save in 1969, the year the term got its official baptism, if a reliever merely entered the game with his team in front and held the lead for the remainder of the game. What this meant is that, by *The Sporting News*'s definition, a reliever in 1967 who came into a game with his team ahead 4–1 and worked three perfect innings would not get a save, but the major-league rule in 1969 gave a save to a reliever who worked just the final inning of a 10–0 blowout.

Over the years, these inequities have been eliminated. In 1973, the rule was amended to give a reliever a save if he either found the potential tying or winning run on base or at the plate during his stint or else worked at least three effective innings. Two years later, the current save rule was adopted.

In determining retrospective saves for pitchers active before the concept was born, researchers applied the 1969 rule. Hence many early day pitchers are now credited with specious saves. An unfortunate example is Ted Conover, a one-game major leaguer with a career 13.50 ERA, who earned a retrospective save some eighty years later for his effort on May 7, 1889, when he replaced Cincinnati rookie starter Jesse Duryea in the eighth inning of a 16–4 Cincinnati blowout win over last-place Louisville and surrendered all four Louisville runs in his two-inning stint. Why was Conover called on at all by Reds manager Gus Schmelz? Probably to save overtaxing Duryea's arm, but to little avail. As it was, Duryea not only lost his chance for a shutout but worked 401 innings in his frosh season and won 32 games. He won only 27 more in his brief five-season career.

When center fielder Stevie Wilkerson took the hill at Anaheim for the pitching-depleted Orioles on July 25, 2019, in the bottom of the 16th inning and notched a save in Baltimore's 10–8 win over the Angels, the media made much to-do of his being the first position player ever to record a save. That may have been the case ever since the save became an official stat in 1969, but is otherwise untrue. In 1883, Cap Anson finished two games in the box for Chicago and collected a retrospective save in one them. But unlike Ted Conover's save six years later, Anson's emanated from a solid performance. In two relief appearances that year, he logged an 0.67 WHIP. Two years later, Anson's teammate, second baseman Fred Pfeffer, bagged two saves and two wins in five appearances. Prior to 1887, when the pitching rules tightened, making it problematical for a non-pitcher to enter the box and throw with whatever delivery he pleased, Anson frequently used his position players in relief or even as spot starters. Wilkerson's save may be the last of its kind if MLB's roster-size increase to 26 in 2020 enables teams not to have to use position players as pitchers in crucial situations.

Here goes:

9.20 Statistics

The League President shall appoint an official statistician. The statistician shall maintain an accumulative record of all the batting, fielding, running and pitching records specified in Rule 9.02 for every player who appears in a league championship game or postseason game.

The statistician shall prepare a tabulated report at the end of the season, including all individual and team records for every championship game, and shall submit this report to the League President. This report shall identify each player by his first name and surname and shall indicate as to each batter whether he bats righthanded, lefthanded or both ways, and as to each fielder and pitcher, whether he throws righthanded or lefthanded . . .

Any games played to break a divisional tie shall be included in the statistics for that championship season.

Before each major league had an official statistician, tabulation errors were often made that resulted in the wrong players being awarded batting titles, stolen base crowns, etc. The most blatant error was perpetrated by an unidentified statistician, probably from Philadelphia, in 1884. From the data furnished by American Association officials at the close of that season, the loop batting crown belonged to Philadelphia A's first baseman Harry Stovey with a towering .404 average. Stovey's heady figure stood uncontested for a century until researchers in the 1980s carefully scrutinized the 1884 AA season and discovered that his true mark was .326 and the real winner of that season's batting crown was Dave Orr with a .354 average. A blunder so gargantuan seems as if it must have been perpetrated deliberately to steer the honor to Stovey, one of the AA's most popular and highly esteemed players, rather than Orr, a nonentity at the time.

In 1901, at the close of the American League's inaugural season as a major league, Nap Lajoie was awarded the loop's fledgling batting title with a .422 average on 220 hits in 543 at-bats. A statistician noticed in 1918 that 220 hits in 543 at-bats produced only a .405 mark, and all the record books then reduced Lajoie's 1901 average to the lower figure. Following a story on Lajoie in *The Sporting News* in 1953, attention was again drawn to his 1901 season. The official American League records for that year had long since been destroyed, but baseball historian John Tattersall's examination of the 1901 box scores unearthed 229 hits for Lajole in 543 at-bats. Tattersall's research again restored Lajole's average to .422, where it remained until another search through the 1901 box scores in the 1980s confirmed that Lajole had actually collected 232 hits in 544 at-bats that year, for a twentieth century–record .426 average. Among the three newly discovered hits were a triple and a home run that also raised Lajole's slugging percentage to .643, a 13-point hike.

Is it now safe to assume that at least all the serious discrepancies in batting, pitching, and fielding records in the so-called post-1900 "Modern Era" have been eliminated? Far from it. In fact, Nap Lajole's .426 batting average in 1901 has yet to gain universal acceptance, and several other significant discrepancies that have been revealed remain intact in record books sanctioned by the major leagues, including Baseball-Reference.com.

One is the 1910 American League batting race, for years food for violent controversy, which was seemingly resolved some while ago when it was incontrovertibly established that Ty Cobb hit .383 rather than .385, giving the crown to Nap Lajole with a .384 mark.

The problem radiated from a Detroit box score that had inadvertently been included twice in the season-end calculations, the duplication resulting in Cobb being credited with three extra at-bats and two unearned hits. However, major-league officials continue to recognize Cobb as the 1910 American League batting leader, believing that history should not be rewritten. Many baseball analysts concur, albeit for a different reason. In a doubleheader on the last day of the 1910 season, to help Lajole overtake the unpopular Cobb, St. Louis Browns manager Jack O'Connor ordered rookie third baseman Red Corriden to play deep on Lajole, enabling the batter to bunt down the third-base line at will and collect six "baby" hits in the twin bill. Cobb still won the bat title by a single point—or so it was then thought—but O'Connor and Browns coach Harry Howell were later banned from the majors for their role in the plot to deprive Cobb of his honor. In any case, Baseball-Reference.com now lists both Cobb's and Lajoie's 1910 averages in bold, designating league leadership, even though the averages differ.

National League statisticians also have a longstanding cross to bear. Chicago Cubs third baseman Heinie Zimmerman was retroactively awarded the Triple Crown in 1912 when he seemingly paced the senior loop with a .372 batting average, 14 home runs, and 103 RBIs. It has since developed that Zimmerman had only 99 RBIs that year, leaving him three behind Honus Wagner, the true leader, with 102. But the final Macmillan encyclopedia in 1996 continued to assign Zimmerman 103 RBIs in 1912, even though other major reference books by then were crediting him with only two legs of the Triple Crown (batting average and home runs).

Meanwhile, recent developments have given statistics sticklers good reason to doubt that even post-expansion statistics are 100 percent free of errors. The most significant one uncovered since the turn of this century is that Orioles first baseman Jim Gentile was deprived of an aforementioned RBI in 1961 that would have put him in a tie with Roger Maris for the American League lead that year with 141.

9.21 Determining Percentage Records

To compute:

    (a) Percentage of games won and lost, divide the number of games won by the sum of games won and games lost;

Never in major-league history has a team with the highest winning percentage in its league not won the pennant. But prior to 1882, the rules made such an event possible—and it happened on one occasion in the top minor league of its time.

At the finish of its 1878 season, the International Association standings listed the Syracuse Stars with 29 wins and 11 losses for a .725 winning percentage. Meanwhile, Buffalo ended with 32 wins and 12 losses for a .727 winning percentage. Early day record books credited the pennant to Syracuse, while more modern reference works give the crown to Buffalo. This in effect would be counter to the current philosophy to concur whenever possible with the statistical rules of the time rather than those in our day were it not for modern researchers' consensus that Buffalo's true record was 27–10 (.730) in league play while Syracuse finished half a game behind at 26–10 (.722).

9.22 Minimum Standards for Individual Championships

To assure uniformity in establishing the batting, pitching and fielding championships of professional leagues, such champions shall meet the following minimum performance standards:

Only once in major-league history has a player been denied a batting crown even though he met the minimum performance standards then in existence. In 1938, rookie Washington Senators outfielder Taft Wright hit .350 in exactly 100 games. At that time, a player customarily had to appear in at least 100 games to be eligible for a batting title. But because Wright collected just 263 at-bats, an exception was made and the crown instead went to the far more deserving Boston Red Sox first baseman Jimmie Foxx, who finished a point behind Wright at .349.

Because there was no at-bat minimum in 1938, Wright theoretically could have won the crown with just one at bat as long as he somehow got into 100 games. The 100-game minimum became the unofficial standard in 1920 and remained in effect until 1945, when a 400 at-bat minimum was formally introduced. For the next dozen seasons, the rule for determining batting and slugging leaders fluctuated wildly, with a new twist added almost yearly. In 1957, the major leagues at last adopted the current standard that a player must have 3.1 plate appearances per every game his team plays to qualify as a batting or slugging leader.

9.22 (a)

The individual batting, slugging or on-base percentage champion shall be the player with the highest batting average, slugging percentage or on-base percentage, as the case may be, provided the player is credited with as many or more total appearances at the plate in league championship games as the number of games scheduled for each club in his club's league that season, multiplied by 3.1 in the case of a Major League player and by 2.7 in the case of a National Association player. Total appearances at the plate shall include official times at bat, plus bases on balls, times hit by pitcher, sacrifice hits, sacrifice flies and times awarded first base because of interference or obstruction. Notwithstanding the foregoing requirement of minimum appearances at the plate, any player with fewer than the required number of plate appearances whose average would be the highest, if he were charged with the required number of plate appearances shall be awarded the batting, slugging or onbase percentage championship, as the case may be.

Taft Wright was denied the American League batting title in 1938 in part because Jimmie Foxx finished right on his tail. If no other hitter had been within 30 points of Wright's .350 mark, quite possibly he would have been the first rookie in American League history to wear a batting crown.

Supporting this is the fact that several other batting leaders prior to 1957 who would not have qualified for their crowns under the current rules were allowed to continue to reign largely because their averages stood alone at the head of the pack. Since 1901, the two major leagues have crowned five batting champs—some say six—with inadequate credentials by current standards. The two American League winners who would not qualify now are Ty Cobb in 1914 and Dale Alexander in 1932. In addition, some current reference works—Baseball-Reference.com among them—credit Nap Lajoie with the 1902 crown even though he had only 352 at-bats and played just 87 games of a 140-game schedule. The three National League champs with far fewer than 3.1 plate appearances per game their teams played are Bubbles Hargrave in 1926, Debs Garms in 1940, and Ernie Lombardi in 1942. Lombardi won with just 309 at-bats, and Hargrave had only 326. Both were catchers, accounting somewhat for the willingness to overlook their skimpy plate totals. Because of the position's harsh demands, catchers have generally been given special dispensation with regard to appearance requirements in determining league leaders. In fact, for many years they were only required to catch half their team's games to qualify for the fielding crown.

Since Lombardi's triumph in 1942, no National League catcher has won a batting title, and only Joe Mauer, with three titles, has won in the

Bubbles Hargrave reached base via a hit, walk or hit by pitch only 144 times in 1926 but won the National League batting title.

American League. But had the same 100-game-minimum rule that governed in 1942 still applied a dozen years later, the 1954 NL batting crown
would have gone to Smoky Burgess, a backstopper with the Philadelphia
Phillies. In 108 games and 345 at-bats, Burgess swatted .368—23 points
better than Willie Mays, the recognized leader in 1954.

The 1954 season saw another batting-title first when a player who
would have won his league's title under the current rule failed to qualify under the standard then in existence. On the surface, this seems an
impossibility. How could a player accumulate 3.1 plate appearances for
every game his team played and yet fail to have enough at bats to qualify
as a leader? And yet, incredibly, it happened.

In 1952, a rule was enacted that a player had to have 2.6 official at-bats
for every game his team played to win a batting title. The rule was still
extant in 1954, when Ted Williams posted a .345 batting average, slugged
at a .635 pace, and had a .516 on-base percentage after he collected 136
walks in just 117 games. But because Williams got so many free passes,
he had only 386 at-bats. His total was 20 short of the 406 he needed to
give him 2.6 at bats for each of the 156 games the Red Sox played, and
the crown instead went to Cleveland's Bobby Avila, who finished the season with a .341 average. Williams was awarded the slugging title, however, largely because his .635 mark was 100 points higher than runner-up
Minnie Minoso.

When Williams's walks, sacrifice hits, and hit by pitches in 1954 are
combined with his at-bats, his total number of plate appearances is far in
excess of the number needed today, let alone in 1954 when the schedule
was eight games shorter.

But although Williams surely felt an injustice had been done to him,
few members of the baseball public were aware of it at the time. By 1954,
most fans were thoroughly befuddled as to what credentials a player
needed to win a batting title. The confusion persisted until expansion
lengthened the schedule to 162 games and made it imperative that a player
whose team played a full slate accumulate at least 502 plate appearances
to qualify as a leader. In 1959, many Clevelanders were baffled when Tito
Francona of the Indians entered the last day of the season with the highest
average in the American League and yet was said by the media to have no
chance to win the batting title even though he was just a couple of at-bats
shy of 400. Only then did Tribe fans discover that at some point (back

in 1957, to be exact) the rule had been changed from 400 at-bats to 3.1 plate appearances for every schedule game. Francona finished with 399 at-bats and a .363 batting average—10 points higher than winner Harvey Kuenn. But since he needed some 30 more plate appearances to meet the minimum standard, his average would have fallen below Kuenn's had the requisite number of plate appearances been added to his total.

One final note: In 1996, Tony Gwynn fell four plate appearances short of the required 502 when injuries held him to just 116 games, but when four hitless plate appearances were added to his total of 498, his .353 mark still finished well ahead of Colorado's Ellis Burks at .344.

9.22 (b)

The individual pitching champion in a Major League shall be the pitcher with the lowest earned-run average, provided that the pitcher has pitched at least as many innings in league championship games as the number of games scheduled for each club in his club's league that season . . .

Before 1951, qualifications for ERA leaders were fuzzy. Generally, any hurler who either hurled 10 complete games or else worked at least 154 innings—the number equaling the amount of games scheduled prior to expansion in 1961—was considered to be a qualifier, but sometimes the ERA champ would be a real eye-opener.

In 1940, after being called up from the minors with less than eight weeks to go in the season, Ernie Bonham of the New York Yankees tossed 10 complete games in 12 starts and compiled a 1.90 ERA, easily good enough to win the crown . . . until someone pointed out that he had pitched only 99⅓ innings. A number of record books recognized Bonham anyway (and a few still do), whereas others gave the honor to Bob Feller, who finished the season with a 2.89 ERA. The unofficial complete-game minimum of 10 was otherwise firm prior to 1952, however, including in 1943 when Howie Pollet was recognized as the NL ERA leader with a 1.75 mark despite having toiled only 118 innings. Incidentally, Baseball-Reference.com continues to recognize Pollet, and not his far more deserving Cardinals teammate Max Lanier, who finished with a 1.90 ERA in

213⅓ innings as the 1943 NL ERA king, while refusing to recognize Bonham as the 1940 AL ERA leader.

Until recently—just once before 1951, when the one inning for each game played by a pitcher's team went into effect—was there an exception to the unofficial complete-game minimum: in 1927, when New York Yankees rookie Wilcy Moore, working as a combination starter-reliever, posted a 2.28 ERA in 213 innings, but had only six complete games in his 12 starts. Ironically, exactly ten years earlier, Fred Anderson of the Giants—who had eight complete games—was not recognized as the 1917 NL ERA champ (though he now is by Baseball-Reference.com) even though he hurled 162 innings and had an ERA 0.39 less than the leader, Pete Alexander. The Moore and Anderson cases pointed up the most serious flaw in the then-existing qualification standards: Unless an exception was arbitrarily made, as in the case of Moore, a pitcher frequently used in relief had no chance to win the award regardless of how many innings he hurled because he could never collect a sufficient number of complete games. Significantly, in 1952, only the second season the new rule was in place, the National League ERA crown went to Hoyt Wilhelm with a 2.43 ERA in 159⅓ innings and 71 games, all in relief. Whether Wilhelm would have been awarded the ERA title if his performance had occurred prior to 1951, we will never know.

Along with embracing the increasing importance of relief pitching, the new rule in 1951 paraded a certain prescience in another way when it made a minimum number of innings pitched the only criterion for eligibility. Were 10 complete games still a criterion, no pitchers would have qualified for an ERA crown since 2011 when Tampa Bay's James Shields became the last pitcher to date to log a double-digit complete-game total with 11.

9.23 Guidelines for Cumulative Performance Records

(b) Consecutive-Game Hitting Streaks

A consecutive-game hitting streak shall not be terminated if all of a batter's plate appearances (one or more) in a game result in a base on balls, hit batsman, defensive interference or obstruction or a sacrifice bunt. The streak shall terminate if the player has a sacrifice fly and no hits. A player's individual consecutive-game hitting streak shall be determined by the consecutive games in which such player appears and is not determined by his club's games.

Rule 9.23 (b) answers whether Joe DiMaggio's 56-game hitting streak in 1941 would have been terminated if he had been unable to play in a game during his skein. It would simply have been put on hold and then resumed when DiMaggio returned to action regardless of how many games he missed. Some other significant hitting streaks have nearly gone unrecognized, though, when their perpetrators sat out games. In 1922, first baseman Ray Grimes of the Chicago Cubs set a then major-league record when he collected at least one RBI in 17 consecutive games. No one was aware of it at the time, not even in Chicago, because the streak did not come in a continuous 17-game stretch—Grimes was idled by a back ailment for nine days in the middle of his skein. But even if his feat had been accomplished in a single 17-game burst, it still might have gone unremarked until long after the fact. In 1922, RBIs had only been an official statistic for two seasons, and as yet few cared all that much about records anyway. When Pete Rose established a new record for career base hits in 1985, virtually the entire sporting world was aware of it, but Ty Cobb's landmark 4,000th hit in 1927 received so little attention that even Cobb failed to realize what he had done until he read about it in the newspaper the following day.

Unrecognized altogether for over half a century was Bill Joyce's record of 69 consecutive games reaching base safely in 1891 as a member of the American Association champion Boston Reds (in what evolved into the AA's final season as a separate major league). Joyce's record, begun in 1890 while with Brooklyn of the Players' League, was tied in 1941 by by Ted Williams (69) and broken by Joe DiMaggio (74), but at that time no one even knew he had held it. Joyce's streak was frozen at 69 when he broke an ankle sliding on July 2, 1891, at Boston in a 12–4 win over Washington. His skein ended on October 3, 1891, his first game back in the lineup after his injury interruption, when he went 0-for-3 in a 6–2 win at Boston over Washington's Kid Carsey.

The current mark is 84 consecutive games, set in 1949 by Ted Williams, the only player in history to compile two such streaks lasting 60 or more games.

9.23 (c) Consecutive-Game Playing Streak

A consecutive-game playing streak shall be extended if a player plays one half-inning on defense or if the player completes a time at bat by reaching base or being put out. A pinchrunning appearance only shall not extend the streak. If a player is ejected from a game by an umpire before such player can comply with the requirements of this Rule 9.23 (c), such player's streak shall continue.

This could almost be called the "Lou Gehrig Rule." In Gehrig's day, there was no formal rule regarding the minimum amount of time a player had to appear in a game to extend a consecutive-game playing streak beyond that his name had to appear in the box score. The present rule was instituted before the 1974 season in conjunction with legislation on what terminates a hitting streak.

One must think that the rulemakers had Gehrig's shadow on their minds when they decreed that a single plate appearance—even in a pinch-hitting role—would not terminate a consecutive-games-played streak, but a pinch-running appearance would. Obviously a pinch-runner is often in a game longer than a pinch-hitter, who may be around for only a single pitch. Gehrig, however, had a day on July 14, 1934, at Detroit when his back was suffering so bothersome a bout with lumbago that it seemed his streak was at an end. Fortunately, New York was on the road, allowing Yankees manager Joe McCarthy to find an ingenious way around Gehrig's temporary disability. On his lineup card that afternoon McCarthy penciled in Gehrig as the Yankees' shortstop and leadoff hitter in place of Red Rolfe.

The record books thus show Gehrig as having played one game at shortstop in 1934, making him one of the rare lefthanders to play a keystone position, even though he never actually served as a short fielder. After opening the game with a single, Gehrig was removed for Rolfe as soon as he touched first base. His streak was thereby preserved, never to be seriously jeopardized again until early in the 1939 season when he began showing symptoms of the incurable neuromuscular disease that would soon claim his life.

Little remembered, however, was that this game just so happened to be the turning point of the season for both clubs. Pinch-running for Gehrig, Rolfe scored the first run of the game as the Yankees took a 4–0 lead after the opening frame. The contest quickly evolved into a free-swinging affair. Heading into the bottom of the ninth, the Yankees led, 11–8, but fell prey to a last-ditch four-run rally that sent the Tigers home with a 12–11 victory, catapulting them into first place ahead of the Yankees by two percentage points. After Detroit won again the following day over the Yanks to take a one-game lead, Mickey Cochrane's club eventually romped home by a seven-game margin.

Gehrig, of course, held the American League record for consecutive games played as well with 2,130, until Cal Ripken Jr. broke both his career and league records on September 6, 1995. The National League record prior to expansion was much more modest, but also took a bizarre twist along the way. Stan Musial, from April 15, 1952 through August 22, 1957, set a new NL record for consecutive games played with 895, break-ing Gus Suhr's old mark of 822 (Musial's skein was subsequently broken by Billy Williams.) But if not for a suspended game, Musial's streak would have ended at 862 games. Musial intended to sit out the second game of the July 21, 1957, doubleheader at Pittsburgh. The *St. Louis Post-Dispatch* reported he had not played because "the combination of the doubleheader and the hot humid weather was too formidable." With one out in the top of the ninth and the Cards ahead, 11–2, Ken Boyer singled and the game was suspended to comply with a Pittsburgh curfew.

When the game was resumed on August 27, Musial immediately pinch-ran for Boyer and then played first base in the bottom of the ninth. The full half inning on defense extended his streak, even though it offi-cially ended after the August 22 game against the Phillies at Connie Mack Stadium in which he tore a muscle and chipped a bone swinging at a pitch from Jack Sanford. The following day, Joe Cunningham replaced Musial at first base.

Definitions of Terms

A BALK is an illegal act by the pitcher with a runner or runners on base, entitling all runners to advance one base.

Imagine a fanatical discussion on the history of the balk rule and its many ramifications. There may have been one, but no inking of it has ever been found. Yet a form of the rule has existed since the Knickerbocker rules of 1845. Spectators and players alike were as confused by it then, as most are now. The current rule book dwells at several different junctures on all the movements a pitcher can make—or fail to make—that constitute a balk. Rather than treat each juncture separately, let's try to abridge our subject by doing a short overview.

We start by saying that the first balk rule in 1845 was created for the same purpose each new version of it has served in the years since. Which is simply to prevent a pitcher from unfairly deceiving a batter or a baserunner so as to keep either or both off balance by enticing the batter to show his hand as to whether a sacrifice bunt or hit-and-run play is in the offing and by curtailing base stealing.

Forty years later, the first season that overhand pitching was universally legalized, the term had already begun to acquire its present meaning. A balk in 1885 occurred in any of the following instances according to then Rule 29:

(1) If the Pitcher, when about to deliver the ball to the bat, while standing within the lines of his position, makes any one of the series of motions he habitually makes in so delivering the ball to the bat, without delivering it. (2) If the ball is held by the Pitcher so long as to delay the game unnecessarily; or, (3) If delivered to the bat by the Pitcher when any part of his person is upon the ground outside the lines of his position.

The second type of violation was a matter of the umpire's judgment, whereas the third referred to the boundaries of the pitcher's box, which in 1885 was a 4 x 6 foot rectangle.

In 1893, the first year that the pitcher's plate was established at its present distance from home plate, a pitcher was judged to have committed a balk if he did any of the following:

1. Made a motion to deliver the ball to the bat without delivering it;
2. Delivered the ball to the bat while his pivot foot was not in contact with the pitcher's plate;
3. Made a motion to deliver the ball to the bat without having his pivot foot in contact with the pitcher's plate; or
4. Held the ball so long as to delay the game unnecessarily.

Before the 1898 season, three more ways for a pitcher to balk were added:

5. Standing in position and making a motion to pitch without having the ball in his possession;
6. Making any motion a pitcher habitually makes to deliver the ball to a batter without immediately delivering it; or
7. Feigning a throw to a base and then not resuming his legal pitching position and pausing momentarily before delivering the ball to the bat.

Contingency 6 might seem unnecessary, since even if a pitcher somehow managed to delude a batter into swinging at a phantom pitch, it could not be counted as a strike. Generally, the ploy was not an effort to dupe the batter, however, but a baserunner for the purpose of getting him to stroll off the bag and then nailing him on the hidden ball trick. Before 1898, a pitcher could pantomime his entire delivery routine without having the ball in his possession. Further restrictions on what a pitcher could do while one of his infielders tried to pull off a hidden ball play were imposed in 1920, bringing the rule closer to 6.02 (a) (7) and 6.02 (a) (9), mandating that a balk be called whenever a pitcher stands empty-handed on or astride the rubber.

But though the 1898 balk amendments took a giant step toward the present rule, there was still one more important stride to be made. It was taken in 1899, when for the first time a balk was assessed if a pitcher threw to a base in an attempt to pick off a runner without first stepping toward that base. Prior to then, pitchers had been free to do just about anything they wished in trying to hold runners close to their bases, including suddenly snapping a throw to a base while looking elsewhere. Helped by the new balk rule, National League teams stole nearly 600 more bases in 1899 than they had the previous year, and the Baltimore Orioles set a modern single-season stolen base mark with 364 thefts. Before 1899, pitchers not only could fake throws to first, they could also twitch their pitching shoulders, swing their legs every which way, and utilize many other maneuvers that are now considered balks.

Until the 1954 season, the ball was dead as soon as a balk occurred. There were no exceptions. Regardless of what happened, the runner or runners on base moved up one rung, a ball was assessed if the pitch had been released, and that was that.

The old rule cost an offensive team on many occasions but none more dearly than in 1949, when it played a hand in deciding the National League pennant race. In a Saturday night game at St. Louis's Sportsman's Park on August 6, the Cardinals had Red Schoendienst aboard and cleanup hitter Nippy Jones at bat with two out in the bottom of the first against the New York Giants. On the mound for the Giants was lefty Adrian Zabala, one of the numerous players banned from Organized Baseball for five years after jumping to the Mexican League at the start of the 1946 season. The ban had been lifted by Commissioner Happy Chandler two months earlier, allowing Zabala to rejoin the Giants, for whom he had last pitched in 1945. During his forced vacation from the majors, he had acquired some bad habits while pitching in the outlaw Provincial League. Working out of the stretch with a runner on first, Zabala was caught in a balk by second-base umpire Jocko Conlan as he delivered the ball to the plate. Jones, not seeing the signal, concentrated only on the pitch and proceeded to belt it into the bleachers for an apparent two-run homer. However, the prevailing rule at the time canceled the four-bagger and allowed the runner to advance only from first to second. Forced to bat over, Jones flied out to end the inning.

Zabala was subsequently charged with two more balks that night, giving him three in the game to tie the then-existing single-game major-league record. But he was otherwise almost completely in command. The Cardinals managed to scratch out only one tally against him after being robbed of Jones's two-run dinger, and lost the game, 3–1. Had that defeat wound up in the victory column instead, St. Louis would have finished the 1949 season in a tie with Brooklyn, forcing a best two-of-three pennant playoff.

In a final note of irony, Zabala won just two games in 1949 and never again pitched in the majors.

For all the attention lavished on fine-tuning the various references to balks in the rule book, we are still left to inquire if a pitcher can be charged with a balk if something totally out of his control occurs to interrupt his delivery with men on base. The perfect pitcher to ask would have been Stu Miller. In the first of two All-Star Games in 1961, on July 11 at San Francisco's Candlestick Park, Miller held a 3–1 lead for the National League stars in the top of the ninth when he ran afoul of the infamous "'Stick wind." With runners on second and third, Miller all of a sudden felt himself being blown off the mound as he prepared to deliver the ball. After the second American League run came home on the balk, the tying tally crossed moments later when the gusting wind spun a roller out of third baseman Ken Boyer's grasp.

The Americans went ahead, 4–3, with another wind-aided run in the top of the 10th, but then fell victim themselves to the elements. In the bottom of the frame, the NL rallied for two runs when the wind sabotaged Hoyt Wilhelm's knuckleball and made it easy pickings for first Hank Aaron and Willie Mays and then Roberto Clemente, whose single drove home Mays from second with the winning run.

Despite committing the most famous balk in a midsummer classic and giving up three runs in the 1⅔ innings he worked in relief, Miller got credit for the victory.

The rule that a pitcher, following his stretch, must come to a complete stop before making his delivery was intended to prevent pitchers from quick-pitching in order to hold runners closer to their bases, but through the years it has meant chaos each time a campaign is waged to enforce it to the letter.

In 1950, when it was first expressly stated that a pitcher had to pause a full second after his stretch with a runner on base, 88 balks were called in the first two weeks of the Triple-A Pacific Coast League season after there had only been 54 balks in the two major leagues combined the previous year. Nonetheless, prior to expansion in 1961, the post-1893 record for the most balks in a season belonged to three pitchers with six apiece, last done by Vic Raschi in 1950. Another crackdown in the late 1970s saw Frank Tanana set a new American League single-season record for balks in 1978 with eight and Steve Carlton shatter the National League mark the following year by committing 11. In 1984, with enforcement of the complete-stop rule again more relaxed, Tanana tied for the AL lead in balks with just four and Carlton and Dwight Gooden shared the NL balk title with seven. Then, four years later, MLB moguls decided umpires were not uniformly calling balks and changed Rule 8.01 (b) from:

The pitcher, following his stretch, must (a) hold the ball in both hands in front of his body and (b) come to a complete stop; to:

The pitcher, following his stretch, must (a) hold the ball in both hands in front of his body, and (b) come to a single complete and discernible stop, with both feet on the ground.

The difference between the two rules is that the 1988 version replaced "complete stop" with "single complete and discernible stop, with both feet on the ground." This slight change, designed to make balk calls uniform, instead kindled one of the most exasperating springs ever experienced by major league pitchers. Just six weeks after Opening Day in 1988, the Braves' Rick Mahler perpetrated the 357th balk of that season, setting a new MLB record for most balks in an *entire* season, and it was only the middle of May! Not long afterward, Yankees skipper Billy Martin threatened to upset the applecart by having his pitchers come to a complete stop for five minutes between pitches. By the time the rule was once again relaxed after it threatened to make the game a travesty—junior circuit hurlers alone were assessed an all-time record 557 balks in 1988—A's ace Dave Stewart had committed 16 balks, still the ML season record, and Rod Scurry of the Pirates racked up 11 in only 31⅓ innings, effectively destroying his bid to come back from a year in the minors after becoming involved with cocaine.

The culprit for the sudden balks explosion was thought without any evidence to support it to be then Commissioner Bart Giamatti, Pete Rose's nemesis. Whether Giamatti, who banned Rose for gambling on baseball games, was the driving force that propelled balk totals through the roof in 1988 is still a matter of conjecture today, but all individual, team and league balks records set that season still stand and are highly unlikely to be seriously threatened in the near future.

A BASE ON BALLS is an award of first base granted to a batter who, during his time at bat, receives four pitches outside the strike zone or following a signal from the defensive team's manager to the umpire that he intends to intentionally walk the batter. If the manager informs the umpire of this intention, the umpire shall award the batter first base as if the batter had received four pitches outside the strike zone.

Alexander Cartwright and his cohorts made no reference in their playing rules to a base on balls. The omission exists because until 1863 there was no such thing in baseball as a free trip to first base. To reach base, a player had to hit the ball, even if it took 50 pitches before he got one to his liking.

In the 1863 season, both balls and strikes were called for the first time, with a batter being granted his base after receiving three pitches that were adjudged balls. However, before an umpire was permitted to call a pitch a ball, he was first obliged to warn a pitcher an unspecified number of times for not delivering "fair" pitches or for delaying the game. In essence, far more than three pitches had to be delivered outside the strike zone before a batter received a walk.

In 1874, umpires were instructed to call a ball on every third unfair pitch delivered, meaning that nine balls in all were needed to draw a walk, though technically it came after three called balls. The rule was again amended five years later, allowing umpires to call every unfair pitch a ball until nine were reached. In 1880, a walk was pared to eight called balls and then to seven the following year.

The 1884 season saw the National League shrink the number of balls needed for a walk to six, but the American Association still required seven balls. In 1886, the AA dropped to six balls, only to have the NL again demand seven. The two leagues adopted a uniform code of rules in 1887, including a reduction to five balls. Finally, in 1889, the figure was set at four, where it has remained ever since.

In 1879, the last year that nine balls were required to walk, Charley Jones, at the time the game's leading slugger, topped the National League with just 29 free passes, and there were only 508 walks issued throughout the loop. The league total more than doubled in 1881, when a walk came after six balls, and the figure continued to climb all during the 1880s—peaking in 1889—the first year that a batter could stroll to first base after only four called balls. That season, National League pitchers handed out 3,612 free tickets, 1,519 more than in 1888.

*The **BATTER'S BOX** is the area within which the batter shall stand during his time at bat.*

Cartwright *et al* also made no reference to batter's boxes in their playing rules. In all forms of baseball prior to 1874, a batter had to stand with either his forward foot or his back foot on a line drawn across the center of the home-plate area. If a batter struck a pitch without having a foot on the line, the umpire simply called the resulting blow "no hit" and called the batter back to the plate. There was no other penalty.

The 1874 season introduced a 6 x 3 foot rectangular box for the hitter to occupy, thereafter known as the "batter's box." The dimensions were increased to the present 6 x 4 in 1886.

Unlike the early game, nowadays when a batter steps out of the box—causing a pitcher to pause in the middle of his delivery—the plate umpire will not call a balk. Instead, the arbiter will just signal that time is out and then resume the game as if the incident had not occurred. If in the umpire's judgment the disruption was deliberate, he can take further action, including tossing the batter out of the game.

Before 1957, as a pitcher was about to deliver the ball, a batter was free to step out of the box and take his chances. The absence of an equivalent to current Rule 5.10 (f) opened the door to incidents like the one in Rule 5.10 (f) that occurred in a 1952 Western International League game. It also enabled a batter to try a ruse that is now regarded as unsportsmanlike conduct and may result in the transgressor being called out. With a runner on third base a batter in earlier times could drop his bat as the pitcher went into his windup in an effort to induce a run-scoring balk.

By the way, there is still nothing in the rule book to say that a player must have a bat in his hands as he awaits a pitch. Three is not even an edict that he has to be accompanied by a bat when he steps into the batter's box.

A BUNT is a batted ball not swung at, but intentionally met with the bat and tapped slowly within the infield.

Hits that we now call bunts were originally known as "baby" hits. No one has a clue who coined the term "bunt." It is even impossible to say for certain who laid down the first deliberate bunt. Some historians credit the gambit to Dickey Pearce, a stocky little shortstop active from the mid-1850s until 1877. A weak hitter even against underhand pitching, Pearce learned to bunt out of necessity, but whether he was the first to master the art will always be arguable.

*A **CATCH** is the act of a fielder in getting secure possession in his hand or glove of a ball in flight and firmly holding it; providing he does not use his cap, protector, pocket or any other part of his uniform in getting possession. It is not a catch, however, if simultaneously or immediately following his contact with the ball, he collides with a player, or with a wall, or if he falls down, and as a result of such collision or falling, drops the ball. It is not a catch if a fielder touches a fly ball which then hits a member of the offensive team or an umpire and then is caught by another defensive player. In establishing the validity of the catch, the fielder shall hold the ball long enough to prove that he has complete control of the ball and that his release of the ball is voluntary and intentional. If the fielder has made the catch and drops the ball while in the act of making a throw following the catch, the ball shall be adjudged to have been caught.*

(Catch) Comment: A catch is legal if the ball is finally held by any fielder, even though juggled, or held by another fielder before it touches the ground. Runners may leave their bases the instant the first fielder touches the ball. A fielder may reach over a fence, railing, rope or other line of demarcation to make a catch. He may jump on top of a railing, or canvas that may be in foul ground. No interference should be allowed when a fielder reaches over a fence, railing, rope or into a stand to catch a ball. He does so at his own risk.

If a fielder, attempting a catch at the edge of the dugout, is "held up" and kept from an apparent fall by a player or players of either team and the catch is made, it shall be allowed.

A runner was not permitted to tag up and try to advance on a caught fly ball until 1859. Until then, an "air" ball was dead as soon as it was caught and remained dead until it was back in the pitcher's hands. But the 1859 amendment merely said that such balls were no longer dead. Four years later, the rule put into words that a baserunner had the right to advance after returning to his original base as soon as the ball had been "settled into the hands of a fielder."

For many years the phrase "settled into the hands of a fielder" spelled trouble, especially for some umpires who took it to mean that a ball had to be firmly secured before a runner was free to tag up and advance. A number of outfielders became deft at juggling routine fly balls in order to hold a runner to his base while they jogged toward the infield until they were close enough to throw the runner out if he attempted to advance a base. Tommy McCarthy was supposedly a whiz at this trick when he patrolled the outfield with Hugh Duffy for the great Boston Beaneaters teams of the 1890s. But if McCarthy and other gardeners of his era were really so crafty, why was this apparent loophole not sealed up while they were still active (McCarthy, for one, finished in 1896)? In 1897, a rule at long last was created to thwart McCarthy et al, but only on balls that an umpire judged were juggled intentionally . . . not always easy to determine. In actuality, it was only in 1920 that the rule was finally altered to explicitly allow a runner to advance on a fly ball as soon as it touched a fielder, regardless of whether or not it was held secure. Meanwhile, two years earlier, a batting title was decided, owing largely to two umpires who were unfamiliar with the 1897 rule. But more about that in a moment.

Since the adoption of the 1920 amendment, on many occasions runners have advanced two and sometimes even three bases on a fly when an outfielder has juggled the ball or else fallen down or crashed into a wall after making a catch. At times a sacrifice fly has scored more than one run even though no errors or mishaps occurred on the play. Rocky Colavito, reputed to have one of the strongest arms in history, was once so victimized. Playing right field for Cleveland in the second game of a doubleheader with the Chicago White Sox on August 30, 1959, Colavito decided to showcase his arm in the top of the second inning on Barry Latman's fly ball to deep right with John Romano on third and Al Smith on second. Knowing that Romano, a slow runner, would tag at third and try to score, Colavito put his all into a heave homeward and to his embarrassment saw the speedy Smith tally right behind Romano when his throw rainbowed and seemed to hang suspended in the air forever before it finally descended after both White Sox runners had crossed the plate.

As for the controversial batting title, it emanated from a game at Cincinnati on April 29, 1918, involving the Reds and the Cardinals. In *The Complete Book of Forfeited and Successfully Protested Major League Games*, Nemec and Miklich profile the key event, a deep fly ball to Reds center fielder Edd Roush in the top of the eighth inning of a 3–3 game with one out and Bert Niehoff of the Cards on third base. Niehoff tagged up at third, expecting to score the go-ahead run after Roush made the catch.

But the *Cincinnati Enquirer* reported that "just as [Roush] reached the ball he stumbled and fell to the ground. The sphere bounced out of his glove as he fell, but Edd twisted around and caught it in one hand as he hit the sward."

Niehoff had left third base as soon as Roush touched the ball, and crossed the plate standing up. But Roush rose and threw the ball to second baseman Lee Magee, who fired it to third "where Heinie Groh was hollering for the ball. Groh tagged the bag and then appealed to umpire-in-chief [Hank] O'Day, who ruled that Neihoff had left third before the catch was completed and was thereupon the third out rather than the go-ahead run. The *Enquirer* said, "Hank's decision on this play was a most unusual one, but eminently correct under the rules."

Center fielder Edd Roush cost himself the 1918 National League batting crown when he caught a fly ball. Had he dropped it instead, as events played out for the remainder of the season he would have won the title.

The *St. Louis Post-Dispatch* was not so sure, especially after Cards skipper Jack Hendricks announced he was playing the game under protest when he failed to convince O'Day's partner, [Bill] Byron, that Neihoff had every right to vacate third the instant the ball first touched Roush's glove. It concluded: "It was a peculiar tangle, one that is now up to President [John] Tener to decide which is right, Manager Hendricks or Umpire Hank O'Day," upon learning that Hendricks had made good on his threat and filed a formal protest immediately after the Reds tallied a run with two out in the bottom of the ninth off Cards starter Lee Meadows to win, 4–3.

On Sunday, May 12, Tener notified Cardinals president Branch Rickey that Hendricks's protest had been allowed and the game of April 29 would have to be replayed in its entirety. Tener's decision was based principally on O'Day's frank admission that Neihoff had waited until the ball first touched Roush's glove, but O'Day continued, wrongly, to maintain that "he should have remained on the sack until Roush entirely completed the catch."

Plate umpire O'Day's ignorance of the 1897 rule that favored the runner—even when a ball was not blatantly juggled intentionally (compounded by base umpire Byron's ignorance of it as well)—is appalling coming from one umpire with over more than two decades of major-league service and another who was a future Hall of Famer. As for Roush, writer/researcher Tom Ruane discovered that his protested catch and assist on the inning-ending double play in essence cost him the NL batting title. He went 2-for-3 in the disallowed game. When it was replayed as the second game of a doubleheader on August 11, he got only one hit in four at-bats. Had the protested game not been thrown out, Roush would have finished with a .336 BA, one point ahead of the actual crown wearer, Brooklyn's Zack Wheat, and five points ahead of Wheat if another protested game in 1918 (in which Wheat went 0-for-5) had not also been thrown out.

A considerably more famous debatable catch occurred seven years later in a World Series game. The rules as to what constitutes a legal catch make it clear that if an outfielder sees that a batted ball is headed for home run territory and catches it after jumping into the stands, it will still be a home run. If, however, he *falls* into the stands when jumping to make a catch, it will count as an out provided he catches and holds onto the ball. Any runners who are on base at the time will be allowed to advance one base.

The umpire can only make an educated guess sometimes whether an outfielder who disappears into the crowd in pursuit of a ball actually caught it. Probably the most classic example of an arbiter who was put in this unenviable spot came on October 10, 1925, during Game Three of the World Series between the Washington Senators and Pittsburgh Pirates, played at Washington's Griffith Stadium—where temporary bleachers had been installed in right-center field to provide added seating. In the top of the eighth, with two out and the Senators ahead, 4–3, Pittsburgh catcher Earl Smith laced a long drive toward the temporary seats off Senators reliever Firpo Marberry. Washington right fielder Sam Rice (who had been moved from center to right earlier in the game) raced back for it, jumped to his limit, and toppled into the seats. For some 15 seconds Rice was lost to view, but at last he emerged from the crowd, holding the ball triumphantly over his head. Umpire Cy Rigler ruled it a catch, and thus began a furious argument. Eventually even Pittsburgh owner Barney Dreyfuss bowled through the crowd of players on the field to make his voice heard in the protest. Commissioner Judge Kenesaw Mountin Landis, in attendance, was at last persuaded to confer with Rice, hoping for clear directions, but Rice would only say, "The umpire said I caught it."

In the end Rigler's ruling stood for the lack of any contradictory evidence, and the Pirates lost the game, 4–3. Ironically, the game had earlier featured a sixth-inning home run by Washington's Goose Goslin that *bounced* into the temporary stands. Rice lived nearly fifty more years without ever saying anything more definite about his play on Smith's long drive than he had offered on October 10, 1924. It seemed that his epitaph would be: "The umpire said he caught it." When Rice passed away, however, it emerged that he had left behind a letter to be opened upon his death. The letter averred that he had made the catch but provided no explanation for why he had refused to settle the issue while he was still alive.

*A **DOUBLEHEADER** is two regularly scheduled or rescheduled games, played in immediate succession.*

On September 9, 1876, the Hartford Blues and Cincinnati Red Stockings played two games against each other in the same day, the first such occurrence in National League history. But the pair of games was not a doubleheader in the strict sense. The first contest took place in the morning and then, after a dinner break, a second game was played in the afternoon. The first true major league doubleheader, wherein two games were played in immediate succession, came on September 25, 1882, when the Providence Grays split a pair at Worcester just four days before the Massachusetts club played its final game as a member of the National

League. Worcester's 4–3 win over Charley Radbourn in the first game of the September 25 twin bill was the last victory by a team representing that city in a major league.

Technically, purists insist the first doubleheader was a morning-afternoon affair that occurred at Boston on July 4, 1873, between the pennant-winning Red Stockings and the Elizabeth Resolutes, the weakest entry in the National Association that season. Amazingly, the New Jersey team—which left the loop a month later with a horrific 2–20 record—won the morning contest, 11–2, over Al Spalding, universally regarded as the top pitcher in the 1871–75 NA era.

As is still true in most minor leagues, the second game of a doubleheader was often scheduled for only seven innings in both major leagues prior to World War I. Much of the reason for the abbreviated second contest was because games in those days often did not start until mid-afternoon, making it a constant challenge to end before darkness. None of the parks as yet had lights, nor had Daylight Savings Time yet been imposed in the summer months. It need be mentioned that a number of seven-inning no-hitters that once were counted as complete-game no-nos are no longer listed among no-hit games because they went less than nine innings.

*A **FORCE PLAY** is a play in which a runner legally loses his right to occupy a base by reason of the batter becoming a runner.*

Even veteran umpires can be momentarily stymied as to whether a play is a force play. One such moment occurred in a June 28, 1998, interleague clash between the Mets and Yankees at Shea Stadium. With the game tied, 1–1, in the bottom of the ninth with one out, Carlos Baerga was on third and Brian McRae on first for the Mets. Baerga tagged up when pinch-hitter Luis Lopez skied a fly ball to Paul O'Neill in deep right. Recognizing that he had no chance to get the winning run at the plate, O'Neill simply lobbed the ball toward the infield after making the catch. But shortstop Derek Jeter noticed that McRae was almost standing on second base and winged the ball to Tino Martinez at first to double up McRae. The umpires then had to confer before ruling that Baerga's winning run counted because, in their estimation, he crossed the plate before Jeter's throw reached Martinez and McRae had not been retired on a force play. At the time there was no rule allowing video replay to confirm their decision.

If umpires are occasionally confused about this rule, players are even less informed on its complications. On June 10, 2010, in a night game at Minnesota's Target Field between the Twins and Kansas City Royals, the home team had Denard Span on second and Nick Punto on third with one out in the bottom of the third inning when Joe Mauer hit a shot to deep center. Punto properly tagged up at third and started for home when Royals center fielder Mitch Maier caught the ball at the base of the fence. But Span, thinking the ball would hit the fence, took off at full tilt and was nearly at third when Punto glanced back and saw Maier make the catch. Punto yelled at Span to get back to second and then slowed to a jog upon realizing it was too late and that Span would be doubled off second for the third out. When Span was indeed doubled off, Punto was still a few yards short of the plate. Few in the park, least of all Punto, knew that he would have scored a run that counted had he crossed the plate before Span was retired. Even many sportswriters in attendance had to look up the rule later on after Kansas City won the game in 10 innings, 9–8.

Punto is somewhat unfairly singled out here; his mistake is a common one and often goes undetected by fellow players, sportswriters, managers, and broadcasters alike.

A *FOUL BALL is a batted ball that settles on foul territory between home and first base, or between home and third base, or that bounds past first or third base on or over foul territory, or that first falls on foul territory beyond first or third base, or that, while on or over foul territory, touches the person of an umpire or player, or any object foreign to the natural ground.*

A foul fly shall be judged according to the relative position of the ball and the foul line, including the foul pole, and not as to whether the infielder is on foul or fair territory at the time he touches the ball.

Prior to the twentieth century, a ball hit foul by a batter with less than two strikes was not deemed a strike. As a result, the American League record for the highest batting average was established in a season when the new loop did not yet recognize the foul strike rule. In 1901, while Nap Lajoie was hitting .426 to set an AL mark that looks unbreakable, the National League for the first time was counting any pitch fouled off by a batter with fewer than two strikes as a strike. The AL did not grudgingly follow suit until two years later. Hence Lajoie's record—already suspect because the AL in 1901 was operating for the first time as a major league and many of its teams were stocked with marginal players—was further tainted by the fact that he was not charged, as were NL players that year, with a strike for hitting a foul ball.

In 1901, the AL outhit the NL by 10 points and upped the margin of difference to 16 points in 1902. The following year, the first in which both leagues counted foul balls as strikes, the NL outhit the AL by 14 points, seeming to support the argument that hitters had appeared to be superior in the AL during the previous two campaigns only because they were given the equivalent of an extra strike or two in many of their at-bats.

The history of the foul pole is a story unto itself. In the nineteenth century, although some parks had foul poles, there was no rule that one had to be equipped with them to help umpires determine whether a batted ball leaving the park was fair or foul. There was only this: "When a batted ball passes outside the grounds, the umpire shall declare it fair should it disappear within, or foul should it disappear outside of the range of the foul lines."

Not until 1931 did the rule book say: "When a batted ball passes outside the playing field the umpire shall decide it fair or foul according to where it leaves the playing field." By that time, there were foul poles in all major-league parks to help umpires gauge whether a ball was fair or foul as it left the park. Where it eventually landed was no longer of any relevance.

So how important are foul poles? In Pittsburgh's final game of 1908, a makeup at Chicago on October 4 of an earlier tie game, the Pirates' Ed Abbaticchio hit what appeared to some spectators to be a two-run homer in the top of the ninth into the right-field stands at Chicago's West Side Park off a tiring Three Finger Brown to bring the Corsairs within one run of Chicago. But with no foul pole to guide him, Hank O'Day ruled the ball foul. Abbaticchio then struck out, Chicago won, 5–2, and the Cubs claimed the pennant three days later after winning a makeup contest for the famous Merkle tie game against the Giants by a one-game margin over the Pirates and the New York club. A female spectator later sued the Cubs for damages alleging that she was struck by Abbaticchio's blast and swore the ball had been fair, citing the area she had occupied. But she made a hazy witness under interrogation and her claim was denied. Had it been true and ruled a home run on October 4, 1908, if Pittsburgh had won this game, Fred Merkle would be nothing more than a journeyman first baseman today and O'Day would have umpired his last game of the season and perhaps not reside now in the Hall of Fame, for Pittsburgh would have won the 1908 National League pennant with a 99–55 record.

An **INNING** *is that portion of a game within which the teams alternate on offense and defense and in which there are three putouts for each team. Each team's time at bat is a half-inning.*

No one can answer who first brought the term "inning" to baseball. In his original playing rules, Alexander Cartwright made no mention of innings, calling a team's stint at bat a "hand" and stipulating that even after one club achieved 21 runs or aces, a game could not end until an equal number of hands had been played. In Cartwright's day, however, it was already common parlance to say a nine must be given its innings. The word inning is thought to have been borrowed from cricket and to signify a period of prosperity or luck. Certainly every team, from the dawn of baseball history, has looked to prosper when it took its turn at bat, but inning actually predates cricket and comes from the old English "innung," which meant a taking in or a putting in.

INTERFERENCE
(a) Offensive interference is an act by the team at bat which interferes with, obstructs, impedes, hinders or confuses any fielder attempting to make a play.
(b) Defensive interference is an act by a fielder that hinders or prevents a batter from hitting a pitch.
(c) Umpire's interference occurs
  (1) when a plate umpire hinders, impedes or prevents a catcher's throw attempting to prevent a stolen base or retire a runner on a pick-off play, or
  (2) when a fair ball touches an umpire on fair territory before passing a fielder.
(d) Spectator interference occurs when a spectator (or an object thrown by the spectator) hinders a player's attempt to make a play on a live ball, by going onto the playing field, or reaching out of the stands and over the playing field.

Of the four types of interference, spectator interference—especially on a fly ball—was the last to be specifically addressed in the rule book. This hazard did not appear there until 1954. That was the first season in which an umpire was licensed to declare a batter out on a foul or fair fly even when the ball was not caught, if in his judgment a fielder would have made the catch had a spectator not hindered the play. The key word here is judgment. Baltimore fans seated in the right field stands in Game One of the 1996 ALCS on October 9 at Yankee Stadium took vehement exception with right-field umpire Rich Garcia when Orioles gardener Tony Tarasco camped under Derek Jeter's long fly to right in the bottom of the eighth inning and then watched helplessly as twelve-year-old Jeffrey Maier leaned over the outfield wall and spiked the ball into the stands. After seeing a postgame TV replay, Garcia acknowledged that he been wrong in awarding Jeter a home run to help give the Yankees a come-from-behind 5–4 victory, but AL president Gene Budig nonetheless denied Baltimore's protest.

Seven years later, in Game Six of the NLCS on October 14, 2003, at Wrigley Field, Cubs loyalists nearly rioted when several spectators tried to snatch the Marlins' Luis Castillo's long foul fly down the left-field line in the top of the eighth inning that Cubs left fielder Moises Alou appeared to have lined up for a catch. Even though left-field umpire Mike Everitt ruled no fan interference, the blame after Alou failed to make the catch soon settled eternally on Chicagoan Steve Bartman when the Marlins rallied from a 3–0 deficit after Castillo reached on a walk and eventually won, 8–3, forcing a Game Seven. In both of these instances, the team that fell prey in front of millions of TV viewers to possible fan interference that was not then reviewable went on to lose the LCS and the pennant. For those of our readers who don't yet know, the Cubs gave Bartman a World Series ring in 2016 after breaking the 108-year drought since

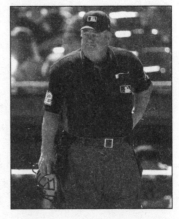

Joe West celebrated his record forty-first year in blue in 2019 and is second only to Bill Klem in the number of major league games he has officiated. In 2020, he in all likelihood will surpass Klem's mark of 5,375 games.

their last world championship in 1908 and Bartman in turn broke his thirteen-year public silence since the incident.

Even though possible fan interference is reviewable now, events with game-changing and even postseason outcome implications still occur that are beyond the current scope of video review and may always be so.

A quintessential example came on October 17 2018, in Game Four of the ALCS at Houston. In the bottom of the first with a runner aboard and the Astros down, 2–0, Jose Altuve rifled a shot to deep right field that Boston right fielder Mookie Betts got in his sights at the base of the right field wall after a long chase. But when Betts leapt to make the catch, his glove was jostled by a spectator and the ball escaped his grasp and went into the stands for an apparent two-run homer. Right-field umpire Joe West promptly took the two runs off the board by ruling that Betts's glove had been interfered with before it had crossed the railing above the wall. Houston fans in the immediate vicinity vigorously booed the call. A video review of the play was inconclusive because the view from the one camera angle in the right-field corner that would have clearly captured the location of Betts's glove at the moment of spectator impact was blocked by other spectators who were on their feet to better observe the play. Consequently, West's decision—even though many observers maintained he was poorly stationed to make the call—was perforce allowed to stand because there was insufficient evidence to overturn it. It would likewise have stood if he had ruled Altuve's blast a home run. As it was, Houston lost the game, 8–6, and eventually the series, four games to one. As for West, he celebrated his record forty-first year in blue in 2019 and is second only to Bill Klem in the number of major-league games he has officiated. In 2020, he in all likelihood will surpass Klem's mark of 5,375.

THE LEAGUE is a group of clubs whose teams play each other in a pre-arranged schedule under these rules [of baseball] for the league championship.

The first baseball teams to band together and play under the rules of the game—then in existence for a so-called "league championship"—were a group of sixteen New York clubs who gathered in 1857 to form the National Association of Base Ball Clubs. The fledgling loop played its games at the Fashion Race Course in Jamaica, New York, assessed spectators a 50-cent admission fee, and adopted the nine-inning format to replace the old first-team-to-score-21-runs-wins rule. All the players in the NABC were simon-pure amateurs, however, or at least that was the circuit's claim; the notion of openly paying players to perform for one's team was still more than a decade away from being popularly accepted.

The first all-professional league did not organize until 1871. Calling itself the National Association, it fielded nine teams and played its first game on May 4, 1871, with Cleveland (Forest Citys) facing Fort Wayne (Kekiongas) at Fort Wayne. The Fort Wayne club played just 19 championship contests before it folded, and no team played more than 33. By 1875, its last year of existence, the NA had swollen to fourteen teams, but only the top three—the Boston Red Stockings, Hartford Blues, and Philadelphia Athletics—played anywhere near a complete schedule. Rife with weak clubs, corrupt players, and lackadaisical team officials, the loop gave way the following season to a new circuit that christened itself the National League, and has remained alive under that name ever since.

A LIVE BALL is a ball which is in play.

BUT can more than one live ball be in play? Oh, yes. Throughout the rule book there is much discussion and many comments about what can happen while a ball is in play, but all of them skirt one of the umpire's greatest nightmares: a situation in which there is *more* than one ball in play. Perhaps the most memorable occasion when this occurred came on June 30, 1959, in a game at Wrigley Field between the St. Louis Cardinals and Chicago Cubs. With one out in the fourth inning, Stan Musial of the Cardinals walked on a pitch that hit Cubs catcher Sammy Taylor and home-plate umpire Vic Delmore, and then skipped to the backstop.

Taylor thought the pitch had ticked Musial's bat for strike two and began to argue with Delmore. When Musial saw that Taylor was otherwise absorbed, he rounded first and headed for second. Realizing what was afoot, Cubs third baseman Al Dark sped to the backstop to retrieve the ball. But before he could reach it, a batboy picked it up and flipped it to field announcer Pat Pieper. Surprised by the toss, Pieper muffed it and the ball bounded toward Dark, who scooped it up and flung it to shortstop Ernie Banks covering second base.

Taylor, meanwhile, had absently been given a second ball by Delmore as the two continued to argue. Cubs pitcher Bob Anderson, by then also part of the debate, grabbed the ball from Taylor when he saw Musial streaking for second and threw it over Banks's head into center field. Musial, who had slid into the bag, picked himself up when he saw the wild heave thinking he had third base cold. But to Musial's dismay, with almost the first step he took off second, Dark's throw arrived at the bag, and before he could retreat Banks put the tag on him.

After a 10-minute delay while all four umpires—Delmore, Al Barlick, Bill Jackowski, and Shag Crawford—conferred, Musial was ruled out. The Cardinals lodged a protest, but it was withdrawn when they won the game, 4–1. We will never know what the ruling would have been had they lost.

The pitcher's **PIVOT FOOT** *is that foot which is in contact with the pitcher's plate as he delivers the pitch.*

Prior to the 1887 season, there was no such designation as a pitcher's pivot foot and prior to 1893 there were no pitcher's plates. As of 1887, the first season that the National League and American Association agreed to play by the same rules, the pitcher's box was 5½ feet long (home to second) by 4 feet wide. Before delivering the ball, pitchers were required to have one foot on the back line of the pitcher's box at all times, face the batter, hold the ball so the umpire could see it, and were allowed only one step or stride in their delivery. The pitching distance was now 55½ feet from the rear line of the pitcher's box to the center of home base, but the front line was still 50 feet to the center of home base as it had been since 1881, thereby restricting a pitcher's single stride forward to 5½ feet—a distance greater than most pitchers could manage with a single step. Hence most were no longer pitching 50 feet distant from the plate but as much as a foot or so more. Each corner of the pitcher's box still retained either a 6-inch square iron plate or a stone marker.

In 1893, the pitcher's box was abolished and replaced with a whitened rubber "pitcher's plate," that measured 12 inches (third to first) by 4 inches and lay even with the playing surface. The back of the pitcher's plate was centered on an imaginary line drawn from the intersection of the third and first base foul lines to the center of second base. The new pitching distance of 60-feet, six inches was measured from the front of the pitcher's plate to the intersection of the third and first base foul lines. The pitcher was required to keep his rear foot in contact with the rubber when he released the ball, but many hurlers found ways to fudge that requirement, especially when only one umpire was working the game. Some, like Pittsburgh's Frank Killen, kicked dirt over the rubber, hiding it from view, and then pitched from several inches in front of it. Since the vast majority of games in the mid-1890s still had only one umpire, violations like Killen's were seldom caught.

*A **QUICK RETURN** pitch is one made with obvious intent to catch a batter off balance. It is an illegal pitch. Rule 6.02 (a) (5) Comment describes it in detail: A quick pitch is an illegal pitch. Umpires will judge a quick pitch as one delivered before the batter is reasonably set in the batter's box. With runners on base the penalty is a balk; with no runners on base, it is a ball. The quick pitch is dangerous and should not be permitted.*

Ever since 1887, when a pitcher first had to anchor his back foot before delivering the ball to the batter, there has been a rule of one sort or another against quick-pitching a batter, though it has not always been deemed a balk. In most cases, the pitch was disallowed. Babe Ruth once benefited enormously from such a judgment. In the final game of the 1928 World Series, the New York Yankees and St. Louis Cardinals were knotted at 1–1 in the top of the seventh when Ruth stepped into the box. Ruth already had one homer on the day, accounting for the Yankees' only run. Lefty Bill Sherdel was on the hill for St. Louis. After getting two strikes on Ruth, Sherdel slipped a pitch past the Babe that everyone in St. Louis' Sportsman's Park thought should have been a called third strike. But plate umpire Cy Pfirman, a National League official during the regular season, waved it off, saying it had been agreed before the Series that there would be no "quick returns"—pitches that were unacceptable in the American League but condoned by National League arbiters. Given a reprieve, Ruth clubbed a home run and Lou Gehrig followed with another four-bagger to put the game out of the Cardinals' reach.

Quick pitching is seldom called by an umpire at the major-league level anymore, even though it's been used on occasion in the past few years. But before the 1887 pitching rule change described earlier under **Pivot Foot** it was a staple of a number of prominent pitchers. Perhaps its leading exponent was southpaw Ed Morris—especially when he was caught by Fred Carroll. The pair were batterymates for seven seasons in the majors, beginning with Columbus of the American Association in 1884 and subsequently with Pittsburgh entries in three different leagues (the American Association, the National League, and the Players' League). They mastered the quick pitch to a point where as soon as Morris's delivery struck his mitt, Carroll would wing the ball back to Morris and the lefty would snag it barehanded and instantaneously fire it in again. In the days before advanced scouting, hitters seeing Morris for the first time were intimidated by this type of pitching. The two batterymates were also among the best of their time at holding runners; Morris had an excellent pickoff move (albeit no doubt an illegal one nowadays) and Carroll an extremely swift release on steal attempts.

In its early years, the National League put the batter at an even larger handicap to avoid being quick-pitched. Writer/researcher Richard Hershberger found the following discussion in the May 20, 1877, *Chicago Tribune* regarding an interlude the day before in a game between Chicago and St. Louis, which featured George Bradley and Cal McVey working the points for Chicago in its 7–1 win.

> A question of rules arose yesterday which should not cause a moment's doubt . . . It is well known that Bradley [pitcher] and McVey [catcher] have at times a trick of sending the ball back and forward with lightning rapidity . . . Yesterday they were putting [Jack] Remsen through this exercise, when he had two strikes in succession called and utterly losing his head he demanded "time" without alleging any reason, but clearly because he was being outwitted. The fact is, he didn't know whether his head was under his arm or where it was, and he wanted to collect himself . . . The new clause of Sec. 7, Rule 2, which was introduced to cover such causes, is: "The umpire shall suspend play only for a valid reason, and is not empowered to do so for trivial causes at the request of a player." It can hardly be said to come within this rule to stop play to throw the other side off their balance, or to give time to a rattled player to collect his thoughts. It is doubtful whether any excuse can be found for Remsen's conduct in standing astride of the plate so as to stop the game until he got ready to have it go on again.

Unfortunately, little discussion of early-day quick pitch exponents can elsewhere be found.

*A **RETOUCH** is the act of a runner in returning to a base as legally required.*

This rule is seldom strictly enforced on a long foul ball down the line that, say, sends a runner on first base scampering almost to third before it is called foul so long as the runner passes in the neighborhood of second in returning to first. In any case, any missed base or failure to tag it is an appeal play by the defense; the umpire cannot initiate it. Nor can the team on defense initiate an appeal once the next pitch has been thrown. In the event a runner on any base does not tag his base of origin after a foul ball has been hit, he cannot be thrown out on an appeal in any case because the umpire-in-chief cannot put the ball in play again until every runner has properly tagged his base.

*The **STRIKE ZONE** is that area over home plate the upper limit of which is a horizontal line at the midpoint between the top of the shoulders and the top of the uniform pants, and the lower level is a line at the hollow beneath the kneecap. The Strike Zone shall be determined from the batter's stance as the batter is prepared to swing at a pitched ball.*

In theory, the strike zone was changed in 1969 when it was reduced at its upper limit from the top of a batter's shoulders to his armpits and at the lower limit from the bottom of a batter's knees to the top of his knees. The truth, however, is that umpires subsequent to 1969 gradually shrank the upper limit of the strike zone until it became the beltline. To halt this practice, the Official Playing Rules Committee rewrote the definition of the strike zone prior to the 1988 season. But some older arbiters allegedly ignored it and still went by the pre-1988 strike-zone configuration, whereas others found it easier to picture the armpits as the upper limit rather than an imaginary midpoint between the beltline and the top of the shoulders. In 1995, the definition of the strike zone was again rewritten. Though umpires were strongly advised to adhere to it, some current players and managers still contend that too many umpires continued to fall into three groups: those that presume a pitch to be a strike unless there is a reason to call it a ball; those that presume a pitch to be a ball unless they deem it to be a strike; and the worst group of all, those that appear to have no regular approach at all to making ball-strike decisions. In recent years, however, to the displeasure of most umpires, electronic pitch-calling devices have been installed in many parks. Controversial as these devices are, their presence appears to have resulted in the strike zone becoming more uniform since, as we have already pointed out, they may otherwise one day strip this task from plate umpires.

Until the National Association came into existence in 1871, the strike zone was nebulous. Beginning in 1858, when the concept of calling strikes was first introduced, umpires were authorized to assess a strike on any pitch that was "within fair reach of the batter." In 1871, the National Association adopted a rule that originated several years earlier, allowing a batter to request either "high" or "low" pitches. The strike zone for a high ball was between a batter's waist and forward shoulder, whereas the low strike zone ranged from the waist to the forward knee. A batter was required to declare verbally his choice of pitches when he stepped up to the plate, and was not permitted to change his mind during his turn at bat. If a batter did not declare himself, the strike zone then became the entire area between the shoulder and the knee.

Quaint as the notion of a high and a low strike now seems, it endured for the first 16 seasons of professional play, from 1871 through the 1886 season. Prior to 1874, however, pitches in the wrong strike zone were not called balls but simply no pitches. In 1887, when the number of balls needed for a walk was pared to five and the number of strikes hiked to four, the high-low rule was eliminated. Confronting hitters with a strike zone double in size seemingly ought to have resulted in markedly lower batter averages, but quite the opposite occurred. Along with some major changes to the pitching rules, giving batters an extra strike and granting a walk after only five balls instead of six apparently more than compensated for the larger strike zone, at least in 1887.

By 1892, however, it was clear that a contrary adjustment was compulsory to restore a balance between hitters and pitchers, as the NL batting average that season plummeted to its 1880 level of .245. After considerable debate, the rules committee once again increased the pitching distance.

To compensate hurlers when the pitching distance was lengthened in 1893, groundskeepers followed an innovation that teams like the St.

Louis Browns developed on the sly in the 1880s, claiming it quickened drainage of the infield after a rainstorm and began to raise the pitcher's plate, centering it in a circular mound. There were no restrictions at first on how high a mound could be built. Teams like the New York Giants, with speedballers like Amos Rusie, consequently strove to have them tower above the batter, whereas clubs that were about to face Rusie in their home parks would shave their mounds the night before beginning a series with the Giants.

These sorts of shenanigans went on for a full decade since there was nothing in the rules to prevent it. Indeed there was nothing at all in the rules about mounds! Then, in 1904, all organized professional leagues adopted a rule that the "pitcher's plate shall not be more than 15 inches higher than the baselines or the home plate . . . and the slope . . . shall be gradual." The new rule was the first even to acknowledge that a pitcher's plate did not have to be level with the surface of the playing field.

In the late 1960s, the game's moguls faced a similar crisis that had forced their brethren to lengthen the pitching distance in 1893. After Carl Yastrzemski set an all-time nadir for a major-league batting leader when he won the American League hitting crown in 1968 with a .301 average, Bob Gibson topped the majors with a microscopic 1.12 ERA, and Cincinnati was the only major-league team to average as many as four and a half runs a game, one of the changes instigated in an effort to restore the balance between hitters and pitchers was to pare five inches off the mound and reduce its maximum height to ten inches.

Batting averages rose in 1969, but not nearly as much as they had in 1893 after the pitching distance was increased. Continued experimentation with the rules was necessary in order to procure more offense. Among the changes that eventually impacted on the balance between hitters and pitchers were reducing the strike zone and, in the American League at least, legislating that a hitter could be designated to bat in place of the pitcher.

To many observers, the strike zone seems to have expanded in recent years, but MLB authorities insist it has not (even though team and individual batting averages have shrunk to alarming proportions and strikeouts have soared). In actuality, by some accounts pitchers in 2019 put the ball in the strike zone less than 50 percent of the time, relying on their speed and free-swinging batters to chase pitches—particularly high and low ones—that are well out of the zone. Additionally, with two strikes on a batter, the number of pitches in the strike zone dropped below 40 percent. Whatever the truth of the matter is, it is a deeply disturbing reality that in 2018, for the first time in major-league history—in addition to there being a record number of batter strikeouts for the 13th straight season—the number of batter strikeouts (41,210) exceeded the number of base hits (41,019). It should also be duly noted that MLB conducted a novel experiment in the independent Atlantic League, its pet testing ground, in 2019. To coax pitchers back into the strike zone, particularly when the bases are empty, the Atlantic League allowed batters to run to first base and remain there if they reached it safely not just on a dropped third strike but on any mishandled or wild pitch regardless of the count.

A TAG is the action of a fielder in touching a base with his body while holding the ball securely and firmly in his hand or glove; or touching a runner with the ball, or with his hand or glove holding the ball (not including hanging laces alone) while holding the ball securely and firmly in his hand or glove. It is not a tag, however, if simultaneously or immediately following his touching a base or touching a runner, the fielder drops the ball. In establishing the validity of the tag, the fielder shall hold the ball long enough to prove that he has complete control of the ball. If the fielder has made a tag and drops the ball while in the act of making a throw following the tag, the tag shall be adjudged to have been made. In 2019, the following was added to the definition of Tag: "For purposes of this definition any jewelry being worn by a player (e.g., necklaces, bracelets, etc.) shall not constitute a part of the player's body." The same stipulation regarding jewelry worn by a player was added to the definition of **Touch***.*

Again, we cannot be sure when the word "tag" became part of baseball lingo. In the infant forms of baseball, a fielder did not retire a runner by tagging him with the ball or tagging a base before he reached it but by hitting or "soaking" him with a thrown ball. This barbaric method had vanished by the time the Cartwright rules were adopted, but the idea of requiring a fielder to tag a runner was not embraced until 1848. Prior to that season, it had been possible to nail a runner at any base—including home—simply by tagging it before he got there. Runners in the pre-1848 era were tagged only when they clashed between bases with a fielder who happened to have the ball. As of the 1848 campaign, however, it became necessary to tag a runner coming into a base on any play except a force out.

*A **WILD PITCH** is one so high, so low, or so wide of the plate that it cannot be handled with ordinary effort by the catcher.*

Many games have been decided by a wild pitch. Perhaps the most renowned instance in postseason history came in decisive Game Five of the 1972 NLDS (when LCS's were still best-of-five affairs) on October 11 at Cincinnati's Riverfront Stadium. The Reds entered the bottom of the ninth trailing the Pirates, 3–2, with relief ace Dave Giusti on the mound. After Johnny Bench led off the frame with a homer to tie the game, Giusti surrendered two more hits before giving way to Bob Moose, normally a starter. Moose retired Cesar Geronimo and Darrel Chaney, bringing up Hal McRae, who was batting for Reds reliever Clay Carroll. Moose unleashed a pitch in the dirt that eluded Pittsburgh catcher Manny Sanguillen, allowing George Foster to score the pennant-winning run from third base. It is still the only occasion in MLB history when a team trailed in the bottom of the ninth in a decisive winner-take-all postseason game and won it on a wild pitch.

Note that the final game of the 1886 World's Series between the National League champion Chicago White Stockings and the American Association champion St. Louis Browns was also decided by Curt Welch's purported "$15,000 Slide" (he actually scored standing up) in the bottom of the 10th inning after Chicago's John Clarkson delivered a wild pitch with Welch on third to give St. Louis a 4–3 victory in Game Six of the Series. But it was neither a decisive winner-take-all game (as St. Louis was leading three games to two at the time), Nor was St. Louis behind when it took its final at bats.

WRENCHES IN THE WORKS

A term that is not yet in the rule book but ought to be. MLB contends that the game is healthier than it's ever been, but attendance has been on a steady downward trend for several years and was at its lowest since 2003 in 2019. Instead, fans are following the game more and more on their cellphones or staying home to watch it on TV, where they get replays of almost every moment of interest they may have missed. And what are major league owners doing to bring people back to the parks? They are raising ticket and parking prices, constantly trading favorite players or letting them become free agents, tinkering with the rules after decades of almost no changes, and either eliminating, truncating, or discouraging former staples like the intentional walk, the squeeze bunt, the hidden ball trick, and the hit-and-run that have generated excitement and surprise ever since the dawn of major league ball. In addition, this decline also came when MLB players hit more home runs than ever before, with two clubs (the Minnesota Twins and New York Yankees) becoming the first clubs to ever hit 300+ dingers in a single season. If the game thought that the long ball would solve all its problems, attendance totals said otherwise.

And the players? Who wouldn't be the first to reject a three-year offer of $18 mil per annum from a perennial contender whom you've served loyally for a year or two to grab a five-year contract for $20 mil per annum from a team that hasn't sniffed postseason play in over a decade?

In 2018, the Gallup Poll concluded that the 9 percent of Americans who mentioned baseball as their favorite sport to watch was the lowest percentage for the sport since Gallup first asked the question in 1937. Americans named baseball as the most popular sport in 1948 and 1960, but football claimed the top spot in 1972 and has been progressively the public's favorite ever since, currently by nearly a 5-to-1 margin over baseball even though its popularity, too, is slipping due to issues unrelated to the rules, style or tempo in which the game itself is played. In fact, according to data compiled by the *Sports Business Journal* in 2016, baseball has the oldest average player age of any of the major American sports.

Former New York Mets second baseman Wally Backman, the manager of the independent Atlantic League's Long Island Ducks—MLB's preferred petri dish—bemoaned in 2019 the many ways the game has departed from the style in which it was played while he was still active. At the same time, Backman, guaranteed by nature to introduce a cataclysmic element in any major-league team that would ever dare to hire him as its dugout chieftain, acknowledges a new generation has taken over the game. "If you don't want to do it," he proposes, "then you just get out of the game. Because things are going to change—that's obvious."

Backman understates the situation: Things have *already* changed. And skeptics have already connected the dots. To rekindle fan interest after the toxic 1994–95 strike, baseball moguls chose to ignore the herculean stats being posted by strongly suspected PED users. To win back the many fans whom the PED users soured on the game, MLB has introduced a ball that brings the same thrill, and even more often than the gigantic home run totals the PED users produced. Only it's the ball that's been 'roided now that the PED users have been weeded out to a large extent, and the public isn't buying.

On August 10–11, 2019, the *Wall Street Journal* ran an article entitled "Juiced Ball Hits Triple-A." The article categorically stated that, as promised in April 2019, the two Triple-A leagues—the International League and the Pacific Coast League—have switched to the same baseballs now used in the major leagues, unlike the less expensive balls used in the other minor leagues. The two top minor leagues were set on a pace to hit an astounding 2,100 more home runs combined than in 2018.

The official major-league ball is manufactured in Costa Rica and has higher specifications than minor-league balls. It also is constructed of slightly different materials than the minor-league ball. Minor-league baseballs are made in China and cost around half as much as the major-league balls, albeit their price is likely to go up owing to new tariff laws. the *Wall Street Journal* article confirmed that the current major-league baseballs have less air resistance and are more aerodynamic than the previous baseballs used.

Bob Nightengale wrote in *USA Today* on August 19, 2019: "The game is still played with the pitchers' mound 60-feet, 6 inches from home plate, the bases 90 feet apart, three outs per half inning and nine innings in a regulation game. Those are about the only constants resembling the game of baseball as we once knew it." Nightengale went on to cite the similar viewpoints held by former Cubs manager Joe Maddon (recently hired by the Angels) and longtime big-league fixture Lou Pinella among the several disgruntled baseball lifers he interviewed. He furthermore quoted Hall of Fame pitcher Goose Gossage as having said, "I can't watch these games anymore. It's not baseball. It's unwatchable. A lot of the strategy of the game, the beauty of the game, it's all gone. It's like a video game now. It's home run derby with their [expletive] launch angle every night."

Don Malcolm, the provocative creator of *The Big Bad Baseball Annual*, recommends countering the game's "escalating malaise" either by fixing the ball (extremely unlikely) or installing screens in all major-league parks, making home runs from "foul line to power alley distances achievable only with three or four times the present loft." To his mind, the ideal configuration for the extra-base hit paradigm per game for each team is 1.7 doubles, 0.5 triples, and only, 0.9 home runs. If put to a vote among lifelong fans from all walks, a surprisingly high number may agree with Malcolm's quotients, but among major-league players probably only pitchers, who are in the minority, would concur.

Baseball historian and critic Ev Cope observes that baseball is no longer "chess on grass" but "has become another sport of brute force—on the mound and at the plate. If 'Inside Baseball' is not yet dead, it is in intensive care." Cope thinks this may simply represent "how American society has evolved. We seem to be more aggressive and not be as patient as we used to be, nor as sentimental. That proof is clearly evident in our or 3Ms: Media, Movies, and Music."

Is all of this lamenting about the disappearance of so many treasured features of the pre-modern game even necessary, much less constructive? After all, every other major sport in America has undergone massive rule and equipment changes—including free agency—since baseball magnates shaved the mound to its present height in 1969, and none are the worse for it in the eyes of most of their ardent followers. Who is to say that in another few years the pitching distance won't have altered, batters will no longer be able to get credit for an out-of-the-park home run (only a double) if they've previously struck out during the game, batters won't automatically be deemed to have "fouled out" of a game when they whiff for a fourth time, and spectators won't be able to place bets at their seats as to what a batter will do on every pitch?

Just too crazymaking? Maybe not.

Our only unequivocal assertion is that by 2025 a new edition of *The Official Rules of Baseball Illustrated* will be vastly different than this one.

Photo Attributions

Ned Williamson (p. 5): Library of Congress (LLCN 2007680755)
Pitching Mound (p. 9): Public Domain
Harry Taylor (p.13): Public Domain
Cy Seymour (p. 17): Public Domain
Mike Tiernan (p. 17): Library of Congress (LCCN 2007686864)
Ichiro Suzuki (p. 20): Getty Images
Michael "Doc" Kennedy (p. 24): Public Domain
Bid McPhee (p. 25): Library of Congress (LCCN 2007686981)
George Crowe (p. 52): Public Domain
Ned Hanlon (p. 55): Library of Congress (LLCN 2014686465)
Steve Bilko (p. 58): Public Domain
Paul Richards (p. 59): Public Domain
Tim Hurst (p. 60): Public Domain
Ezra Sutton (p. 63): Library of Congress (LCCN 2007680723)
Zack Wheat (p. 66): Library of Congress (LLCN 2007683861)
Jay Faatz (p. 69): Public Domain
Jose Canseco (p. 70): Getty Images
Roger Bresnahan (p. 75): Library of Congress (LLCN 2007683749)
Hooks Wiltse (p. 75): Library of Congress (LCCN 2014691745
Tommy La Stella (p. 80): Getty Images
Clyde Milan (p. 82): Library of Congress (LCCN 2008678508)
Fred Sanford (p. 88): Public Domain
Stuffy McInnis (p. 94): Library of Congress (LLCN 2014718712)
Tony Mullane (p. 97): Public Domain
Christy Mathewson (p. 99): Library of Congress (LLCN 2008677495)
Duke Snider (p. 102): Public Domain
Hunter Pence (p. 111): Getty Images
B. J. Surhoff (p. 114): Getty Images

Marv Throneberry (p. 119): Public Domain

Howard Ehmke/Bob Shawkey (p. 120): Library of Congress (LLCN 2014715926)

Ted Kluszewski (p. 144): Public Domain

Hank O'Day (p. 150): Library of Congress (LCCN 2014696896)

Burleigh Grimes (p. 169): Public Domain

Ronald Acuna Jr. (p. 172): Getty Images

Al Rosen (p. 175): Public Domain

Eddie Stanky (p. 193): Public Domain

Dick Nallin (p. 200): Library of Congress (LCCN 2005676982)

Wes Curry (p. 209): Public Domain

Jocko Conlan (p. 212): Public Domain

Tom Lynch (p. 222): Public Domain

Eddie Collins (p. 223): Library of Congress (LCCN 2007685740)

Whitey Herzog (p. 227): Getty Images

Dick Howser (p. 228): Getty Images

Armando Galarraga/Jim Joyce (p. 229): Getty Images

Amanda Clement (p. 232): David Nemec Collection

Jimmy Ryan (p. 235): Library of Congress (LLCN 2007683704)

Cap Anson (p. 235): Library of Congres (LCCN 2007680738)

Ernie Lombardi (p. 242): Public Domain

Tommy Henrich (p. 250): Public Domain

Gil Hodges (p. 251): Public Domain

Rube Marquard (p. 264): Library of Congress (LLCN 2014706848)

Bubbles Hargrave (p. 272): Library of Congres (LCCN 2014696904)

Edd Roush (p. 288): Library of Congress (LCCN 2014716308)

Joe West (p. 295): Getty Images

Index

Page numbers in italics state the entry's image location.